THE SEED
OF THE CHURCH
IN CHINA

Photo of painting of Bishop William J. Boone,
about 1859, while on furlough in the United States.

The Seed
of the Church
in China

by MURIEL BOONE

A PILGRIM PRESS BOOK
from United Church Press, Philadelphia

Library of Congress Cataloging in Publication Data

Boone, Muriel, 1893-
 The seed of the church in China.

 "A Pilgrim Press book."
 1. Boone, William Jones, Bp., 1811-1864.
2. Missions—China. 3. Protestant churches—
Missions. I. Title.
BV3427.B57B66   266′.3′0924 [B]   73-13815
ISBN 0-8298-0264-9

The scripture quotations are (unless otherwise indicated)
from the *Revised Standard Version of the Bible*, copy-
righted 1946 and 1952 by the Division of Christian Education, National Council of Churches, and are used by
permission.

United Church Press, 1505 Race Street,
Philadelphia, Pennsylvania 19102

To my sister, Frances,
without whose help
I could never have made this salute
to the Christian church in China

CONTENTS

Presented by C.Y. Sha of Bloomfield Conn. and received by post on Tuesday, 3 June 1986

INTRODUCTION

I never saw my grandfather but he saw me! He died long before I was born but I remember, as a small child, the portrait in oils which hung over the piano in the family sitting room in Shanghai, China. The artist had painted the eyes so that they looked directly at one. They were kind eyes, full of wisdom and understanding and I was not afraid of them, yet I used to make a game of hiding from them. Under the piano was the only place where they could not see me. I always felt that he loved me and was asking me to do something for him.

As I grew older and myself became a missionary in China, as he, William Jones Boone, had been, I too loved my Chinese associates and learned an appreciation of their wonderful heritage in the long history of their country. William Boone delved deeply into Chinese classical literature and contributed largely to future generations of missionaries and to the Christian church in China through his translations of the Bible, both in the Wu dialect and in the Wen-li or classical style. His emphasis was on Christian and classical education for boys and girls, and the two schools which he founded in Shanghai later grew into Saint John's University and Saint

Mary's Hall. Boone was sent out to China in 1837 by the Foreign Committee of the Protestant Episcopal Church of the United States.

He arrived just as China was undergoing a profound shock from outside countries who were forcing themselves upon her reluctant attention by their insistence upon opening up trade relations. Great Britain was the most insistent, for she wished continued access to China's tempting stores of tea, silks, ceramics, and other commodities which had become known to Europe through the accounts of returned travelers and Roman Catholic missionaries. China had long grown opium, and Great Britain saw a potential market there for the quantities of the drug easily obtainable in India, where the British East India Company already had a firm foothold. Roman Catholic missionaries, especially those from France, had been able to reside in China for centuries, ever since the time of Marco Polo in the thirteenth century; they were tolerated because of their knowledge of science, in demand at the court of the emperor in Peking. But no Protestant missionary had worked in China until the coming of Robert Morrison from England in 1807. In 1837 William Boone from America arrived in Batavia, Java, en route to China, just three years after the death of Morrison, the first Protestant missionary.

The Manchu or Ching dynasty was a long one, lasting from 1644 A.D. until 1912. For the first century of its rule it proved able and energetic, expanding China's borders and unifying its people. But after the death of the great emperor Chien Lung, in 1799, the dynasty began its decline. Proud and isolationist, in the end it had to bow to the pressure from without and admit foreigners for residence, trade, and missionary activity inside its domain. William Boone, along with a good number of missionaries with the sincere desire to open to the Chinese the one thing which they considered was the very best the West had to offer them, the Christian gospel, went to China.

My father, Henry W. Boone, M.D., was also a missionary to China. His work and my grandfather's were both largely confined to Shanghai and its environs. Henry admired his father and we children grew up hearing of his life and work. But if it had not been for a surprising incident which happened while I was on furlough in the United States, being a missionary in China myself, this book would not have been written. My sister and I, residing in California at the time, decided on a sentimental journey to William Boone's home state, South Carolina, where we had never been, having been born in China. We made for Charleston, where we felt sure we would find relatives. One among the several cousins whom we did locate was elderly and in a nursing home. We visited her there. When she became convinced that we were the granddaughters of the Rt. Rev. William J. Boone she surprised us by asking us to pull out from under her bed a small trunk. This she opened and it proved to be full of old letters —all from our grandfather, each of his two wives, or our father when he was a boy—plus other papers pertaining to China. These, she said to our astonishment and joy, she would present to us as being those of the family most closely related to William Boone. The old lady, Miss Isabel De Saussure, felt she had not much longer to live and wished to give the papers to someone who might use them.

So, at long last, now being retired and having some leisure, I am attempting to write this book, largely based on these very many letters, which I frequently quote in trying to reconstruct the life and times of my grandfather. I have leaned heavily on the histories of China by Kenneth Scott Latourette, under whom I had the privilege of studying at Yale University, and of H. M. Vinacke.

It is a remarkable thing how the Christian church, at least in the hearts and minds of its adherents, has survived in China over the centuries, in spite of recurrent waves of persecution. There is a germ of life and truth in the seed of God's word which, though buried in the earth, refuses to die and springs into visible life when God's season rolls around again.

The Christian message may possibly have been carried to China even before the monk Alopen, probably from Syria, founded the Nestorian Church in China in 635 A.D. For two hundred years the church flourished and its members were spread throughout China. But Alopen had put his faith in the emperor for protection and government failed him. In 845 A.D. a Taoist emperor ascended the throne and ousted both the Buddhists and the Christians. But when Marco Polo was leaving the country four hundred years later, he ran across Chinese Christians! On his way home Polo crossed paths with the first Roman Catholic missionary, John of Montecorvino, going in to China. The pattern was repeated. When the new Ming dynasty ousted the Mongols and ascended the throne, again the Christian missionaries were thrown out. They had made the mistake of relying too much on foreign priests and not on Chinese leadership, so the church suffered a serious setback. But it was not stamped out.

A long period elapsed until, in the fifteenth century, a wave of exploration hit Europe. Spain sent Columbus westward and Vasco da Gama, sent by Portugal, rounded the Cape of Good Hope and proceeded eastward. These two governments and others of the day labored under the delusion that any land they discovered was theirs by right of discovery— disregarding local governments which might be in power. It was because of this belief that Spain claimed all the Americas except Brazil, and Portugal claimed all her discoveries in Asia. Priests accompanied their soldiers, and missionaries were left behind as the army marched on.

Not long afterwards, in 1534, Ignatius Loyola organized his band of young friends who took the vows of chastity, poverty, and obedience in an attempt to cleanse and renew the church. The Society of Jesus (the Jesuits) resulted. Almost immediately they began sending out missionaries—Ricci and other famous Jesuits penetrated China even to Peking, where Ricci was welcomed because of his knowledge of mathematics and astronomy. The Jesuits were followed by the Franciscans and Dominicans. Latourette says that by 1705 there were probably 200,000 Christians. But again there was severe persecution, missionaries all had to leave, and the church was without leadership. It did not die. After the Treaty of Tientsin in 1858 between China and Great Britain, France, Russia, and the United States permitted Christianity to be propagated in China, Roman Catholic and the first Protestant missionaries began to pour in. Again Chinese Christians, not always with any very clear idea of the faith of their fathers but willing to be called Christians, were found. Truth lies dormant but it does not die. Nor will it die in the China of today.

The day of the "foreign missionary" should be over. Today there are many dedicated Chinese Christians scattered throughout the world. When the time is ripe they will again carry God's word to their own people. May God speed the day.

Santa Fe, New Mexico   *M. Muriel Boone*

CHAPTER 1

CLIPPER SHIPS AWAY

S ummer rested lightly on Boston that morning of July 8, 1837. It was one of the peak years for the U.S. Merchant Marine, and sailing vessels of every description lay in the bay and the inner harbor. Man still had the delight of watching the lift of straight masts, the intricate tracing of lacy rigging, and white sails as they billowed and filled and carried a ship out into the bay. It was hard for the watchers to resist the longing to be on her deck, sailing away into the blue unknown. Boston harbor was filled that morning with vessels from many ports. A three-masted bark, evidently from South America, was unloading its cargo of wood, wool, and coconuts at the dock. A fast-sailing schooner about to depart for Liverpool was weighing anchor while other ships lay at rest— their names, *La Gloire, Royal Tar,* and *Lobo,* suggesting their places of origin. Small fishing smacks lay sleeping while jolly boats like busy beetles, men pulling at the oars, scurried from ship to shore and shore to ship carrying seamen, passengers, and luggage.

On land the wharf was an equally bustling place. Sailors scrambled ashore after many months at sea, eager to be home once more or to have some fun before shipping out again for another long voyage. Boardinghouse agents rushed up to entice them. Ship's agents waited to board craft, customs officers lay in wait to perform their function, and longshoremen unloaded cargoes. Friends waited to see people off or to get news of the arrival of ships.

On that morning one such group of friends stood on Boston quay under the bright sunlight. They had come to bid Godspeed to a young couple, William and Sarah Amelia Boone. Farewells had already been said, and the travelers had just crossed the narrow strip of water between the quay and the sailing packet *Louvre* and had scrambled aboard to start on a very long journey indeed. The friends standing on the wharf could still distinguish William, standing stalwart and handsome at the rail, with his wife, Sarah Amelia, beside him dressed in her yellow dimity gown and summer bonnet.

Among those who had come to see the Boones off were wellwishers from Saint Paul's Church in Boston where William, as guest speaker, had preached for seven consecutive days on his conviction that God was calling the church to carry the gospel to all mankind and had led him to embark for China. Two of the gentlemen had come up from New York; they were the Rev. James Milner and Mr. E. A. Newton, who represented the Mission Board of the Protestant Episcopal Church. It was they who had persuaded the board to accept young Boone's earnest application to be sent out to unknown China.

A few close friends and relatives from William and Sarah's home state, South Carolina, had made the difficult trip to Boston to see them off. John Huff, William's friend and confidant of seminary days, was there and William's elder brother, John, with Benji standing beside him. It was especially hard for Benji to see Master Willie go. He could not remember the time when the two of them had not played together on the plantation. What fun they had fishing or, in summer at Walterboro, creeping through the piney woods over deer trails playing Indian! Of course Master Willie had

had to go away to college and seminary and then to medical college, but he came home sometimes then. But now he was going away across all that deep water to someplace very far away. No telling when he would come back.

Sarah Amelia's brother and sister, Charles and Frances De Saussure, were gazing across at their little sister—Sally as they called her—with both love and sorrow. They had never gotten over the shock of seeing her, so gay and popular, suddenly change the whole pattern of her life when she fell in love with and married this zealous young man. Sally had gone from Columbia, South Carolina, which was home, on an infrequent visit to her eldest brother, Henry, in Charleston. There she had met again William Boone, one of her father's former students at the university. He was a frequent visitor in her brother's home and felt much at home there. William was at that time studying medicine in Charleston and, of all things, preparing to go as a missionary to China. They had fallen in love, had been married last April, and now here they were actually embarking on the perilous journey to the Orient! Their sadness at parting was deepened by their father's remark that he had no hope of ever seeing Sally again on this earth.

There were others besides Sally's father, the Hon. Henry William De Saussure, who were thinking of the young couple that day, though they had not been able to make the trip to see them off. There was Mary Jones Boone, William's mother, at her summer cottage at Walterboro, South Carolina, with the younger children. How she wished her husband, Tom, were still living—seven long years he had been gone. He was a religious man and would be proud of William. And yet perhaps he would have thought, as she did, that this was a foolhardy venture. China was a very long way off and how could Willie hope to influence the Chinese? Still, she mustn't forget God's goodness and mercy. She must trust him to protect Willie and Sally just as he had protected her and the children through the years. Ten of them growing up and John doing well in his medical practice! She should be thankful. And now she had her first daughter-in-law, little Sally. It was good that William had a wife. She could only hope and pray that they would help each other, be led of God, and by his mercy be brought back to her safe in his own time.

On the *Louvre* the ensign was flying at the mast, a sign that the ship was about to sail. Sailors in their summer outfits of red shirts and duck trousers were active on deck and up in the rigging. A land breeze was blowing, and Captain Grey hoped soon to be out in the bay where they would drop anchor again and ready everything aboard for the long voyage ahead. He felt utterly at home with a deck under his feet and was known for a skillful sailor and just master under whom men liked to serve. The order was given to weigh anchor, the light sails filled, and the graceful clipper slipped out past other ships still at anchor and became a white bird to those watching from the shore. William and Sally were off at last on their long adventure.

For William this was a moment of almost delirious excitement as he felt the deck lifting under his feet and heard the gentle slap of the waves against the side of the ship. He remembered his boyhood dream of sailing away someday on one of these proud birds, as he watched them skim into Charleston harbor with white wings tipped forward like a gull coming in for a landing. The waterfront had been a place for dreams with its mingled smells of fish, oakum, tar, spices, coffee, and tea. It must have been the tea that added the elusive hint of flowers. Tea came from China in big wooden boxes lined with lead foil and decorated on the outside with pictures of flowers. How he had longed to visit the countries from which all these wonderful things came. And now he was off!

William broke off his thoughts and looked down at his young wife standing beside him. A pang of remorse struck him, for he sensed that Sally was suffering. As he put his arm protectingly around her she turned away, that he might not see her distress. She wanted so desperately to be a help and

not a hindrance to her husband. But her father! She saw him
so clearly as he sat alone now in his study. Chancellor of the
state and trustee of the South Carolina College he had helped
to found, admired and respected, but so alone. Bereft now not
only of mother but of Sally, his youngest. She reached into
her pocket and took out the precious five-dollar gold piece
her father had given her in parting. President Washington
had given it to him when, as director of the U. S. Mint, her
father had produced the first "Gold Eagles" at Washington's
request. Sally fingered the coin lovingly and found comfort.
But thinking of his parting words she wept. He had said that
he never expected to see his dear Sally again. Oh, she loved
William and would go anywhere with him—but if she could
only reach out and comfort her father.

The ship drew steadily into Boston Bay and the captain
gave the order to lower the anchor. Commands were being
shouted by the first mate, and sailors seemed to be running
in every direction going to their several tasks. Sally felt that
she was in the way and turned to William, asking him to take
her down to the cabin. He escorted her toward the poop and
down a short flight of steps. It landed them in a square room,
evidently the dining salon. Beyond it were the passengers'
quarters. William opened a door and stood back for Sally to
enter. This was her first sight of the cabin which was to be her
home for a long time. She was glad to be where she could stay
awhile, for she was so weary of traveling about. Almost ever
since their wedding in April they had been on the go, carrying out orders from the Mission Board. William was to speak
in as many churches on the East Coast as he could before
sailing for China. Sally had traveled with him.

The tired girl looked about her. The room was small. She
saw two bunks on the inner wall, one above the other. On
these their hand luggage was piled. A high wooden rail enclosed each bunk, and she saw with distaste that a small tin
receptacle whose use she could guess was attached to the rail.
Beneath the lower bunk drawers were fitted. There was a
small stand on which a tin pitcher in a basin stood and be-

yond that a long settee. A square porthole faced the sea. A small desk and narrow wardrobe made up the rest of the furniture. There wasn't much space left in the room! William was already at work loosening the straps from the shawl case and shaking out a steamer rug. He supposed that Sally would like to rest, as they had arisen very early that morning.

She smiled at him as she lay down, saying, "Come and wake me at lunchtime, dearest."

William bent and kissed her, replying, "Rest well, my Sally. Never fear, I'll call you in plenty of time. Adieu, my love. I'm going on deck to see what all the hustle and bustle is about."

Both of them were looking forward to quiet days together, for there had been precious few of them since their wedding. Immediately after it they had gone from Sally's home in Columbia to visit William's mother on the plantation at Edmunsbury. Sally loved her mother-in-law, Mary, so forthright and courageous, and was glad to get acquainted with her new brothers and sisters, the youngest of whom was only eight. William then took her on a sentimental journey to his beautiful ancestral home just eight miles north of Charleston. He hired a phaeton, and Sally caught her breath as they drove up the long avenue of noble oak trees bannered with moss leading up to the stately white-pillared mansion.

"Oh, why did you ever leave here?" she exclaimed.

"I had nothing to do with that," her husband replied, laughing. "My august grandmother, Sarah Gibbes Boone, decided to sell it a few months before I was born. I suppose the seven hundred and fifty acres of cotton fields left of the original grant to my ancestor, John Boone, in 1676 were just too much for her and my young father to manage, so they sold it and bought the smaller place. But the present owners, the Holbecks, have kept the old name and still call it Boone Hall, you know. Well, that's what everyone in the state called it anyway. We are passing great-grandfather Thomas's grave. Shall we stop and pay our respects? Thomas Boone, who lies here, is the one who planted this avenue of oaks."

Their honeymoon was exceedingly short, for William had to go back to his medical studies in Charleston. Final exams were coming up. He left Sally at her father's in Columbia, since she said she would simply have to have a chance to decide what she wanted to take to China. She gave away most of her books and all her jewelry except the precious set of pearls which had been her mother's. After William received his degree in medicine they started off at once on the speaking tour. It had not been an easy period, for many of their friends and relatives were much opposed when they heard of William's decision to go to China. As a start for his speaking trip William approached Bishop Bowen of Charleston, his own bishop. It was a shock when his request to preach at Saint Michael's met with a flat refusal. The bishop stated that he did not want anyone to preach in his church on foreign missions because it might draw interest away from domestic missions, which had a prior claim! But William was comforted when the Rev. W. H. Barnwell of Saint Paul's in the same city gave him a hearty invitation to speak. His church pledged a thousand dollars to start the China project, undertaking its support for twenty years to come. In many of the cities where he spoke—Beaufort, Columbia, Philadelphia, Baltimore, New York, and Boston—William met with an enthusiastic response.

William was not the first young Episcopalian who had started off to China. Two years earlier two young men, the Rev. Henry Lockwood and the Rev. Francis Hanson, had set out as the first missionaries to China from the Episcopal Church. While these young men were attending the theological seminary in New York, they came under the influence of two fellow students who were an inspiration to them, as they were to prove later to William Boone. They were Augustus Lyde and Daniel Cobia. The Episcopal Church had but lately opened mission stations in Liberia, Turkey, and Greece, and they and their classmates read with interest reports coming from these stations. They organized a missionary society and a prayer group in the seminary and prayed much for the mission work. They read of the work of that intrepid English trailbreaker, Robert Morrison, as he lived dangerously in Canton, China, and was trying under enormous difficulties to translate the scriptures into Chinese. They read also the exciting *Journal of Two Voyages,* published in 1833, telling of the Prussian missionary Dr. Karl Gutzlaff's adventures along the coast of China! Daniel Cobia had a gift for writing. He felt that the church at large should know of these stirring events and sent a series of articles on missions to the church paper, *The Churchman.* William Boone, attending at that time the Virginia Theological Seminary, was one of those who read these reports with growing interest and excitement.

One spring morning in 1834 Augustus Lyde happened to be on a train going from New York to Philadelphia. He noticed that two churchmen, Mr. Milner and Mr. Newton, with whom he was acquainted, were on the same train. Lyde entered into conversation with them and learned that they were on the way to a board meeting of the Foreign Committee of the Episcopal Church. This was an opportunity for Lyde to press the point of the need and opportunity of opening mission work in China. His eloquence and sincerity impressed the two gentlemen, and they presented the matter at the board meeting. A resolution was passed establishing a mission in China. The board's first candidate was the same Augustus Lyde! His classmate Cobia desired to go too, but his friends dissuaded him on account of his frail health. He gave up the idea and became rector of a church in his native state, South Carolina.

Augustus Lyde, too, met with disappointment. Accepted for China by the board, he went as directed for a medical examination. It was discovered that he was a victim of the all-too-prevalent "consumption." It was said that upon hearing the verdict he exclaimed, "If I cannot go to China, I will do all I can for her here." Thereupon he set out on a tour of churches and seminaries to arouse interest in missions. It was at Virginia Theological Seminary, where he was a senior student, that William Boone met and listened to this burning brand for Christ and was stirred by his message. Lyde said a great deal about the ancient land of China and the need and right of her people to hear the message of God's love in sending his son to be the Redeemer of all men. William was moved, and when he returned to his room his roommate, Charles Pinckney, reported that he paced up and down with his hands clasped behind him, as was his habit when excited.

William exclaimed, "I believe I will offer myself to the Foreign Committee to be sent to China."

Pinckney remonstrated, pointing out that foreigners were not wanted there, the language was impossible, and the time not ripe.

Boone replied, "Jesus said, 'Go ye into all the world and preach the gospel.' Surely he could not have meant to exclude the three hundred fifty million people of China. If by going to China and working there I could but oil the hinges of the door, so that those who come after me could enter and work, gladly would I go." Perhaps he was remembering the remark by Robert Morrison who also found opposition when he attempted to embark for China in 1807. The British East India Company flatly refused to take him on any of their ships. So the young man, sent by the London Missionary Society, made his way over to the United States. There he was given passage, but the owner of the ship on which he was about to sail said to him sneeringly, "And so, Mr. Morrison, you really expect to make an impression on the idolatry of the great Chinese Empire?"

"No sir," he made reply, "but I expect God will."

But of course William Boone was as yet a student, and it was too early to apply to the Mission Board for appointment. After the disappointment of Lyde and Cobia the board looked for other candidates ready to found the newly projected China Mission; Henry Lockwood, a classmate of Cobia and Lyde, offered himself. The board sought a companion for Henry, and after an interval the young rector of a church in Maryland, Francis Hanson, declared himself willing to go. On June 2, 1835, the two young bachelors boarded the good ship *Morri-*

son, on which they had been given free passage by the owner, Mr. Oliphant, who was to prove a friend to missions all down the years. Their voyage on the clipper ship was a lengthy one, taking 126 days, and it was a happy day when at last they went ashore at Canton. At last they were actually on China's soil!

In the first issue of the Episcopal Church's new monthly *The Spirit of Missions* William Boone read with consuming interest a paragraph which stated,

> The Secretary has intelligence of the safe arrival of the Messrs. Hanson and Lockwood in Canton. They speak in kindest terms of the kind attention of the Captain and of facilities for the conduct of religious exercises on board, not only on the Lord's Day but on week days. They have distributed Bibles and Prayer Books among the seamen and are much pleased with the response.

As he read this notice William Boone longed for the day when he might follow them to the Orient.

In Canton the new arrivals were surprised to find a colony of nearly one hundred foreigners in residence. But they were restricted to a narrow strip of land along the Pearl River bank lying outside the walled city of Canton and were forbidden to go into the city. Almost all the foreign residents were traders in the employ of the British East India Company and were there without their wives, as the entry of women into "the factory," as the area where they lived and carried on business was known, was forbidden by the Chinese emperor. There were a very few missionaries: the Rev. Elijah Bridgman and Dr. Peter Parker of the American Board Mission, (the Congregational denomination), and Dr. Gutzlaff who went back and forth from Macao, and a few others. They gave the young men a warm welcome. But their hosts all agreed that the two would-be missionaries would do much better to find a less uneasy place to live, where they could pursue the study of Chinese in peace and thus prepare themselves for work in China when the Lord should open the way. Dr. Robert Morrison had died only the year before, and they quoted his words with strong conviction:

Throughout all China, wherever Chinese is spoken, however dialects may differ, the Chinese written language is understood by all. The voyager, the merchant and the traveler, as well as the Christian missionary, if he can write Chinese, may make himself understood throughout the whole of Eastern Asia.

Mr. Bridgman explained that that was the reason he was attempting to follow Morrison's example and had devoted his time to literary work. He had brought out a lithographic press from America and was printing the Bible which Morrison had translated into Chinese and also some tracts of his own composing. He explained that though missionaries could not as yet travel and distribute the word of God in the interior of China, Chinese citizens who accepted the literature would in the natural course of events circulate it when they returned home to their native districts. It would be a forerunner of the message of the gospel which they all hoped someday they would be permitted to carry into China.

Singapore, Malacca, and Java were suggested as places where the young men might reside temporarily, but Gutzlaff strongly advocated Batavia, Java, as the best for their purpose. He said many Chinese merchants were in residence there and that it would be easy for them to find a teacher of Chinese. Ways might open up whereby they could be of service to the people, too, and he was sure that they could openly distribute Christian literature. Lockwood and Hanson decided reluctantly to accept this advice, of which they could see the wisdom. Mr. Bridgman gave them a quantity of tracts and Bible portions with which they could start both their own study and their work, Dr. Gutzlaff presented them each with Morrison's English-Chinese dictionary, and they departed for Macao, down the river. There they were so fortunate as to find a Dutch brig leaving for Java. They reached there on December 22, 1835, and looked about for a place to live.

Lockwood and Hanson were surprised at the extent of the island. It stretched before them lush and green and they were to learn that it covered as much territory as the state of New York. Dutch and English missionaries gave them a warm welcome; not so the Dutch colonial government. After they assured the authorities that they hoped to work only with the Chinese colonists and not with the native Malay people, they were given permission to stay. They were guided to the Chinese quarter of the city of Batavia and found that it was the business center. Practically all the shops, countinghouses, warehouses, and other business enterprises were in the hands of the Chinese. The number of Chinese living in the city was astonishing—between thirty and forty thousand!

The newcomers decided that their first step must be to find a dwelling place in the Chinese quarter. After some negotiation they moved into an empty shop building on the main street. It was built of bricks in the Chinese style of architecture, with an open shop front facing the street and small living quarters behind. It seemed ideal, for the larger front room could be used as a schoolroom and chapel, while the four small rooms opening onto a courtyard would do the bachelors as living quarters.

They had not counted on the climate. From October to April the southwest monsoon blows, bringing a heavy shower every afternoon. The air was hot and oppressive, and everything felt wet and turned moldy. There seemed to be no air in their tight little house and they felt stifled. Insects abounded, and geckos and other wall lizards clung to the matting ceilings. Mosquitoes were thick. First Francis and then Henry Lockwood succumbed to violent chills followed by fever and head-splitting pain, which indicated malaria. Doses of quinine relieved Henry, but from the start Francis could not seem to get over the debilitating effects of the fever.

In their misery they were greatly befriended by Dr. and

Mrs. Walter H. Medhurst of the London Missionary Society, who had gone out to the Malay Archipelago as early as 1828 and were well acquainted with the vagaries of a tropical climate and how to dodge them. They had built a modest home after the open Malay style in a new suburb outside the old confining city wall. Well ventilated, this dwelling was an airy delight, in sharp contrast to the cramped and dank rooms of the two young men. Lockwood and Hanson took to visiting the Medhursts frequently, especially since they had a fair young daughter, Sarah Sophia!

Dr. Medhurst, a great linguist, understood Chinese and helped the newcomers engage two Chinese scholars, one to teach them and the other to help them open a small school for Chinese boys. From the first they were convinced, and Dr. Medhurst agreed with them, that literacy was the foundation for the understanding of the Christian message. The Chinese merchants who were approached greeted enthusiastically the idea of a school teaching Chinese to their sons. Some of the men had been in Java for several generations, and since Chinese women had been barred from leaving their native land, the children's mothers were all Malay or part Malay. That language was spoken in the home, but the fathers had maintained a deep-seated loyalty to China, their fatherland, and even though they may never have been there themselves wished their sons to be heirs of its ancient culture. So there was no difficulty in finding pupils, and twenty enrolled almost from the start, which was as many as the room could hold and the teacher discipline. From the first the boys were taught Chinese characters, simple mathematics, and geography. Neither Henry Lockwood nor Francis Hanson yet had the language to tell them Bible stories and decided they had best start at once to take lessons in Malay as well as in Chinese, as it was said to be an easy language to learn and all their pupils knew it.

The frequent calls of Henry Lockwood on the Medhursts turned into courtship of their delicate daughter, Sophia, and in 1836 they were united in marriage with a simple service conducted by the bride's father in the English Chapel in Batavia. Her parents planned soon to return to England on furlough, so they urged the young couple to remain in the parents' bungalow and then continue to live there after the Medhursts' departure. This they were grateful to do, but Henry and Sophia were not destined to enjoy each other and their beloved home for long. Within a year Henry's able and beautiful wife died. He was inconsolable, and Francis Hanson, seeking to divert him, proposed that they take a trip into the interior to see something of the countryside. They had met a Dutch pastor whose station was the village of Depok, about twenty miles from Batavia. He had issued a cordial invitation to the two young men to visit him, so they made Depok their goal.

They struck off toward the Blue Mountains and were soon out of the city and almost immediately walking between the green lawns of rice fields. It was still steamy and hot, but the green fields around them gave an immediate lift to their spirits. Little villages nestled among clumps of bamboo. There were tall palms and small evergreen cacao trees hung with red-brown pods rich with chocolate. They did not stop, though the Malay inhabitants were friendly and smiling— they were too anxious to reach the hill country. As the ground began to rise the air became perceptibly cooler and fresher. Rice fields gave way to cacao plantations, slopes planted to tea and coffee, and everywhere the tall and graceful palms. As they drew near Depok evening was approaching, and the hills ahead were half shrouded in a soft lazuli haze. Beyond loomed the sharp bulk of Mount Salak, its volcanic violence now peacefully sleeping.

Their Dutch host gave them a warm welcome, and the two Americans were at once glad that they had come. Healing days followed for both. Since his wife's death Lockwood, always a conscientious student, had immersed himself more than ever in mastering the Chinese language, always mindful that his hoped-for goal was China itself. The rest from study was a refreshment which he accepted gladly. But for Hanson it was a welcome yet somewhat uneasy vacation, for to tell the truth he was dodging study and had been doing so for some time. He was utterly discouraged about ever learning Chinese, and Lockwood's progress in both reading and speaking only made him feel the more hopeless. He simply could not get his tongue around the strange *ng* and *tz* sounds with which the language seemed to bristle. And the characters made his head swim! It was no use and he knew it. He had been considering the idea of giving up China entirely, and thought perhaps since the Malay language was so much easier he might ask to stay and work here permanently among the pleasant Malay people. But upon discreet inquiry he had been given to understand that none but Dutch missionaries, and very few of them, were welcome and that the Dutch colonial government was not at all interested in the education of native children. The natives were rightfully farmers. Holland now owned the farms by right of conquest and therefore, in a way, the farmers. There was no sense in encouraging them to become "uppity" through education. Everything was going smoothly and there was no need for Americans, with their notions of democracy, to infect the Malay mind with subversive ideas. As long as these two Americans confined themselves to educating the Chinese in the city, who after all were businessmen and had to know how to read and write, it would be tolerated, but hands off the Malays! They did not need so-called progress.

The two vacationists delighted in taking long walks and went on trips into the hills, even venturing as far as the cool and beautiful hill station of Buitenzorg, seat of the colonial government, where they spent a few enjoyable days in the European-style hotel built on the bank of a rushing mountain stream. The whole countryside, even the mountain slopes, seemed like one continuous well-kept garden. They spent a whole day in the interesting botanical gardens, already world famous, where plants from all over the world were growing and where the great kanari trees towered above their heads. While they were relaxing in this lovely environment they spoke of their pleasure in the knowledge that their friends and future colleagues, Dr. and Mrs. Boone, were already somewhere on the ocean on the way to join them. But they had no way of knowing the position of the ship nor when it would arrive at the port of Batavia.

Henry Lockwood hoped that his stay in this lovely spot, free from all responsibility, would help his friend Francis to come to a decision on the problem which was troubling him. They returned to Depok, but when, after three more weeks, Henry suggested that they return to Batavia, Francis was apologetic. He said he did not feel ready to leave Depok. His companion was understanding and suggested that Hanson write to the board in New York asking to be allowed to return home for a season. Francis said he would like to remain in Depok for a little while longer, as he did not think he would be able to pray for God's guidance in the heat and confusion of the city. Henry returned to Batavia alone. And so it turned out that upon the arrival of the Boones in Batavia some weeks later Henry Lockwood was the only one there to receive them.

CHAPTER 2

BEFORE
THE WIND

A sense of exultation in the knowledge that at long last he was actually on his way to join Lockwood and Hanson welled up in William Boone on that first morning aboard the *Louvre,* making him take the steep steps up to the deck at one bound. His heart turned in gratitude to God, who had brought him to this day of fulfillment. Surely Java would prove to be only a temporary interlude, and then they would all go to China and learn to know and love the Chinese and share with them the message of God's great love.

As he stepped out onto the deck he found it wet. A seasoned sailor was directing two young apprentices—how very young the lads looked—in swabbing and holystoning the decks. This was a job which would be theirs, no matter what the weather, each dawn as long as the ship was at sea. William approached the man and asked him if he would be so kind as to show him where the two steamer chairs he had sent aboard were stowed. He guided William down a companionway and into a compartment where baggage and some freight consigned to California were stored. On the way he told the passenger that he was the ship's carpenter and that his name was Anderson.

William liked the tall Norwegian. They found the chairs and carried them on deck, where Anderson advised that they be set up just aft of the wheelhouse, where they would be somewhat shielded from the heavy sprays near the bow. William suspected that they would spend a good deal of time in those chairs, for they could not stay down in the cabin all the time.

With the sounding of one bell he went down to warn Sally that it would soon be lunchtime. She was asleep and looked so relaxed and childlike that he hated to disturb her. She had loosened her hair and the red-gold tresses were tossed back over the pillow. Damp curls clung to her forehead, for the room was hot. There were traces of tears on her cheeks. William awakened her gently. Sally opened her eyes sleepily, confused for the moment as to where she was. Her eyes lit on the spittoon fastened to the edge of the bunk, and she sat up and laughed. On the stroke of 12:30 the steward tapped on their door, and they went along to the dining salon just beyond the cabin. Captain Grey was already seated at the head of the one table. He arose when he saw Sarah Amelia and motioned her to take the chair on his right and invited William Boone to sit next to her. Just at that moment another of the few passengers, Mr. Andrews, entered the room. He was a ship company's agent, on his way to California to replace an agent there. He was invited to sit across from William, leaving an empty seat on the captain's left for the chief mate, who only at times had the leisure to be present. When all were seated the only two other passengers appeared—a couple of Venezuelan dignitaries whom the captain remarked would disembark at Port of Spain on the island of Trinidad, where he intended to put in for fresh water. When they had been introduced and seated the meal commenced with a huge covered soup tureen, which was set before the captain to dish out. Sally was pleased with the meal which followed, there being plenty of fresh meat, vegetables and fruit, and an excellent plum duff for dessert. She inquired who the cook was and was delighted to learn that he was a Negro from the South.

Captain Grey proved most pleasant. He was a man in his fifties, trim and alert. His most noticeable feature was his eyes, as blue as the sea and with that far-seeing look of the true sailor. They were set in a face made ruddy through exposure to the weather, a face which showed both strength and kindliness. Both of the young people liked and trusted him on sight. He reminded William of his father, Tom Boone. He had the same outdoor quality, though Tom Boone had been a planter and not a seaman. When William asked him what course he intended to take, Captain Grey replied that in a sailing vessel the exact course cannot be plotted ahead but depends very much upon the wind, weather, and currents. However, definite goals could be set. Trading ships such as this often changed their plans according to what cargo was available at any given port. While docked at Macao a sea-captain friend of his once got a rumor of a relatively unknown island among the Spice Islands where pepper was grown. Knowing that there was a market for pepper in China, he headed his ship there on the spur of the moment, loaded his ship with the spicy condiment, which was both plentiful and cheap, returned to Macao, and made a fortune out of it. Once the ship left soundings there was no way in which it could readily get in touch with the home office, so the captain had the say in trade as well as in all other things. The length of their voyage to Java, he said, would depend on the wind and the waves. They might be kind and speed the ship on its way, or the wind might drop and leave them becalmed for days or even weeks. "So the best thing for you to do," he said looking at Sally with a twinkle in his eye, "is to settle in as if you were at home and enjoy it as best you can." William and Sally exchanged glances and wondered if they would be able to accept his advice. They left the table feeling somewhat wiser.

The next day being Sunday, Captain Grey asked William at breakfast if he would preach at a service on deck at ten o'clock. He said he himself would read the prayers as he was in the habit of doing. William accepted and retreated to the desk in the cabin to prepare for it. At the appointed hour the sailors and other members of the crew, of whom there were about thirty in all, gathered on the forecastle. Chairs had been set out for the passengers and a small table for the leaders. The men stood about in a loose group. The unconventional congregation regarded the passengers, especially Sally, with interest. It was most unusual to have a woman aboard and was generally considered bad luck. But this one was young and pretty, and they would cross their fingers and hope it would work the other way for once. The service itself was no surprise to any except the new hands, for they knew of the captain's habit of conducting a Sunday service if conditions permitted. Prayers they were used to, but this was a brand-new experience, having a preacher aboard. They saw a young man of twenty-six, of medium height, with broad shoulders and a look of determination and strength. He had an unusually high forehead from which the brown hair was combed back. His blue eyes showed liveliness and interest. His expression was pleasant yet serious. The surplice and stole which he had donned made him look dignified and ecclesiastical in spite of his youth.

The preacher was looking at the men. He noticed how young most of them were. One of them looked no older than his brother, George Fraser, at home! He felt a surge of kinship with them and a great longing to be a help to these brothers with whom his daily life would be bound up for many days. Laying aside his notes he began simply:

Men, here we are all in the same boat! I mean not only in the sense of being shipmates, but in many other ways. We are all committed, whether by necessity or choice, to a long voyage whose outcome depends on the mercy of God. "Our times are in his hand." Each one of us, I suspect, has but lately parted with someone he loves and our hearts are sore at the parting. We face days that will hold hard work and sometimes loneliness. But take heart! We know with certainty that there is a heavenly Father watching over us. He made the earth, the sea, the sky and all that in them is and he made you and me. He longs for us, each one, to turn to him in simple faith, humility, and gratitude, much more than any earthly father longs for the return of his wayward son.

He spoke in a voice ringing with conviction and sincerity and the men were listening. He went on:

There is another thing which makes us all sharers of a common experience. There is not a man among us who will not admit that sometimes he has seriously grieved his earthly father and fallen far short of what was expected of him. How much more have we offended our righteous heavenly Father! If God were a tyrant we would be constrained to justify ourselves for not loving him. But no, he has never done anything but good to us and yet we have never made him any return but ingratitude. This is sin which we pile on top of our many other offenses. Should not this consideration cause us to abhor ourselves and seek pardon from him who loved us so much that he sent his beloved Son into the world to live the life of love—which is God—on earth and then to die for us? Jesus himself said, "Come unto me all ye that are weary and heavy laden and I will give you rest." Come asking pardon, for he will forgive you; come asking cleansing, for he will make a new man of you; come with joy and thanksgiving, for he will be your companion, your strength, and your song. In the name of the Father and of the Son and of the Holy Ghost. Amen.

The preacher concluded with the benediction. "The grace of our Lord Jesus Christ and the love of God and the fellowship of the Holy Ghost be with you all now and forever more. Amen." The service was over and the men returned to their various stations. From that time on they looked upon the young preacher as an approachable friend, and many of them had profitable conversations with him when they had time off.

It was calm and beautiful on the bay, and for a while after the short service William and Sally tried out their steamer chairs and enjoyed the caress of the gentle breeze and the sound of ripples as lazy waves slapped gently against the ship's side. Then it was lunchtime. After the meal they decided to explore their new home. As they passed the galley they heard the cook singing lustily, a hymn which they learned was his favorite:

Eternal Father, strong to save, whose arm hath bound the restless wave,
Who bidd'st the mighty ocean deep its own appointed limits keep,
Oh, hear us when we cry to Thee, for those in peril on the sea.

He stopped singing and invited them into his tiny but spotless domain, which he showed them with pride. As soon as Sally spoke the cook knew that they were from the South and was doubly pleased. He was a tall black man and told them that his name was Jerry. He hailed from Georgia. He offered to show them about the ship. On deck they found a busy scene. Men were at work checking every bit of equipment and testing every inch of sail and rope. It occurred to William that putting a ship out to sea was a lot of work and a tremendous responsibility for the captain who sailed her.

Jerry explained to Sally how to tell time by the ship's bells, pointed out where the seamen's quarters were, and indicated the names of the masts and sails. But there were so many of them that it was as much a maze to her as ever when he finished. Then he asked shyly if they would like to see his animals. Sally was astonished, for she did not know that live animals went to sea. All she could think of was the owl and the pussycat until they reached the sheltered pens on the aft deck. There were several cows in the cattle pen, a coop of chickens, and a straw-strewn pigpen. Jerry explained that when they reached California they would take on sheep and that they all made up the ship's fresh meat supply. Sally shuddered but at the same time was glad that they would not have to survive on beef jerky. Jerry gave them a bit of advice which proved valuable. He said. "If you alls feels sick Jerry will fix you a mess of salt beef and rice. It be mos' salubrious for puttin' a calm on the troubled stummik."

About midnight both William and Sally were awakened by the sound of many feet running across the deck above their heads. There were shouted orders, the creak of a wind-lass, and crack of hoisted sails. It was obvious that they were about to get under way. It was an exciting moment! They were actually on the way. There was a strong breeze. The sails popped as they filled and the vessel began to buck the the waves. Sally actually enjoyed the roll and toss, but poor William began to feel seasickness coming on, as well as symp-toms of one of his dreaded migraines. By morning he was a very sick man.

It was five days before William managed to stagger on deck, looking very wan indeed. The tang of fresh air refreshed him, and a day spent in the deck chair gave him the stimulus to attack that for which he had been impatient of the delay—a start in the study of the Chinese language. The following morning he dug out a package which had been sent, at his request, from Java by Henry Lockwood. It had taken a long time to reach him by the hand of an obliging sea captain and had been delivered only a couple of days before the *Louvre* sailed. It contained Robert Morrison's Chinese dictionary and a copy of the Bible in Chinese, the life work of that great and dedicated scholar. Without a teacher William developed a method of study all his own. He began by reading the first verse of the Gospel of Mark in English. He then looked at each Chinese character in the corresponding verse and, finding it in the Chinese dictionary, memorized it, together with the meaning, although he had no way of knowing how the character was pronounced. It was a laborious process but he stuck to it, and it laid for him the foundation of being outstandingly proficient in the Chinese written language. Sally thought his method too involved and contented herself with trying to pick up a few characters from her husband. As recreation they invented a game with characters—a sort of character Lotto. Sally had another form of recreation: petting the cat. For a long time she had not known there was one on board. Then one day a sleek tabby walked daintily into the cabin. Sally was delighted and made it welcome. The captain explained at her inquiry that it was a pet of Jerry's and was tolerated on board to keep the rat population under control.

The clipper headed south with the wind in her favor, bound for the island of Trinidad off the coast of Venezuela, where her two South American passengers would disembark. The ship had been at sea for nearly two weeks, and it was a pleasure to all on board to draw near to land and see rocks and trees once more, if only in the distance. None went ashore except the two Venezuelan gentlemen, the sailors who rowed the longboat, and Jerry, the cook. Upon the boat's return, the large casks the sailors had taken along were filled with fresh water, and Jerry was fortified with baskets heaped with fresh fruits and vegetables and a bag of coffee. Captain Grey headed the vessel east again almost as soon as the longboat had been hoisted into place. They had a long and tough way ahead of them down the coast of South America to the dreaded Cape Horn and around it to the Pacific.

The vessel took nearly a month to battle its way against the current around the bulge of Brazil and down the coast. They kept well out to sea. The southeast trade winds seemed determined to blow them off course, but by tacking and the skillful manipulation of the sails the clipper made it—but only at the rate of five or six knots. After they crossed the equator and drew southward the weather grew steadily colder. Sally was surprised, for she had taken it for granted that the farther south they went the warmer it would be. William went to the baggage room and unpacked his warm jacket and Sally's shawl.

As they approached the Horn at the southern extremity of South America the sea became rough. William did not mind the tossing of the ship this time for he had found his sea legs. A cold, driving rain kept the passengers in their cabins. William sensed approaching peril and wished he might be of assistance, but knew all he could do at the moment was to pray for strength, skill, and courage for all on board.

Finally William could stand no more inactivity in the

cabin, and wrapping up warmly he ventured on deck and found conditions worse than he had imagined. The sky was leaden gray and the sea dark and running high. The vessel was rolling so much that he could scarcely keep on his feet. He looked up and saw that most of the sails had been furled and that men were still aloft close-reefing them. The ship that had been a flying white bird was now reduced to a skeleton of stark masts and taut ropes. Even as William stood there a squall of wind hit the ship, bringing with it rain and hail. He turned to go down the hatch but not before he had been drenched and his face cut by stinging particles of ice.

The three passengers went to the dining salon for meals, but neither the captain nor chief mate appeared at the table. Conditions worsened, and the ship pitched and tossed. Chairs and other movable objects slid across the floor or crashed from their shelves. It became almost impossible to walk down the corridor to meals, and bunks seemed the safest places in which to stay. There was a knock on the cabin door and when William shouted, "Come in," it was opened by Jerry, who stood clutching a hamper. He said, "Cap'n's compliments and he say you all stay in the cabin 'cause Ah cain't cook with no fire an Ah bring you all some dry vittles fo' the next few days. Don' worry none, Cap'n's a mighty good sailor-man an' we come thro' all right." He set the hamper in the corner and staggered back into the corridor. When William opened it he found it contained bread, hardtack biscuits, two or three pounds of salt beef, canned fruit, and a bottle of wine.

That day and night became a prolonged nightmare. Nothing was visible from the porthole but a blur of water and foam. The one oil lamp swinging from the ceiling batted violently to and fro and finally went out. They were left in total darkness. They could hear the sound of orders being shouted from above, but could not distinguish the words. At times the ship plunged so sharply it seemed she must be heading straight for the bottom of the sea. Again she shuddered, and they could hear sharp cracks and deep groans. It was a frightening experience. Sally was comforted by Wil-

liam's nearness but presently that was denied her. He began
to wonder if his medical skill might not be needed for the
men and told Sally of his resolve to go above. Bundling up
as best he could he pulled the heavy mahogany medicine
chest which held his equipment from its corner and took out
such things as he thought he might need. He hated to leave
Sally alone and held her close, reminding her that they were
on their heavenly Father's mission and underneath were his
everlasting arms.

William reported to the captain's cabin in the forecastle and
found the decks awash and a mighty spray shrouding the
whole forepart of the ship. In spite of his advice that William
stay below, the captain was glad to see him, for an accident
had just occurred. A lad had been sent aloft to secure a flop-
ping rope on a yard and, unable to hang on because of the
numbness of his half-frozen hands, had fallen forty feet to
the deck. Fortunately he had struck a coil of rope which probably kept him from sliding overboard, where he would have
been swallowed up without hope of rescue in the angry sea.
His mates had just carried him in unconscious and had laid
him on the floor. The poor fellow undoubtedly had a broken
leg and probably other injuries. William was occupied at once
and the boy, being a strapping lad, pulled through. Afterwards Captain Grey told William that he had forgotten that
he was a doctor as well as a preacher and, as is the captain's
duty, would have tried to patch up the boy alone if William
had not appeared. His responsibilities for sailing the ship
safely through this hell were so great that he begged William
to remain and attend to the many cuts and bruises which a
good many of the sailors had sustained in one way or another.
It was a good twenty-four hours before he returned to Sally
in the cabin.

When William thought it safe to take Sally on deck again
a sight amazing to a southern girl met her eyes. The ship
seemed to be thoroughly coated in ice—hull, masts, rigging,
and spars. The deck had been like glass but had been liberally
sprinkled with ashes to keep the men from slipping. The sun

was in and out of flying clouds, for the wind was still high, and caused a glitter that was almost blinding as it shone on the ice. Bobbing about in the sea were humps and bergs of ice. The sea was deep ultramarine blue; the ice, frosty at the top, took on indescribably beautiful tones of azure and delicate forget-me-not blue as it met the horizon. There were still lookouts posted at every quarter of the ship, and they seemed to be as entranced as the passengers. The storm was over and in their relief the men, those who were not on duty or asleep, joked and sang as they wrung and spread out wet clothing to dry in the sun. Regular meals were served again, and life aboard gradually came back to normal. They had rounded the Horn!

The ice began to melt, and soon only a casing around the base of the masts remained to remind them that ice had been everywhere. The sailors stowed away their thick boots and southwesters and came out in ordinary garb. The wind moderated and they were called out to hoist the topsails and sheet them home. Soon the ship was a gallant bird again flying over the waves. The sea was still choppy and cold, and the young couple, standing at the bow one day, noticed some dark forms whose sleek bodies slid along beside the ship on the leeward side. They asked a sailor engaged in coiling rigging what they were. He took a look and said, "Seals. They have probably come out from the Straits of Magellan, where they gather in great numbers." Sally and William watched them for a long time, fascinated by their sportive grace.

At dinner the captain told them that he would stop briefly at the Galápagos Islands, six hundred miles off the coast of Equador. They were wafted along by the pleasant southeast trade winds, and the weather grew steadily warmer until, as they again approachd the equator, it was distinctly hot. All three passengers spent most of their waking hours on deck, William still studying several hours a day at unraveling verses from the Chinese Bible. Sally began to notice birds dipping and wheeling on long, pointed wings. She thought she recognized them as terns and was delighted to see old friends so far from home. But in the course of the same afternoon she was given a close-up of a strange-looking bird, the Mexican cormorant. Rising from the water unwarily with a large fish in its hooked beak, it flew against a line from the studding sail and fell stunned to the deck. Its dark body was all of two feet in length and there was a patch of red at the base of the beak. Presently it revived, stood up, and stretching out its long black neck gazed in surprise and with no sign of fear at the people surrounding it. Then it expanded its three-foot wings and stood there looking ludicrous. A sailor gave it a push from behind and it slid off to alight on the sea, and would soon return, no doubt, to its nesting island. A sailor remarked that the Equadorian farmers depended on the huge stores of guano on those islands for fertilizer, for sea birds had been nesting there for centuries.

They put into the harbor of San Cristóbal but, as at Port of Spain, did not go ashore. Again a boat was sent for fresh water and returned shortly with full casks. Although it was still a long way off, everyone felt a stir of excitement when Captain Grey announced that he intended to put in at San Diego on the coast of California and stay there for a couple of days. It would be wonderful to step once more on solid ground! The vessel stood well out to sea until it reached the latitude of thirty degrees. At that point the captain ordered a swing toward the east. On the afternoon of September 22 there was suddenly a great shout from the lookout: "Land ho." Everyone boiled up on deck and strained their eyes to see land. At last they could discern a low line of hills to the northeast. Topsails and studding sails were reefed as the ship approached nearer to the land. As they approached San Diego a wooded headland appeared and opposite it a stony point. The narrow channel running between the two looked too small for a ship to negotiate, but the current was strong and bore it along swiftly into the harbor, where two other ships already lay at anchor. One was a small brig from the Sandwich Islands, the other a graceful clipper, the *Ann McKim,* out of Baltimore. She carried an ensign at her mast.

Captain Grey hailed her and received an invitation to go aboard. Learning that she was about to sail for Monterey, which was his desired haven, Mr. Andrews, the other passenger on the *Louvre,* requested passage. That being granted, he went with Captain Grey in the gig over to the other ship, taking along bag and baggage. Andrews was an agent for the Boston company of Bryant and Sturgis, chief suppliers of goods sent by ship around the Horn to California.

William and Sally gazed at the land spread before them with interest and excitement. For the past few years there had been much in the news at home of young men headed West, of the dangers they encountered on the way, and glowing accounts they sent back of virgin forests and boundless acres of arable land waiting for settlers. As they looked at the rocky beach and brown grass stretching away to a clump of tall trees, they almost expected Indians on horses to break from the undergrowth and come racing toward them. But instead, all they saw were a few cows cropping the dry grass and a line of drab wooden warehouses. Half hidden by the trees were a few barely discernable houses and the outline of a mission, the cross surmounting the church standing out clearly.

Upon his return from the other ship Captain Grey told them that San Diego, though possessing a fine harbor, was as yet only a small trading post, but he predicted a good future for it as a shipping point. The crew was to be allowed to go ashore in shifts, but as there was really nothing of interest to see he suggested that the young couple wait until the next morning to go ashore. So they had to content themselves with watching a very beautiful red-and-gold sunset.

Next morning two sailors rowed them ashore in the jolly boat. It was an exquisite pleasure to step on dry land again after so many days at sea. They made for the houses and saw, as they drew near, that there was a scattering of one-story buildings built of mud bricks, each with a flat roof. In front of a couple of them horses were tethered beneath the trees. They did not look to be very spirited nags, but William suggested that they hire two of them for a gallop. Sally loved to ride and thought it would be a lark. A man dressed in blue cotton with a large straw hat over his eyes stood leaning against a doorpost. They approached him and indicated the horses. He seemed to get the point, and soon William and Sally were mounted and heading toward the range of hills. Rough blocks of stone were jumbled at the base of the slopes, but the horses followed a trail which led to a little stream. They followed the course of it and presently found themselves in a grove of towering pines. Here they dismounted and reveled in the whispering of the pine needles in the breeze, much more soothing than the swish of waves! Birds sang in the branches and a tiny chipmunk dashed back and forth unafraid at their feet. It was heavenly. By the time they returned to the ship they were well content with their earthy interlude.

During the time William and Sally were ashore the *Louvre* had been discharging her cargo for California: hardware, glass, paint, furniture, crockery, kitchen utensils, guns, traps, farm implements, boots, clothing, and all the many articles demanded by pioneers in a new land. It was all unloaded in one day, and on the next, having taken aboard four or five sheep, a crate of chickens, the indispensable fresh water, and such meager supply of vegetables as the place afforded, they set out again to sea. The course was now due west across the Pacific Ocean.

Sally and William, now the only two remaining passengers, found that they were following the captain's initial advice that they settle in and feel at home. The days now slipped by easily and comfortably in familiar surroundings. On a calm day Sally loved to stand at the bow of the ship and watch the slow swells come all the way from the horizon and break in spray against the prow. Above it the bowsprit lifted and lowered like the horn of a charging unicorn. On a breezy day it was quite different. The whole ocean was covered with sparkling blue waves, the crest of each capped with white. And when Sally looked straight down over the side of the ship, the advancing waves rose up and curled over, showing depths of jade green before they broke in a shower of frothy droplets.

One day in the distance she saw a column of white suddenly burst from the surface of the sea. She called William. By that time there were several jets, and he guessed that they were whales spouting. It proved indeed to be a whole pod of whales, and for a long while they watched fascinated as half-seen dark shapes appeared for a moment and then submerged. Often they saw dolphin, seemingly racing the ship, leaping into the air, and sliding into the water again in graceful curves. Flying fish too, with their two stiff fins like sails, skimmed over the waves. In midocean they were aware that a great bird was following the ship. It had a tremendous wingspread and floated effortlessly. Jerry threw scraps to it and it went after them like a gull. Sally loved the evidence that there was so much life in and over the sea and felt a kinship with all of it.

The most precious memories of the voyage afterwards were the long intimate hours spent together on deck, when the beauty and peace all about them drew them very close together. Sunsets viewed together as they stood at the rail were more glorious than anything they had ever imagined. Below lay the deep blue of the Pacific, while above unbelievable shades of green, yellow, blue, orange, and red flamed, merged, and finally faded away. Slowly the gray of the sky deepened to inky blue, and the sea and the sky were one. The majesty of the panorama awed the lovers. They watched in silence.

When the stars began to appear William said softly, "The stars come out as soon as it is dark enough. God has shown us his power and love tonight. You and I do not know what lies ahead. We are going to a strange land and there may be darkness and sorrow to be met with. But let us never forget the wonder of this night and that after the glory of the sunset his stars pierced the dark to show us always that our Father is there and that his is the kingdom, the power, and the glory." They fell silent again and stood for a long while drinking in the deep serenity and sense of the presence of God all about them.

Many a balmy night they lay on the deck chairs sharing incidents of their childhood and felt increasingly one. One evening William said laughingly, "Did I ever tell you about the trouble I got into at college with the dean? I reckon you were off at school that year and maybe you didn't hear about it. You must remember there was a dark age when I scarcely knew you." Sally demurred but he reached over and took her hand and went on. "Oh, I'm not the saint you occasionally think I am. I really got a dressing down from the powers that be that time! You see, the food in Commons was simply unchewable, especially the meat, and we all grumbled about it. One day it was my turn to carve. A roast of beef was set before me. It looked well enough, but when I started in with the carving knife it just bounced off as if I had tried to carve a solid rubber ball. I simply got up, marched to the window, and chucked the whole thing out. The fellows burst into applause and we all signed a petition requesting better food. But the provost wasn't impressed, and I was sent for to give an account of myself. Well, the chancellor didn't expel me and the food did seem to improve slightly. Here I lie, madam, a culprit at your feet. Would you deign to punish me with a kiss?" Sally obliged.

Sometimes they turned grave and confessed to each other their misgivings about their parents. When they had become engaged and their friends and relatives heard of the young people's determination to go to China, they were aghast. Sally's dearest friend had exclaimed, "Why, Sally, I can't see you as a minister's wife any more than I can the queen of Sheba! You must be out of your mind to go to China, of all places! Whatever has gotten into you?" Her sisters had depended on Sally to be a companion to their widowed father and still thought of her as a little girl. Sally herself had grave misgivings about leaving him, though he would be physically well cared for by the house servants, who had been with him as long as she could remember. (In this French Huguenot household there had never been slaves. When her great-grandfather Henri De Saussure came across from France to

America in 1761 he had vowed that he would never own a slave. The family had carried on the tradition. Being professional men and not planters it had been easier for them to do this.) But in spite of sadness at leaving her father and distress at the disapproval of her relatives, Sally had felt strongly that God was calling her to walk this untried path, and she trusted him to make of her life something of use to her fellowmen and to his kingdom.

William, too, was troubled because of his mother. She had looked forward so, he knew, to his becoming a lawyer. And when he was admitted to the bar after his two years of study under Sally's brother, Henry A. De Saussure, she had been proud of him. That was before God stepped in and showed him what he wanted William to do. Once the decision was made, his mother had taken it well and given him her blessing. Brother John was such a bulwark of strength, managing not only the plantation but his own medical practice. And Tom—he still seemed like such a boy but he, too, now had his M.D. degree. Sister Eliza was living at home and teaching and would help her brothers take responsibility for the younger ones, he felt sure. He needn't worry and he knew, too, that God was watching over them. But William couldn't help longing for his family, as he knew Sally was longing for hers.

One evening they were sitting quietly on deck when Sally said rather hesitantly, "William, I wish you would tell me about your wonderful experience in Beaufort and how you came to decide to go into the ministry." Her husband smiled and replied, "That I will, my Sally. There is nothing I would rather talk about, for I think in my whole life I will never have a more wonderful experience. Let's see, I will have to go back to that summer. You know, I hadn't been able to spend much time at home those four years while I was going to college in your hometown and afterwards the two years in Charleston studying law. So I decided that before starting in with the law practice I would spend a little time at home with Mother and the small fry. They were all up at the summer cottage at Walterboro. I suppose that is the spot I love most in all the world, for so many happy memories of my father center there and of great times spent playing in the piney woods with John and Benji. Well, I hadn't been home very long before Mother asked me to conduct the daily family prayers, as Father had always done. I felt like a fool with all those big-brother-worshipers, especially Mary and George-Fraser, gazing up at me and hanging on every word. I knew myself a hypocrite, for I didn't understand what I was reading to them from the Bible. So I took to reading it in private so that I might know what I was talking about. Of course, I had heard it read all my life, but I had just taken it as a string of good stories and hadn't applied it to present-day living, nor to my own life. I read the New Testament and felt a profound respect for Jesus as a man. His love of truth, his courage, and forthrightness impressed me. To be a man like him would be something to strive for. But I had no inkling at that time that he could come into my life to make a new person of me. When my vacation ended I went down to Beaufort to join the law firm and start practice, feeling a bit insecure in a strange place. On Sundays out of habit I went to church at beautiful and historic Saint Helena's."

Sally interrupted. "Yes indeed, I know it well. As you know, my grandfather's home is in Beaufort and I have been there often."

"Yes," William continued, "I know. Well, as I was saying, the Reverend Joseph Walker was the rector of Saint Helena's, and he gave me a warm welcome. Not long afterwards I had the honor to be invited to attend the Whist Club, an exclusive group of young professional men who met once a week for no other purpose that I could see but to have a good time. This was attempted by playing cards and drinking a good deal of brandy. I attended as a good way to get acquainted with young men my own age, but did not much care for their concept of what constituted a good time. One morning at the church service Mr. Walker announced that a series of evangelistic meetings was to be held at the Methodist Tabernacle and urged his congregation to attend. I had no intention of going to any such meeting. I had no understanding then of what I now know, that 'God moves in a mysterious way his wonders to perform.' One evening while the meetings were going on I attended the Whist Club. One of the fellows, a bit tipsy I fear, pushed back his chair after several hands had been played and said, 'This is dull, my hearties. Let's go out and find some fun.' Another spoke up. 'There's some sort of a hell-raising meeting going on at the tabernacle; let's go over and break the thing up for a lark.' We went, but it broke us up instead! The minister preaching was a young man, the Reverend Daniel Baker, a Presbyterian. There was none of the ranting in his speech or manner which we had expected. He spoke quietly but with deep conviction. As I listened a sense of the rightness of what he was telling me gave me a sense of excitement. It came to me as a joyous revelation that salvation through Jesus Christ was meant for me. He spoke of the forgiveness of sin, of reconciliation with God, and of putting oneself wholly in God's hands so he could mold and guide and use each of us, 'Until we all attain unto the unity of the faith and of the knowledge of the Son of God, unto a full-grown man, unto the measure of the stature of the fullness of Christ.' This was indeed a challenge. I went again the next night, as did most of my Whist Club comrades. I took the step of humble confession and experienced the joy of cleansing and acceptance into his love by my Lord and my God. You know what I mean, my beloved, for you have experienced it too. That is the beginning of my story, and from now on we go on together, led and used for the coming of his kingdom by him whom we both love."

Sally breathed, "Now I understand."

They were silent for a moment. Then William exclaimed, "I mustn't forget the postscript. The results of those meetings were amazing. The whole town was stirred to its depths. There had been a formalism in the churches which kept people from each other and from God. This melted away. Feuds were forgotten and pride confessed. New life was born.

On his first visit to Beaufort after the meetings Bishop Bowen of the Episcopal Church found seventy persons, among them many of my friends, asking for baptism or confirmation. Very many more, both Whites and Blacks, joined the Methodist, Baptist, and Presbyterian churches." William's voice was filled with a ringing gladness as he went on. "I felt at once that God was asking me to give up the dry matters of the law and an easy berth in Beaufort. I didn't know how he wanted to use me but I felt he was asking me to take a first step by entering the theological seminary at Alexandria, Virginia, to be better prepared. There was just time to apply and get there for the fall semester. So I went, and those two years gave me a rich experience indeed.

"Friends made there were one of the most gladsome gifts God gave me. And among them there stands out Augustus Lyde, whom I met so briefly but who had such a tremendous influence on the direction my life has taken." William paused, then went on with deep feeling. "How can I let you see him? He was a glowing coal of love for Christ. No one could help feeling the warmth and the light of God in his presence. And yet his life was so short. Do you remember when we were in Philadelphia a few days before we sailed? When I took you to the churchyard of Saint Peter's Church to see his grave? I will never forget the inscription on his tomb: Sacred to the memory of the Rev. Augustus Foster Lyde, a Deacon of the Protestant Episcopal Church in the U.S., who was born in Wilmington, N.C., February 4, 1813. It was in his heart to preach the gospel to the Chinese, and for this service he had offered himself to God and the Church; but it pleased his Heavenly Father to call him home early and he died aged 21. Patient, cheerful, victorious through the faith of Jesus Christ." For a long moment William was silent; then he said in a voice charged with feeling, "Sally, we must never forget nor let others forget that Augustus Lyde was the real founder of the Episcopal Church mission in China."

CHAPTER 3

JAVA, SPRINGBOARD TO CHINA

A feeling of excitement seized all on board the *Louvre* as their course turned from southward to due west. As they drew near New Guinea and the many islands scattered through the Caroline Basin the captain grew uneasy. There were pirates in those parts and tales of headhunters persisted. It would be a bad place to have a shipwreck! Neither Captain Grey nor the first mate appeared at table for several days; they were too busy piloting the ship. But the wind was kind, they were not becalmed, and they threaded their way through the Makassar Strait without incident. The passage had been an exceptionally quick and peaceful one, taking only 106 days to traverse the sixteen thousand miles they had traveled. At its end William wrote to the board:

Mrs. Boone and I were blessed with a remarkably pleasant voyage. After leaving the last port on the U.S. coast we did not encounter a single storm the whole way across the Pacific. The Captain told me that it never blew so hard at any time that he could not have carried top-gallant sails, even though it was the season of the Fall equinox. "After all," said the seamen, "it has been good luck to have a woman aboard. Even the Preacher hasn't done us any harm!"

In the milky light of dawn on October 22, when William and Sally came on deck they were overjoyed to find that the ship lay at anchor near a stone quay built on low-lying mud flats. Beyond the silted harbor stretched a sea of green, and far beyond they distinguished blue cones of volcanic mountains. They had learned that the city of Batavia lay nine miles inland, up the Tjiliwung River. Their friends and forerunners, Lockwood and Hanson, were not there to meet them nor had they expected them to be. They could not know when the ship would come into port. But it was a comfort to know that as soon as they reached the city there would be old friends waiting to welcome them and show them the ropes.

When the moment came, Sally and William found they were strangely reluctant to leave the ship. They had enjoyed the leisurely voyage which was, in fact, their deferred honeymoon. They felt loath to leave all their new friends too, Captain Grey in particular, Jerry, and many of the crew—yes, and even the cat. But when they once got ashore and into the little pony cart, or *sadoe* as they learned it was called, which would carry them the nine miles to Batavia, they soon forgot the ship in the rush of new sensations. The rocking motion they had become accustomed to on the sea was compensated for by the jolting and bumping of the springless cart over the rutty road. As soon as they passed a line of warehouses fronting the quay they emerged into a green world. Lines of tall palms bordered the roadway. Beneath them were clustered cool green banana trees with bannerlike leaves. Beyond stretched swampy ground which soon gave way to cultivated fields, with here and there a group of cottages seemingly built of woven bamboo and looking for all the world like little baskets. They went by one close to the road, and Sally was enchanted to see happy brown children tumbling at play in the dust. A woman sat in her doorway weaving a basket and a group of men in the back yard were working on a new boat. Every instant there was something new to see! Always the houses were shaded by trees whose names they did not yet know: feathery masses, towering trunks, and a tree so aflame with blossoms that all the leaves were hidden.

They eventually came to the edge of town, where the houses started to crowd more closely. People walked barefoot in the roadway carrying produce in to the bazaar, men and women alike dressed in the tight-skirted sarong, variously and beautifully patterned in rich brown, indigo, and white. A long scarf to match the sarong was passed under the arms of the women, crossed, and knotted at the back, thus covering them from the armpits to the waist. Sally saw a woman who had slung the loose end over her shoulder, making a hammock in which she carried her baby. Most of the men wore a square of cloth covering the head and tied at the back to make a sort of cap. There were narrow brick-lined canals running parallel to the street where women were washing clothes. Things went at a leisurely pace, and the people chatted gaily to one another as they moved in little groups or stopped to greet a friend. The newcomers were fascinated.

Before they knew it they had entered a long street of more substantial one- and two-story buildings fronted by pillared and roofed sidewalks. The cart clattered up to a doorway and stopped. Climbing down from his perch the driver announced that this was the Chinese school, to which he had been instructed to take them. Even before William and Sally could climb down from their hard seats they could hear the students chanting their lesson in a high singsong. Entering the rather dark room they saw the backs of some twenty boys, each intent on his book. The Chinese teacher sat facing them at the end of the room. This was a thrilling moment. Neither of them had seen a Chinese before in their lives and here was a whole room full of them! At last they might be of some service to China. It flashed through William's mind that perhaps one of these very boys might grow up to be a leader among his people. The teacher rose and bowed to the guests, motioning them to come forward. The boys turned to look at them, forsaking their printed characters, and the rhythmical chant died away. Intelligent and keenly interested faces were lifted to the two visitors. Everyone guessed who they were, for new people were a rarity and it had been announced that two teachers from America were soon to arrive, although nobody knew just when. The schoolmaster motioned to one of the boys and he left the room, returning almost at once with Henry Lockwood. He gave them a warm greeting and introduced them to Mr. Yang and the pupils, in Chinese. They were led into an inner room where a class of nine little Chinese girls was being taught by a lady of the Dutch Reformed Mission who had volunteered her services. Sally loved the shy little girls on sight. They were so pretty!

By this time the driver had followed and now squatted humbly outside the door, pleading with big brown eyes to be noticed. Henry saw him and stepped to his side. He said something in Malay, and Henry reached into his pocket and got out a florin with which he paid him. After another word or two he bowed politely and left. The driver had reported that the larger cart with their luggage was following and would be along presently. It was nearly noon, so after they had looked about the very simply equipped school, Henry suggested that they go up to the bungalow and have some lunch. On the way he explained that he was still living at the Medhursts', as they had been delayed in England and had written their son-in-law please to consider their home his until they should return. Indeed, plans were uncertain for there was some thought that they might be stationed not in Batavia but in the Portuguese colony of Macao, on the southern China coast. For the present, at least, Henry urged the new missionaries to stay with him.

Sally was excited as she walked up the garden path, fragrant with blossoms. She noticed the fruit trees framing the quaint little house. This would be home. Henry's servant, Amat, a Javanese, came out to meet them and they went up the steps and into the cool, shaded retreat. Henry had long since prepared the Medhursts' large bedroom for them. Lunch was soon ready. There was a bowl heaped with strange and beautiful fruits in the center of the table, and Sally could scarcely wait until the meal was over to sample them. Henry recommended the dark purple mangosteens, which were just coming into season. She cut the thick rind and found the two halves lined with delicate pink and filled with creamy white meat in five distinct lobes. She thought she had never tasted anything more delicious than the perfumed yet delicately tart "ice cream fruit."

In the afternoon there was a heavy thundershower, for the monsoon had begun. The rain came down in torrents and the air was hot and steamy. But when the sun came out everything glistened and sparkled. Sally was eager to get into the garden and track down a delicious yet strange fragrance which filled the air. She found the tree, an ilang-ilang laden with waxen blossoms, growing near their bedroom window. She recognized the name as that of a perfume currently popular in the United States. Both she and William were overjoyed to learn that mail from home had already arrived. A vessel, the *Omega*, had come in a few days before from New York. Although she had sailed later than the *Louvre* she had made better time by not running up the coast of California, but by striking due west from South America. The most precious letter for Sally was one from her father. She read:

Warm Springs, No. Carolina
July 15, 1837

My dear daughter, Sarah Amelia;
Your letter written from Boston followed me to Greenville and thence to these salubrious springs, and I was glad to see your handwriting for I had not hoped to see it for many a long day. One of the greatest pleasures left to an old man is that of frequent communication with those dear to him. But I fear the great ocean which now separates us will let that form of enjoyment come to me sparingly. You are now fairly launched on your distant and perilous jour-

ney. I am praying daily that you will pass through its dangers safely and reach the land where you feel your duty calls you. I have doubts as to your success among those strange people the Chinese, but I respect the fervent piety and devotion to duty which you and William show. I am enduring this separation with patience and resignation. May God's will be done.

The baths here are very salutary, their temperature about 100°. The habitual range of the thermometer is from 60° to 70°. The mountain air is pure and bracing. Through these varying means, by God's blessing, I am very much improved, sleeping and eating better. Do not be concerned about me.

It was a joy to me to see your sister Eliza and brother John when they came home to bid you farewell. Your Uncle John and the boys are with me here. Remember me kindly and affectionately to your husband. May God grant you both his blessings of health and fulfillment.

Your affectionate father,

Henry W. De Saussure

Sally wept as she read it.

William was anxious to start learning to speak Chinese as soon as possible. He was taken to call on Mr. Lin, Hanson's teacher. After a cup of tea and the assurance that Mr. Hanson was staying in the country and would not be studying for the present, he accepted William Boone as his pupil. He chose for him the Chinese surname "Boon" (pronounced Wen in Mandarin), meaning "literary accomplishment." He selected it, of course, because of its similarity in sound to the English surname. William was pleased with it, for it is a graceful and easy character to write and its meaning challenged him to achieve! Since Mr. Lin hailed from Foochow he spoke the Fu-kien dialect, upon which they embarked at once. The characters which William had learned on the boat gave him a head start, and he was glad to learn to pronounce them now.

Sally did not offer to take upon herself the direction of the housekeeping, as she saw at once that she knew almost nothing about procedures and methods in these strange surroundings. She was amused on her first morning there to behold Siti, the wife of Amat, skating over the wooden floor of the dining room before breakfast, half a coconut shell tied to each foot, polishing the floor. Amat was standing by the side door with Henry's shoe in his hand. He was actually polishing it with a piece of purple mangosteen rind. The results achieved by both were excellent. Even at breakfast in the coolest part of the day it was a comfort to have the large linen punkah, like an elongated fan suspended from the ceiling, swung back and forth to stir up the air. Siti sat out on the verandah and pulled the rope with an easy rhythm. The newcomers learned that a ripe papaya half is a good way to begin breakfast, and the straight little trees with the fruit growing directly out of the side of the trunk were pointed out to them outside the window.

It soon became apparent that while William was busy for nine hours a day with his teacher, Sally had best study Malay so that she might both be able to converse with the servants and later take over the class of little girls. It was not long before she met a young German missionary, Mr. Barkenstyne, a friend of Henry's. He assured her that Malay was not hard to learn—a soft musical dialect that had been reduced to an alphabetic Romanized script so it could easily be read. He offered to teach her, and they set up a regular class period. She learned readily and enjoyed the study, practicing each new word on smiling Amat and Siti. Sometimes she tried it out too on the occasional peddler who strayed in to display his intricately woven baskets, lengths of hand-printed *bat tek* or batik which had so captivated her in the sarongs of the women, or almost irresistible carvings in exotic and often sweet-smelling wood. The egg man and fruit man came each day to the door also, but for all else Amat had to make a trip every morning to the *passer* to buy what they needed. Sally occasionally accompanied him and reveled at the riches of the earth spread out before her. There were great round baskets heaped with coconuts, the large balls of breadfruit or the rank-smelling jackfruit, looking like huge green olives. Stalks of bananas and delicious pineapples, mangoes, rose apples (from which her Dutch friend had told Sally delicious jelly could be made as well as from guavas) were heaped up.

But the fish department was the most colorful. Displayed on shallow rattan trays were fish, large and small, of every color of the rainbow. Amat picked out one striped in red and white which Sally dubbed "pajama fish" for want of a better name. They would have it for *riz tavel* or lunch. The vegetable department showed gray taro roots something like potatoes, long slim lotus roots curiously jointed, onions, and a variety of greens. More than all else there were piles and piles of rice and all the condiments used to eat with curry—curry and rice being, as she was learning, the staple diet of the people and the dish Amat most liked to serve them. She watched a woman buy some peppercorns. The trader weighed them out on tiny scales, took up a piece of banana leaf, and deftly made a little bag which he secured with a cactus thorn for a pin, poured the pepper in, and handed it to her. The market so fascinated Sally that she could scarcely tear herself away.

When Francis Hanson learned that the Boones had arrived in Batavia he bid farewell to his Dutch friend and host in Depok and came back to town. He looked bronzed and well, and Henry hoped that he would now be ready to settle in and prepare himself for eventual service in China, as they were all doing. But at his first meal with the three he told them that he had written to the Foreign Board in New York telling them of his inability to learn the Chinese language and saying that he would like to return home for future service there. He had but lately received their reply giving him permission to leave, and they had even arranged passage for him through Captain Richardson of the ship *Brooklyn*, about to sail for Java and points west. They could not tell when it would arrive in Batavia, but Francis should be ready, as the company was granting him a free passage.

He seemed elated about it. When the others heard this they immediately set to work writing letters for him to carry home for them. The ship arrived early in January 1838, and they bid Francis a reluctant farewell.

William and Sally had been in Batavia less than a month when they wrote their first letter to the Mission Board. One paragraph is as follows:

> Mrs. Boone and myself are both happy in the anticipation of being permitted to do our Master's work in these ends of the earth. Far from being chilled by disappointment upon seeing with our own eyes, all our expectations with respect to opportunities of usefulness are more than realized. We need nothing, I am satisfied, but a thorough knowledge of the language to do here all that man can do anywhere else toward the salvation of his fellow creatures, viz. make known to them, with humble reliance on God for his blessing, that Gospel which is the power of God unto salvation to everyone that believeth.

On Saturday his teacher, Mr. Lin, and William took time off from Chinese, and Sally and her husband often made a holiday of it. They went sightseeing and were surprised as they entered the Arab quarter to learn that the cool blue and white mosques had been there since 1475, when the Muhammedans conquered Java. That explained why so many of the Javanese professed the Muhammedan religion, including Amat; but they seemed to take their religion rather lightly. They saw the old warehouse and the walled city and spent hours in the stimulating halls of the Batavian Society of Arts and Sciences, inspired by Sir Stamford Raffles when Britain held a short but successful tenure in Java. They went to the museum on broad Koenig's Plein and marveled at the Javanese antiques, arts, and crafts on display. But there seemed little else of interest to see in town, so they took to packing up a picnic lunch and making Saturday excursions up the river or out toward the Blue Mountains through the wonderful countryside. Sometimes Henry Lockwood and Mr. Barkenstyne accompanied them.

They all reveled in the great variety of trees: the tall straight palms that clattered their fronds at the slightest breeze, making castanet music, kapok trees with pods bursting with their gift of cotton, the green trunks of giant bamboo, which yielded a hundred articles for daily use by the people, including their houses. The birds that called and flitted in the branches caught their attention. They learned the names of only a few—the scarlet minivers like darting flames, the crimson and black orioles, the graceful Java pigeon with the incredible aigrette of sparkling sapphire which swayed on its slender stem like a lovely fan. There were noisy cockatoos too, and once in a while they flushed a multicolored pheasant. They always returned refreshed from these jaunts and ready for the spiritual renewal of Sunday, when they went for worship to the English Chapel or occasionally to the Stadkirche. Once a week they met with others of the small missionary community for a prayer service. Sally was the only American woman in Batavia at that time.

Time passed quickly. On May 17 William wrote a letter to the board telling of his progress. He said:

I am, as you may suppose, almost exclusively engaged in the study of the Chinese. It is indeed most difficult to a beginner; I have not, however, met with any sounds that I cannot make. Some of them are made with great difficulty and after many trials, but practice is diminishing this. The whole class of nasals I have found particularly trying. The tones do not give me so much trouble, but they are exceedingly hard to remember. As yet I have not felt, to any great extent, the debilitating effects of the climate; but am able to study very nearly as much as I did at home.

The acquisition of the Chinese has, I think, in late addresses, been represented as much easier than it is. Mr. Medhurst (whose opinion I respect very highly), in his address published in the London Missionary magazine, says that a man of ordinary ability may speak it fluently in two years and compose in it intelligibly in four. I do not think that the facts sustain such a statement as this. Mr. Medhurst, from peculiar abilities, may have done this himself, but it is surely going too far to say that an ordinary man can do it.

Do not mistake this as the language of disappointment or discouragement. Both Brother Lockwood and myself feel encouraged in trusting to the infinite grace of our adorable Redeemer. We can say with the seventy, "We have lacked nothing, Lord." For myself I feel that if I can acquire the Chinese language, I would exchange stations with no one whatsoever; and I am determined, if God gives me strength to at least not fail my Christian friends. I have never been happier in my life than I have since coming here. I believe I can say with truth that when night comes it affords me as much pleasure to count my Chinese gains as ever a miser enjoyed in telling over his gold.

Sally's time was filling up, now that she was beginning to speak Malay with some ease, and she took on the class of nine little *paranake* or children of mixed blood. They came to her house for lessons three days a week, and she grew to love the gentle and eager little girls. William and Sally were both distressed when they learned of the slavery commonly practiced in Java. Mr. Lin approached them about an eight-year-old Chinese boy whose father had recently died and whose mother was forced into selling him to pay her debts. Mr. Lin said the boy, Tong Liang, was a bright little fellow and it seemed a shame. William felt strongly that the church would never be securely planted in China unless there was to be educated Chinese Christian leadership. Perhaps if this little boy were to be trained from childhood God might bless and use him. So they took the little fellow into their home and soon became very fond of him. It was a great disappointment when after a few months his mother, a Javanese, hounded by her creditors, came and took him away to sell him after all.

In November 1838, after the Boones had been in Batavia just a year, the Walter Medhurst family returned from furlough in England. Sally was particularly glad to see Mrs. Medhurst, for she was pregnant and needed the advice and friendship of an older woman. The Medhursts and Boones soon became very good friends. The younger couple looked at once for another house and were fortunate in finding one quite close by which was a good deal larger than the Medhursts, large enough to make it possible for them to take other boys into their home. William was immersed in his Chinese studies and Sally continued to keep busy with housekeeping and the class of little girls.

On June 8, 1839, she wrote to her father:

My beloved Father:

I write from my bed on my elbow to give you by this vessel the gladsome news that yesterday at 11 o'clock on the seventh of June, I was made the happy mother of a darling little boy after a tolerable time and having been surrounded by kind and affectionate friends and skilful medical aid.

O, my father, in that hour my heart was greatly sustained by our gracious Father and Friend. Oh, how much better to me than I dreamed in my wildest expectations—and if not for that I would have been under such a time of pain and trial.

My dear little boy is quite a fine, fat, fair and healthy child. He is like both families. We have named him Henry William and feel that our dear father will be gratified by our selection. We will send you a lock of his hair—he has a good deal of it and is a precious Boone to us.

I had my dear and excellent husband with me and my friend Mrs. Ennis of N.Y.—the wife of one of the missionaries of the Dutch Society of America, recently returned from Bally and the Eastern coast of this Island and who are staying with us. [Sally did not tell her father for fear of distressing him that Mr. Ennis had recently been captured by headhunters and decapitated while on a trip of exploration with a Javanese who escaped.] She is quite a lady, very pious and an affectionate friend and nurse. Thus, my dear parent, you will feel assured how comfortably I have been provided for in this distant land, away from all my natural friends under this trial. My own health for the last three months has steadily improved and I have been actively engaged in my ordinary occupations up to the night I was taken sick.

O Dear Father, help me to praise the Lord for all his tender mercies. From this period I trust my heart is newly awakened by his loving kindness and tender mercies to consecrate myself and all I have to him. This little darling I will consecrate to him too and endeavor by precept and example to raise him from day to day with a single eye to his external welfare and God's glory. May this world and its allurements be small in my eyes, that the Lord will enable me to do this. I pray you aid me by your prayers.

My dear husband's health is not very good. He has been suffering very much from his head again. But he is very prudent in his studies and is using such faithful means according to the advice of a physician who stands very high here. His mind is so composed that I trust we will be enabled to wait patiently on the Lord's dealings with us, trusting that all of his ways are leading us to Christ our Savior.

I feel very anxious to hear from you, dear Father. Our latest dates [on letters from you] are the 11th of November '38, and the winter and summer have passed, both trying seasons to your feeble frame. My heart often yearns to hear from you and know how your mind is sustained in these your latter days. Give much love to all of our dear brothers and sisters, friends and relatives. I hope soon to be able to write very fully. Now my want of strength reminds me to close my letter with devoted love to and ardent prayers for my dear Father.

Ever your own,

[signed] S. A. Boone

It is doubtful whether Henry William De Saussure received his daughter's letter telling of the birth of his namesake, for he died that same year. Nor was Sally ever to see his tomb in the Presbyterian churchyard of the Round Church in Columbia, South Carolina. He joined that church upon moving to Columbia, and Sally was brought up in it.

Henry Lockwood was not in Batavia when the baby was born. For some time he had been in poor health and decided that a vacation might benefit him. So in May he had gone over to Macao. He found the weather there very hot and did not improve as he had hoped. The wise course seemed to be to take a furlough in the United States, to which he returned, arriving there on September 5, 1839. He had studied Chinese diligently and had made good progress in the language and was most anxious to return, but his health did not permit it and in 1840 he reluctantly sent in his resignation to the board. The Boones felt bereft. They had lost a loved and esteemed brother and colleague. Before leaving Macao he had written a long letter to the Boones. He did not think the time yet ripe for them to transfer to China. He cited one big advantage, however, in living in Macao and that was that the sound of spoken Chinese was all around him. He wrote:

> Here the language is almost constantly sounding in the ears, there being very few moments in the day, and often but few hours in the night that its sounds are not heard, either from servants in the house or crowds on the street. But the dialect spoken in Macao is the Cantonese and if you some day hope to go up the coast of China, it would be best to stick to the Hok-keen [Fu-kien] dialect which you are now studying.
>
> Mr. Bridgman is here, having been in China for eight or nine years, and probably understands as much or more of the people and the language as any other missionary. The course he has pursued has been the only one, probably, in which he could have maintained so long a residence in the Empire. His quiet and unobtrusive labors may yet be found to have done far more for the ultimate benefit of China than those that have been attended with much more noise and eclat. *The Chinese Repository,* edited by him, you are acquainted with. Part of his time is devoted to local societies for the benefit of the Chinese. The influence of *The Repository* on the community has no doubt been beneficial. He has just published a brief compilation of the history of the United States in Chinese. The preparation of tracts and the revision of the Scriptures employ a part of his time. He has also living with him two or three boys, as servants, the only

capacity in which they are allowed to remain, but who are receiving a good English education. One of them has already a considerable acquaintance with the Hebrew, and promises in moral and pious character as well as talent, to become an important instrument in preparing an acceptable translation of the Hebrew Scriptures for his countrymen.

The Ophthalmic Hospital in Canton conducted by Dr. Peter Parker, is another mode of approach to the Chinese, which has been used with great success and has gained much popularity. The extent to which this instrument might be employed, were more men and means possessed, is perhaps almost unlimited. The Medical Missionary Society, formed here, has determined on extending the plan and Dr. Parker has just come down to Macao to commence operations in a fine new building which they have purchased here. I have myself, in particular instances, witnessed the marked contrast in respect and kindness on the part of Chinese manifested toward those in Medical mission work whom they had found to be their friends, instead of the usual contempt and disregard with which strangers are usually received in China. It seems to me imperative to extend these kindly impressions in order to counteract as much as possible the fatally opposing influences of the opium traffic. The annual introduction for some time past, of twenty million dollars' worth of this article, has probably done more, because of its deleterious effects upon the consumers and the consequent moral recklessness with which it does not fail to stamp the foreign character in the eyes of the Chinese and to confirm and perpetuate their unfavorable prejudices, than all the efforts of philanthropy and Christian benevolence will be able to overcome in very many years. The trade, moreover, is rapidly increasing, notwithstanding the efforts of the imperial government to prevent it, and so strong is the hold which the drug has acquired upon the appetites of the people and such the corruption which both its use and sale has effected among the provincial officers from the highest to the lowest, that all efforts to prevent its progress will probably prove to be of no avail. The Mandarins themselves are now the smugglers and foreigners have only to deliver to them the opium. More than twenty vessels of various sizes are said to be employed along the coast in this illegal traffic. When will the same zeal and courage be displayed in dispensing the means of salvation among the Chinese? Not, it is to be feared, until this terrible means of destruction has made an awful progress among them. Truly it is to be wished that those who call themselves Christians had the same zeal! By an American gentleman, Mr. Oliphant of New York, a prize of 100 pounds has been offered for the best essay on the opium trade [in an effort to expose its terrible effects].

With high respect and esteem,

Yours truly, Henry Lockwood

When William read Henry's letter he felt the urgent desire to proceed at once to Macao to offer his skill in medicine and the message of salvation in his heart and mind to the Chinese people, whom he was growing to love and esteem more and more. But that course seemed impossible for the present. With the departure of Lockwood the school and all the rest of Lockwood's responsibilities had devolved upon him. He could not desert them until he was able to find some other organization to whom he could turn them over, and there was none such on the horizon for the present. The school had been running for four years and now had forty pupils, some of them beginners, some more advanced. William felt that the students needed some stimulus to awaken them, for they had been in the custom of reciting their lessons by rote according to the old Chinese method and did not understand much of what they read nor put any thought into it. He commenced compiling a few questions on each day's lesson, which were given the boys the day before they were to recite. The following day he came to the school and asked for their interpretation of what they had studied. The Gospel of Mark in Malay was introduced as part of the daily curriculum. Each Sunday afternoon all the pupils were invited to the Boones' home, and what they had learned from Mark's Gospel was discussed in Malay so that the youngest children and the girls might have a share. Their teachers came too, and all seemed to enjoy and respond in interest to these informal afternoon gatherings.

Dr. Boone's time was still given to the study of Chinese, but he was giving some medical aid to patients who came to the house. Most were cases of "fever and ague," for malaria was very prevalent. He wrote to the board and asked them to forward twelve ounces of quinine, as what he had brought with him was used up. The cinchona was being grown experimentally at the botanical gardens, but no quinine was as yet to be had on the local market. William himself was in need of the drug as much as anyone, for he was suffering from repeated attacks of both malaria and the severe and prolonged headaches which were to plague him for the rest of his life. He felt quite discouraged and wrote the Foreign Board pleading that more missionaries be sent out to help carry the load and expand the work. The church at home seemed to have lost interest in the China mission before it had really begun. He and Sally received so little mail from home and felt quite cut off. Their joy was in little Henry, who was flourishing and who had become the pet of everyone, especially the devoted Amat and Siti.

In 1839, pursuant to William's dream, he and Sally took into their home fifteen promising Chinese boys to be members of their family. In January 1840 he wrote enthusiastically to the board about them. He reported that they were affectionate and obedient and that he was much impressed with the good behavior of Chinese children. The boys were allowed to go home every other Wednesday to spend the night at home so as to keep in close touch with their families. He says:

We are very much gratified to perceive the slow but constant evidence of the influence which the truths they learn are making on their minds. We are daily convinced of the very great importance that should be attached to such schools in those missions which seek to exercise an influence on and in China.

The return from England of the Medhursts, bringing with them new recruits for the London Mission, gave the Boones hope and joy. They moved to a house nearby to relinquish the Medhursts' home for their occupancy. This was a fortunate thing, for there was more room in the new house for their boys. In William's own words in a letter to the board dated January 31, 1840, he said:

> The progress of the boys in English has been truly gratifying and beyond our most sanguine expectations. They have devoted three hours a day to the English language under the tuition of Mrs. Boone and myself and six hours to the Chinese. Much the greater portion of their time, you perceive, is thus spent at the Chinese. This is necessary; the Chinese language is so difficult even to them that they learn more English in three hours than they do of the Chinese in six.
>
> At the close of the Chinese New Year, before dismissing the boys for a short holiday, we had an exam, in the English Chapel, to which Europeans and Chinese were invited. Our boys read, very well indeed, the 5th chapter of St. Matthew's Gospel in the English and translated it into Malay. They recited from memory the first catechism for children, answered questions on the multiplication table, and read from the New Testament in Chinese. The audience was delighted. I hope that this will inform the local community on what our school is doing and that we will soon be able to raise funds for it locally.

It was well that William wrote this letter to the board at home, for interest in the China Mission was definitely lagging. Progress toward actually entering China for mission work seemed so slow as to be almost hopeless. But William and Sally were not at all hopeless. The letter from Lockwood in Macao and now the return of London Mission personnel revived their purpose to be ready when God opened the door. The British East India Company's insistence on continuing to sell opium to China in the light of its demoralizing effect on the people who indulged in the habit seemed terrible. No wonder the impression the Chinese had of the foreigner was that of a barbarous creature, his only purpose seemed to be to get rich at China's expense. It seemed to William that opium as well as Chinese self-sufficiency were the two barriers presently keeping the word of God from being proclaimed in the land his heart longed for. But had not David said in his psalm, "Oh that men would praise the Lord for his goodness, and for his wonderful works to the children of men! For he hath broken the gates of brass, and cut the bars of iron in sunder (Ps. 107:16, KJV)." Surely God in his own time would open the gates to China. One had no right to be discouraged. Indeed, it seemed to him faithless to doubt God's purpose to let the light of the gospel fall on this great land in his own time. William would wait patiently for God's way to reveal itself.

Henry Lockwood's return to New York and his report to the board, as well as William's letters, changed the attitude of the board. They had even written the Boones suggesting that they transfer to another mission, possibly Liberia. But Henry's account of opportunities for work on China's doorstep at Macao changed their viewpoint, and in the fall of 1840 they wrote the Boones that if it could be arranged for the members of the London Mission to take over the work they had started, it was advisable that they proceed to Macao to serve there on a temporary basis in the hope that they might someday be able, by the grace of God, to enter China proper. William talked with Walter Medhurst, who said that while he himself was also awaiting going into China as soon as the way opened, his mission might well leave some of the new recruits in Batavia to carry on. They would be quite willing to add the Episcopal mission school for Chinese boys to the one they themselves had opened and to provide for the boys of the Boones' household. So William and Sally began making preparation for departure.

Packing up was no easy task. Sally felt the tug of parting with her friends even more than William, for her personal contacts had been greater, while he was largely immersed in the study of Chinese. She could not bear to part with the boys in their home or the little girls in her class, all of whom she had come to love. Then, too, what would she and little Henry do without the devoted Amat and Siti? She would be lost without them. When the boys' parents learned that the Boones were departing, in the generous Chinese way they showered them with parting gifts, together with expressions of regret at their departure and good wishes for the future. In February 1841, after three years and three months in Java, they boarded a vessel about to cross the South China Sea to Macao. The journey took them a month, but at last they were on their way to the very threshold of China!

CHAPTER 4

CHINA
MAINLAND

W hen the vessel which was carrying the Boone family from Batavia to Macao entered the great bay where the Pearl River empties into the South China Sea, anticipation rose in the hearts of each of the three. Henry, nearing the age of two, was charmed with the fishing junks near the shores of the many green little islands. Sally and her husband shared the joy of the approaching fulfillment of their dream. China at last! It seemed to them a very long time since they had left the United States in 1837, almost four years ago, with China as their goal. The ship rounded Barra Point and drew into the shallow harbor of Macao. Across the bay lay the rolling hills of southern China. Above them on Barra Hill stood the tall white tower of a lighthouse. William's attention was caught by the imposing façade of a starkly beautiful church, replete with pillars and arches. He had had news of the burning of the Macao cathedral, the Church of Sao Paulo, a few years ago; this must be it. It had been built, strangely enough, by Japanese Christians in 1602—possibly they were refugees from the persecution of Christians in Japan. Topping the miraculously undamaged façade the cross stood undaunted, outlined against the blue sky. William was deeply stirred by the sight. The church behind it lay in ruins but the cross of Jesus was eternal. He felt a sense of prophetic assurance in the fact that the first two things which met his eye in China were a lighthouse and a cross. It was this very sight which, a few years later, inspired Sir John Bowring, first governor of Hong Kong, to write his hymn "In the cross of Christ I glory, Towering o'er the wrecks of time."

While William was contemplating these things his little son, Henry, was crying "Mama, Mama, look!" as he pointed at tiny bamboo huts at water's edge. Inside each one squatted a fisherman manipulating a large net stretched between a square framework of bamboo poles. This he alternately let down into the water and pulled up, sometimes, if lucky, revealing a netful of jumping fish and shrimp. Sally anticipated fish for dinner. William was not to be diverted, for he was remembering bits of history Dr. Medhurst had told him before they left Batavia. It was only a few years after Columbus sailed westward that the Portuguese explorers thrust eastward in their square-sterned caravels flying the green and red flag of Portugal. At Malacca they met with Chinese trading junks and decided to push on to China, where they arrived in about 1514. But their lawless behavior at the ports where they attempted to start trade made them persona non grata. It was not until 1557 that, because they did the mandarin in power there a good turn by helping him fight off pirates, they were allowed to establish a trading post at Macao. On the rocky little peninsula there was an ancient temple dedicated to the goddess of fishermen, Ah-ma, at a tiny fishing village on the bay, (A-Ma Ngao). The name Macao may have originated from their interpretation of this name when they first landed. Trade with Japan was forbidden by the Chinese emperor during that period of history, so the Portuguese stepped into the breach and acted as go-betweens for Chinese merchants, selling their silk, tea, and art works for them and bringing back silver. They also carried the treasures of the Ming dynasty back to Portugal and on returning loaded their caravels with European cloth, clocks, mirrors, and cannon, which became popular items of trade in China. Thus they were granted a sort of leasehold at Macao by China and had managed to keep a foothold on the three-mile-long strip of land to this day.

William's reverie was interrupted by a gentle tug at his arm. Sally was calling his attention to the fact that the ship had dropped anchor. They hurried to the cabin to prepare for disembarking. Chinese coolies soon came aboard to help them with the luggage, and they were hustled ashore. The leisurely pace of Java, it was apparent, did not prevail here, at least not with these competing coolies! Since they had not as yet met any of the resident missionaries, they had decided to go directly to the hotel and stay until such time as they could find living quarters. They engaged a *carroca*. The old brown pony drew the carriage slowly up Avenida Almeida Riberio, where the shops were, and along the stone-paved street on the bluff of the ancient Pousada de Macau. Chinese waiters in white jackets came out to meet them and they were ushered into the high-ceiled lobby, where the manager met them with a warm smile and the greeting, *"Comprimento."* He informed them that *alamoco* would be served between twelve and one and escorted them to their imposing chamber with windows affording a view of the bay. At noon they were served at a round table on the balcony. Two or three other groups, evidently Portuguese, were seated at nearby tables. A delicious shrimp soup, *sopa decamarao*, started the meal, which was followed by a filling chicken and rice dish called *arroz gordo*. The meal was served family style and they were not offered a menu.

The Boones' stay at the hotel was not as long as they expected, for the next afternoon the Rev. Elijah Bridgman of the American Congregational Mission, of whom Henry Lockwood had written them, called. He cordially invited the family to stay with him for the present and indicated that before long a missionary residence now occupied by three families would have a vacancy, as one family was soon to return to England. They accepted his kind offer and were warmheartedly received by Mrs. Bridgman and the three American children: Elizabeth, Mary, and Fred. Henry was delighted to see other children and after a short period of hanging back, let Elizabeth take his hand and lead him away to play. Mrs. Bridgman assured Sally that the children's beloved ayah would keep watch over them.

The Boones were ushered into the Bridgmans' modest drawing room and they all settled down to get better acquainted. After answering questions by their hosts as to their home background and their stay in Batavia, William asked, "Will you be so kind as to tell us, Mr. Bridgman, how things now stand in regard to the friction between the British and the Chinese emperor over the opium trade?"

"That," replied Mr. Bridgman, "is the burning question of the moment. The emperor, alarmed over the drain of silver out of China, the terrible addiction to the drug spreading to rich and poor alike with its easy availability, and most of all, perhaps, because of the death of a prince of the royal house from the effects of opium, has issued several edicts prohibiting its import, sale, and use. But there seem to be no results, for the drug still flows into Canton in a steady stream. I fear some of the very officials appointed by the crown to control the trade are growing rich through condoning it."

"I have heard that British and other foreign merchants are all restricted to carry on their trade at Canton only," put in Sally. "How far is Canton from Macao?"

"Only sixty miles up the river," Mr. Bridgman replied. "There have been attempts made to extend the trade to Amoy, Ningpo, and other places, but these have failed. Since 1757 trade with foreign agents has been confined to a narrow strip of land on the riverbank outside the city of Canton. Nationals of other countries are not allowed to enter the city, and trade can only be carried on with a designated group of merchants called the Co-hong. The British have chafed under these restrictions and under the contemptuous way they are regarded and often treated by the Chinese. The real problem is,

I think, not the opium trade, but a conflict between two powers, each considering herself the greatest. China believes herself to be at the center of the universe, 'The Middle Kingdom.' The earth being square, all other countries are on the mere fringes of China and are inhabited by barbarians. Trade is beneath the dignity of the emperor, and foreign countries are patently made up of small traders, for any who come to China are in search of trade. As for England, since the advances made by the industrial revolution and her colonial expansion overseas, she has become 'Great Britain.' Restrictions and slights, especially from the 'heathen Chinese' are very hard for her to swallow."

"Is Captain Charles Elliot still the British superintendent of trade?" asked William.

"Yes, I know him well," was Mr. Bridgman's reply. "He is often here in Macao. He has tried to pursue a conciliatory policy toward the Chinese, but I hear there are those in parliament who oppose this and I fear he may soon be replaced. Events of the past two years have been warlike enough in any event. Two years ago the emperor of China took a strong stand, though he had opposition at court by the empress and her party, and ordered the opium trade abolished. He sent Lin Tse-hsu as special commissioner to Canton with orders to stamp out the opium trade. Lin was a man of action and proceeded to carry out his orders. Learning that the foreign merchants had much opium on their ships and in the warehouses, he declared it all contraband and demanded that it be turned over to him at once. He surrounded the foreign 'factory,' as the trading post was called, with his soldiers, allowed no Europeans to leave there, and stopped supplies of water and food. All foreign opium dealers were commanded to sign a bond against importing opium—on pain of death. Captain Elliot, wanting to avoid a clash, ordered that the stocks of opium be handed over, and Lin collected 20,291 chests of the drug and had it burned."

"And how did the British merchants react to that?" exclaimed William.

"They were outraged, of course, especially since much of the opium was owned by firms in India for which they were the agents," continued Mr. Bridgman. "Captain Elliot thought the Chinese went too far in demanding that the bonds be signed and refused to let anyone do so. Until British policy could be decided all trade was stopped. To the credit of America, her merchants did sign bonds pledging not to sell opium. This was an embarrassment to the Chinese, for there was other trade besides opium—tea, silk, porcelain, and the like. After six weeks the siege on the factory was lifted and the British all left either for Macao or their ships, some of which were at anchor in a good natural harbor forty miles across the bay from here, off an almost uninhabited island called Hong Kong or 'Fragrant Harbor.' Our Portuguese governor became alarmed when Lin threatened to drive the British from the coast and announced that he could not be responsible for their safety. Hence the Brtish community nearly all took refuge on the ships in Hong Kong harbor."

"Did the British ladies have to live on the ships too?" asked Sally.

"There were very few of them in any case, for women were forbidden at the factory, and few men risked bringing their wives out from England," Mr. Bridgman answered. "Poor Lin was rewarded for trying to do his duty by being demoted and sent into exile in disgrace. He was replaced last year by a new commissioner, Keshen, a Manchu. Elliot tried to negotiate with him a trade treaty and asked for permission to reside on the island of Hong Kong, but it all fell through. Lord Palmerston, then the foreign secretary and connected with trade interests in parliament, was not satisfied with Hong Kong anyway. He called it 'a barren island with hardly a house upon it.' Right now we are at a stalemate and do not know which way the wind will blow. Let us hope and pray with all our hearts that peace will prevail and that each of these great nations will respect the other's rights. Oh, why should the British mercantile interests, through greed, be allowed to present to China such a false picture of England

and, by inference, of all Western nations?" In agitation Mr. Bridgman got up and paced the floor exclaiming, "And to think that we Americans have had a share in it too, albeit small. When the British merchants had to leave Canton after the siege of the factory, Americans who traded in commodities other than opium were able to stay and assisted the British to dispose of their cargoes of varied merchandise from England. So the Chinese picture all Western nations as being in collusion against them. It is all wrong, I tell you. We have good things to offer China, and we offer them this offal of opium!" He glanced at the ladies and resumed his seat, apologizing to them for becoming overwrought.

At this point Mrs. Bridgman observed that Sally was looking anxious. She leaned forward and said to her, "My dear, let us go and see what the children are up to. The men can finish the rest of the talk." Sally was willing to leave, and they excused themselves and went out. It was quite evident that Sally was pregnant and her hostess felt that she had had enough.

The men were so engrossed that they scarcely noticed their departure. "There have been many incidents," Mr. Bridgman went on. "Sailors go ashore and get involved in brawls. While Lin was still here there was a serious one. A Chinese was killed, and heartened by Elliot's conciliatory stance, Lin demanded that the British culprit be handed over to them for punishment. Elliot replied that in a brawl involving sailors of different nationalities he did not know who had actually committed the murder. In any event, Elliot feared that Chinese law would deal harshly and, guilty or innocent, the prisoner would be in for torture and probable execution. Lin, on the other hand, believed he was right in averring that a crime committed on Chinese soil should be tried in the Chinese manner." (Later Lin was rightly regarded by the Chinese people as a patriot.)

"But come, we must stop all this talk. The ladies will expect us in the dining room for a cup of tea. There is just one more thing I want to say," he went on earnestly. "You and I desire to introduce to the Chinese people the glorious gospel of our Lord, Jesus Christ. But first of all we must exert ourselves to understand their minds and their beliefs. They are not children but a race with an ancient culture of high quality behind them. Theirs is a treasury of literary achievement. We will never be able to penetrate their hostility toward us, for which they have ample reason, unless we show ourselves willing to learn from them. Let us pledge ourselves to learn for ourselves what God has entrusted to them before we offer them the gift God is entrusting us to carry to them. That is the reason I have devoted myself these ten years since arriving in China to the study of their literature and philosophy and am now engaged in printing the word of God for distribution." William never forgot these words.

William did not, for the present, look for a new teacher with whom to continue his study of Chinese. In Batavia he had been suffering for some time from severe headaches, and his doctor had recommended a long rest away from study. The trip across the China Sea had already given him some relief, but he decided he must stay away from books a little longer. Sally was glad to be in a household where she had no responsibilities for the time being. Mrs. Bridgman proved a warm and sympathetic friend and urged her young guest to stay with them until after the baby was born. She insisted that nothing would give her more pleasure than to assist Sally at that time. In this kind offer, feeling a stranger as she did, Sally took great pleasure.

So it was that William sallied forth to explore the small city without Sally, taking Henry with him. They walked up the Praia Grande and admired the pastel pink, blue, green, and yellow storybook houses of the Portuguese settlers, many of whom had lived there for generations. Garden walls were draped in festoons of bougainvillea vines laden with masses of magenta blooms. The firecracker vine showered tiny red trumpets hanging down from the branches of banyan trees which reached out over garden walls. Through half-closed gates they caught glimpses of gay flowerbeds. William thought it was like pictures he had seen of the Riviera. He was intrigued too by the grotto named for the Portuguese soldier-poet, Luis Vaz de Camoëns, where he was supposed to have composed one of his great poems. Henry was much more delighted when, on another day, they visited streets of Chinese shops hung with bannerlike signs declaring their merchandise. There was such a happy confusion: hawkers shouting their wares, the staccato clack of wooden sandals, gaily clad children darting between their soberly garbed elders, many of whom carried baskets of produce hung at either end of a pole. It was most exciting! At least 90 percent of the inhabitants of the town seemed to be Chinese, with a sprinkling of Portuguese, a good number of Eurasians, more Britishers than usual perhaps, since they had fled from Canton, a few Dutch and French and—fewest of all—Americans.

William was introduced to several of these foreigners by the Bridgmans and learned that their views of China and the Chinese differed greatly. One English gentleman said to him, "This is not an 'opium war' at all. It is a war to put China in her proper place. What right had she to treat Lord Napier like a common peddler when he came as a commissioner of the British crown? And what right had that antiopium agitator in Canton, Lin, to seize 24 million dollars' worth of British-owned opium, surround our factory with soldiers, and tell us to vow never to sell opium again? What bloody right has he to tell us what we can sell or not sell? The Chinese are responsible for all this mess. It is their muddling that has made this silly row. Their own mandarins have made money out of it and have kept the whole show going, not us." William wondered. It seemed to him it was the British merchant who was making the money.

China, naturally, took a very different view of the matter. The trade itself mainly concerned Canton, the port of entry, and Peking, the seat of government. But those who desired to buy and use opium, the consumers, were increasingly scattered throughout the country. The well-to-do could afford to buy it, and destitute sailors working on junks along the coast were said to be almost universally addicted to smoking opium, as it was easy for them to obtain and sell it. Its effects were devastating. Many stories were spread abroad as to the ruthless barbarians who wished to destroy the Chinese people by spreading this curse. It was told that they pillaged the coast, killed babies to get their eyes, and practiced many other atrocities. Children were frightened by the bogeyman foreigner, and hatred of them was generated by word of mouth and by posters proclaiming them devils. The term foreign devil became the common way of speaking of any non-Chinese. What right had they to impose their presence on a country that was not theirs and had not invited them to come? The surge of expansion of the nineteenth century, washing up upon China's shores, cast up much flotsam and jetsam, some of which proved harmful and some of great benefit to China. Nine-tenths of the population of China, it is safe to say, had never seen a non-Chinese in their lives and shuddered at the thought of ever encountering one. This early bad impression made it hard for foreigners in China all down the years. William gradually became aware of these differing points of view.

On April 27 the baby was born. Sally felt herself in the lap of luxury, for Dr. William Lockhart of the London Mission as well as her friend Mrs. Bridgman attended her. She and William were delighted that the baby was a girl and named her Mary Eliza. She had an animated Parisian look from the start, and Mrs. Bridgman declared laughingly that she looked exactly like her mother. William was extremely proud of his wife and daughter and prayed that they might be kept in safety through these difficult times.

The birth of the baby seemed to mark a fresh outburst of hostilities. The new commissioner from Peking, Keshen, was willing to negotiate a treaty with Captain Elliot, but when it was forwarded to Peking it was indignantly rejected by the emperor. The British again went into action, capturing the Bogue forts guarding Canton. In retaliation the Chinese launched flaming rafts at night, hoping to burn up the British fleet. But unfortunately the wind directed them toward the shore and several villages were set alight. The British fleet destroyed several Chinese war junks at the inner forts protecting Canton and threatened the city. At this point the Chinese retaliated by sacking and burning the British Trade Center, the factory, on the edge of Canton. On May 26 British troops commanded high ground behind the city, but before they could attack Captain Elliot proposed a truce. He did this because he was aware that the number of Chinese and Manchu troops defending the city far outnumbered his men. This did not please the authorities at home. He was recalled and Sir Henry Pottinger sent out to replace him as plenipotentiary. The new commander arrived in August 1841. At the same time Sir William Parker was given command of the British fleet.

When the baby, Mary Eliza, was a month old the Boone family moved into their new quarters, which they shared with the Browns and the young McBrydes. Little Julia Brown was only slightly older than Henry and they soon became fast friends. Sally inherited Dr. Anderson's cook and with the help of a good ayah took up housekeeping duties again. Provisions were in short supply because of the war and it took some contriving to keep the table furnished. The town was crowded with refugees. Not a few of the merchants at the factory in Canton, unable to have their wives with them, had taken Chinese, Malay, or Indian women, and these, together with their children, crowded into Macao. There were Chinese refugees too, especially the villagers whose homes had been so recently burned.

The usual summer diseases—malaria, dysentery, cholera, and typhoid—were rampant. Dr. Peter Parker's little hospital was crowded. He asked Dr. Lockhart and Dr. Boone to assist him and this they were glad to do. William was delighted to have this direct contact with Chinese individuals. He was impressed with their courage and fortitude in the face of tragic circumstances and painful treatments. His Chinese patients, however, did not come until their condition was critical and he was not always able to save them. Quinine, ipecac, calomel, Dover's powder, and castor oil were the chief medicines he had to work with. The three doctors knew of no way to save a cholera patient and had their best results with those suffering from malaria. Dr. Parker had already won much confidence as an eye surgeon and was besieged with applicants for cataract operations and for treatment for the very prevalent trachoma, which caused so much suffering and blindness. William was distressed by the many blind persons whom he met on the street. Often at night he heard the plaintive sound of a one-stringed bamboo violin accompanied by the tap of a blindman's stick as he wandered the streets. Being outwardly blind he was supposed to have inner sight and be able to see into the future. For this gift he was revered and was often called into a home in need of advice to offer them, for a small fee, his wisdom and insight.

This was a period of great joy and satisfaction in William's life. He felt that his days up to this time had been a period of waiting. He still hoped one day, perhaps soon, to get into China proper, where he could establish a permanent work of his own. Above all he would emphasize the spiritual message which he so longed to share with the Chinese. Since he was equipped with the Amoy dialect he could not preach here and be understood. Someday he and the family would proceed to Amoy, where he could preach God's word. But he was content for the present to be of real service in the medical field and realized the wisdom of spending those two years, which had sometimes seemed to go so slowly, at the medical college in Charleston. His observation and contacts, along with bits of Chinese lore and religious belief passed on to him by his colleagues, gave him a sense of gradually entering into Chinese life. Both admiration and compassion burned within him as he came to realize their inherent honesty, their patience and good humor, coupled at the same time with shackling superstitions and much dire poverty. He longed with all his soul to be of help.

But William's greatest joy came in the late afternoon when

he returned home from the hospital. Sally met him with the light of love in her eyes and smile. She was as fresh and dainty as a flower, and to keep her that way he would not let her touch him until he had changed his clothes after his contacts with disease at the clinic. Medical science of that day had no knowledge of disease germs but William did know that some diseases were undoubtedly communicable. When he returned to the drawing room Sally was usually seated at the tea table ready to pour his tea. Henry would come charging into the room riding his stick horse, shouting, "Papa, Papa." The ayah followed with the baby in her arms. William felt that no one could be more blessed than he and offered up a silent prayer of thanksgiving for the joys that gave him such a sense of peace and fulfillment. He was often asked to preach on Sunday at the English Chapel. After the service he and Sally would sometimes go into the adjoining cemetery and stand with reverence before the grave of Robert Morrison. William felt he owed so much to Morrison who gave him a start with the Chinese language through the dictionary and Bible which were William's textbooks aboard the *Louvre*. The graves of many British and American sea captains and men were in the cemetery. Sally felt sad as she read their headstones and realized that many of them had been mere lads, far from home when they died. She and William were both well acquainted with Robert Morrison's son, who came to call on them when in Macao. He was acting as interpreter to the British plenipotentiary, anxious to serve both the Chinese and the British in helping to bring about better understanding between them.

At these services the Boones met members of the British diplomatic community, officers of the fleet and an occasional sea captain who happened to be in port. To the latter they owed gratitude for many acts of kindness in the carrying and delivering of letters and packets. But for their good-heartedness there would have been no way to have news of the homeland or to send letters home. Among others at church they often saw the Gutzlaffs. William remembered with what interest he had read Dr. Gutzlaff's book *The Journal of Two Voyages* when he first thought of going to China. Sally was interested to learn that the Gutzlaffs, as well as the Bridgmans, had taken into their home a small group of Chinese boys to educate and train. While living at the Bridgmans she and William had become fond of their three boys, Ah-shing, Ah-kun, and Ah-foon. Sally had undertaken to teach one of their classes and, now that she was in her own home, offered to continue doing so. The boys were from Canton and they missed their own brothers and sisters. They enjoyed staying after class for a bit and playing with Henry and Julia Brown out in the garden. They made Sally think of her own boys in Batavia, and she often wondered how they were getting along. A letter from Mrs. Walter Medhurst in Batavia was most welcome, but Sally was distressed when the letter reported that the boys were not doing too well. She sensed that they were now on a boarding school type of regime and were not treated as members of the family, as they had been when she was there, and felt sorry. Still, she was glad that their education was continuing.

After the arrival of Sir Henry Pottinger things began to change in the war situation. He was of sterner stuff than Captain Elliot. He realized that the Chinese emperor in Peking, far to the north, had looked on the war as a local affair centered around Canton. Sir Henry and Sir William Parker decided to bring it to the emperor's doorstep. They directed that attacks be made on the coastal ports of Amoy, Chinhai, Ningpo, Woosung, and Shanghai.

These developments had a profound effect on the plans of the Boones and other missionaries waiting in Batavia and Macao and other places. After the British succeeded in taking Amoy, William's long-desired haven, he learned through Mr. Morrison that the people of Amoy did not seem as averse to the presence of foreigners as they were at Canton. They had been somewhat jealous of the trade monopoly held by that city and were anxious to extend their own trade. Many had been abroad to the Malay Archipelago and were not unaccustomed to dealing with people of other nations. When he heard this William decided to try to make an exploratory trip to Amoy as soon as possible. He did. After returning to Macao, where he had left Sally and the children, he wrote on May 11, 1842, to the Mission Board in New York as follows:

I wrote you in my last that the Rev. Mr. Abeel, M.D., of the American Board of Commissioners of Foreign Missions, who formerly worked among the Chinese in Siam, and myself left this place for Amoy on the first of February, at which place we arrived on February 24th. Our friend, Mr. J. R. Morrison, Esq., interpreter to her Majesty's commission, had kindly mentioned our going up to the Plenipotentiary, Sir Henry Pottinger, who offered to give us a letter to Major Cowper, the Commandant at Koo-lang-soo, Amoy, request- ing him to furnish us with a house and give us all facilities for prosecuting our labors. On our arrival, we were very kindly received by Major Cowper and were soon settled in a comfortable Chinese house.

In consequence of our knowledge of the language we were soon able to confer many favors upon the Chinese by inter- preting for them when they got into any difficulties and were carried before the commandant. Our arrival was on this account hailed as a general benefit, and the news of it seemed to spread far and near. Many came to our house daily to enquire about the new religion we came to teach and to ask for books, and in this way many heard of the only name under heaven by which we can be saved. Should this place, in the providence of God, be thrown open to missionary effort by the English taking possession of the Island of Amoy [this was written before the treaty was negotiated], or by the arrangements by which peace is con- cluded, there will not be a more desirable place in the Empire. I propose to go up with Mrs. Boone and the chil- dren at the first good opportunity. Let me entreat you to take advantage of this opportunity by earnestly endeavor- ing to procure some two or three of our younger brethren to come out speedily. I am at present enjoying a comfortable degree of health. Our winter is short and mild and is of inestimable value.

Sally felt William's absence from Macao sorely and wrote to him almost every day, sending the letters by obliging captains or friends. On the day of his departure, February 1, she wrote her husband:

My dearly beloved husband:

I commence this my first sheet to you on the evening of the day of your departure and I trust it will be early received by you and much lighten your heart to hear of us after our separation. This has been a long, long day for me. I have felt much depressed and much comforted at times, and have tried to apply continually to the source, Christ Jesus, for that comfort which must be drawn from Him alone to be sufficient to strengthen us to bear the trials and temptations which we meet here below. My children, my sweet children, oh how dear they have been to me this day! Thank Thee, Lord, for this blessing. Oh, that I may be fully awakened to the responsibility which rests upon me in being their mother, in setting before them by precept and example a Godly, sober and devoted life. Pray for me that this may come to pass.

Henry has been at my side the whole day, talking much of you. He says, "Papa will come presently, Mama. Can I go with Papa to the garden?" Then in the next sentence, "Shall I go to Hong Kong to ship to see Papa?" This day, dear Willie, I have commenced a new pattern before him, setting before me your advice and example of being more cool and attentive to his every wish and answering more carefully the least of his inquiries. Our friends in the house have been most tender and sympathizing to me, and have in the most affectionate manner offered me their services. This evening Mr. Bridgman with Elizabeth, Henry and Fred all paid us a visit and found us all in the garden. Mr. B. proposed that the prayer meeting should be held at our house as he believed more persons would be accommodated by its being here. So it was held here and a most grateful and solemn one it was, conducted by Mr. B. upon the importance of prayer. He used an appropriate passage from James' epistle. He showed the high privilege of meeting and praying for each other and then took a very bright view of the state of China at present, urging on all that most earnest and continual prayer be made for the entrance of the Gospel in China.

I was truly sorry to find your pillow left and was glad to hear that Mr. McBryde had got a pepper box for you. The least of matters concerning you, my dear husband, give me great interest and pleasure. Mrs. Hobson's Chinese teacher said that he would not leave her to spend Chinese New Year with his family in Canton until Dr. Hobson's return! Mr. Brown's teacher has gone to Canton for a few days. A-shing, A-kun and A-foon have returned from Canton saying they were obliged to come back for they could not stand the taunts of their friends, which were continual, for not worshipping the idols. It is better for them to be here. We have all to receive them warmly and to try to make the residue of their vacation, two weeks, a season of improvement and pleasure for them in every respect. Pray for these boys, dear, that this may be the beginning of an abundant life for them.

Sally's first few letters were addressed to Hong Kong, for William was delayed there for some time. But by March first a letter was addressed to Amoy, which reads as follows:

My dear William:

I cannot go to bed though it is quite late without writing to you and talking with you—and is it so that this day closes one month of separation between us? For me, dear husband, it has been heavy though not with discontent for I have been happy in the consciousness that you were doing aright in the Master's cause. I bless God that he has distinguished you and this not for the world's good opinion, though I do not hold that in contempt, as some do, for the good opinion of the good and wise is much to be desired, I think. But for His own good opinion which shall some day be your guarantee for entering into the place where glory and honor and rejoicing will ever pervade because there is the Father, the Son and the Holy Spirit.

The family are all quite well. Mr. J. R. Morrison and Mr. Brown went off yesterday to select a lot in Hong Kong. It is not that they will remove for a year or more, however. I am greatly engaged in the school and all the housekeeping and with my children. I am trying to study the Hokeen dialect daily, and again my good friends the McBrydes will make me judge for them in every matter which occupies me more than you could suppose. However, dear Willie, I must say your good advice has benefited me very much for I keep it all day in my mind and try never to be flurried tho' I may be hurried—and I am trying to feel comfortable in doing things a little more leisurely. You must know, our little darling Mary is in short clothes and greatly pleased is she with her little feet. She is very fond of the looking glass you know and now waves her hand to herself and is so much delighted to witness the action in the glass, all this at her own bidding! She is fatter and looks much more animated and knowing than when you were here, and her flesh is more firm. She has no more teeth though, yet. Henry talks much of you. He has had a very bad cold in his head, not in his chest, of which I am glad. The other day at table he said, "I have a very bad winter in my head." I think there is much association of ideas in this remark for he had often heard me say he had a cold in his head.

All friends are very kind to me here and all enquire most kindly after Mr. Abeel and yourself. Give my kindest regards to Mr. A. All unite in love to you. The little pets send kisses and your own Sally a great deal of affection and many anxious cares for you.

A few days later she added:

Mr. Morrison is very kind, frequently here. He said that he hoped to see me at Amoy. I trust you will find that in a very short time you may send for or come for your own beloved and little ones and may the Lord grant it. My heart is sustained, but oh, how rejoiced I would be could I think that there may soon be an end of this separation.

Late in April William returned to Macao with glowing reports to Sally of the house that awaited her coming on the quiet little island of Kulangsu, across from the busy island of Amoy. The house had been previously occupied by the Chinese military commandant of the island, who had been killed in battle. He had not been in favor with the village for he commandeered provisions for his troops. His family had fled to Amoy and the house stood empty, so Major Cowper had allocated it to them for the present. Mr. Abeel had taken his cook along, which had saved the day for the two men, but William confessed that he would be glad to eat something besides rice and vegetables after Sally took over! There had been a local man on the premises who told them he was the caretaker, and they had been glad to engage him in the same capacity. Sally was reluctant to part with her efficient ayah and hoped she would be able to find one in Amoy.

In May the family, with affectionate farewells to their housemates and many friends, who viewed their departure with great misgivings, embarked for Hong Kong on a British merchant ship. The distance between Macao and Hong Kong across the wide bay was not great, only forty miles, but they proceeded with caution and it took them nearly two days. The weather was lovely, and Sally was filled with rapture in having William beside her again and in drawing nearer to the realization of their long-delayed goal. Fishing junks passed close by, their amber-colored sails reflected in the blue waters of the bay. There were many islands in the distance but as they approached Hong Kong they drew so close that they could see the clustered cottages of fishing villages on rocky shores. At the very entrance to Hong Kong harbor there was a little island clad from top to bottom with the cool green of trees. Sally declared it ought to be named Green Island.

Several British ships lay at anchor in the harbor, most of them former British merchantmen now equipped with guns and part of the British fleet, the flagship of Sir William Parker standing out from among them. There were only a few dwellings to be seen on shore, for occupancy by the British had not as yet been granted by the emperor. There was said to be a Chinese fishing village around on the seaward side of the island. A high hill took up most of the island's area, and it was covered from top to bottom with a green jungle of trees and bushes. There were no accommodations on shore, and Sally was told that they would stay aboard until arrangements could be made for them to board some ship of the fleet going up the coast to Amoy. William went ashore to see if he could contact Mr. Morrison and again enlist his help. Sally rejoiced when he returned shortly with Mr. Morrison who wanted to see his good friends: Sally, Henry, and Mary. He told them they would not have to delay long in Hong Kong, for in two days a ship was proceeding up the coast and would stop at Amoy to put off stores for Major Cowper and his men. He already had permission for the Boones to proceed on board. It seemed to them that God was opening the way and they gave thanks.

So it was that on a hot June day they arrived at Amoy, situated on an island adjacent to the coast of southern China and directly across from the very large island of Formosa. As they passed the southern end of Formosa an officer with whom they were chatting told them that the people of Amoy, being great seagoers, had colonized Formosa and to this day depended upon it for their supplies of rice, their own area being too rocky for rice-growing. Amoy had long been one of the chief shipping ports of China. American clipper ships had been in the habit of stopping here for cargoes of tea and ever since had been dubbed "tea clippers." As they entered the harbor they were saluted by two British frigates lying at anchor and they returned the salute. The ship dropped anchor quite near the shore, and William and Sally could see that the houses of the city crowded right down to the embankment, at the shoreline. Junks seemed to be unloading their cargoes directly into the warehouses from their decks. When Sally asked her husband what he estimated the population of the city to be, he replied, "At least two hundred thousand."

The captain of their ship had papers to deliver to Major

Cowper. He invited the Boones to go with him in the captain's gig, so it was not long after the ship anchored that they were in the boat and alongside the other ship. A wave of excitement seemed to go through the sailors as they helped Sally and the children aboard, for they had not seen a foreign woman or child since they had come to Amoy three months previously. To Sally's delight an old friend, Walter, son of the Medhursts of Batavia, was on deck to meet them. He served as interpreter to Major Cowper, who was not surprised to see them for he knew that William Boone had left a month ago with the hope of returning with his family. The major received them most kindly and offered to help them in any way he could. William was already indebted to him for many courtesies, not the least of which had been finding a house for Mr. Abeel and himself. The major knew his guests were eager to get home and offered to send them across to the island of Kulangsu, which was only half a mile across the bay from Amoy. He said William could arrange for getting their duffle from the other ship at his convenience: Mary took a shine to the major's brass buttons and let him hold her while she tugged at them, to his evident amusement.

After they had partaken of refreshments a sailor announced that the boat was ready, and they were soon being ferried across the narrow stretch of water. The major's farewell was accompanied by the promise that he would pay them a call very soon. Sally liked the bluff but kindly soldier and was glad they would see something of him. She was in a great state of excitement when the boat touched shore, and she realized that here she would make a home for William, where he could do the work for which they had crossed the ocean: preach the gospel of their Lord and Savior, Jesus Christ. She sent up a fervent prayer that many might be saved.

The sailors offered to see them to their door, but William thanked them and said he well knew the way and that the villagers were friendly. It was indeed not far, for they could see the house at the head of the street at the end of a gentle slope. On either side were tiny shops with open fronts offering goods needed in the daily life of the villagers, who were nearly all either vegetable gardeners or fishermen. Baskets of rice, salt, beans, and sugar stood in front of one of the larger shops. The shopkeeper hurried out when he saw them coming, bowing to William and looking curiously at Sally and the children. Soon everyone seemed to have sudden business on the street and a small but curious crowd started to follow them. William turned and bowed to them all saying, "Elders and brothers, I have this day brought my family to live among you, knowing you to be sincere and friendly neighbors. Please come to our humble home at any time and you will be welcome." Sally saw the people smile and drop back a little. Some of them bowed and went back into their shops. Only the children continued to follow right up to the gate of their house. Henry was pleased and clapped his hands and shouted, *"Kung-hei, kung-nei,"* a greeting he had learned from his Cantonese ayah in Macao. The Kulangsu children may not have understood, but they clapped and pranced their delight. Old Wong, the caretaker, opened the gate, called out a word to the children which scattered them, bowed low to William and Sally, closed the gate behind them, and ushered them in. Sally found she was standing in an open courtyard flanked on either side by rooms. Straight ahead was a heavy two-paneled door which stood invitingly open and was evidently the front door. In it stood Mr. Abeel, smiling and extending his hand. He had been alone for the past six weeks and was glad to see William and to greet his family. They all stepped into a wide room with rafters high above their heads and a floor of dirt pounded until it was like cement. Wong had closed the heavy door, and the room was dim and cool after the hot sunshine outside. Sally made out stiff Chinese wooden furniture set in the Chinese manner along the walls, giving the room a look of ceremonial propriety. They were glad to sit down and talk with Mr. Abeel while Wong slipped out to tell the cook in the kitchen at the back to prepare tea, for the learned Si-sang and his Si-niang had arrived.

Sally could not sit still long as she wanted to see the house. Behind the reception room was a sort of pantry and behind that the kitchen, a large room, half of which was taken up by the clay cook stove. On top of the stove were huge black iron pots, fitted into holes over the fire. Sally thought to herself that she doubted if she could lift one of them and was glad that they had a cook. Against the wall were two large wooden buckets for carrying water from the well. A long wooden chopping block on legs occupied one side of the room. On it lay a heavy cleaver and various dippers and strainers. A section of bamboo which served as a holder for chopsticks hung on the wall. That was about all the equipment the cook seemed to have. Sally wondered how she would get along. Best let the cook take the lead in his own way at first.

She learned that the row of three rooms on either side were the bedrooms. She and William would occupy the three rooms on the right of the central reception hall, and Mr. Abeel and the cook would have the three on the left. Old Wong went home at night. Their bed, she discovered, was ornately carved, its wooden canopy rich with red and gold lacquer, linen curtains attached. But instead of springs there were boards over which a straw mat and a quilt were laid. Sally exclaimed, "Oh, my aching back," and laughed. Well, she thought, if the Chinese sleep on boards I reckon I can learn to. But I do believe their bones must be made of sterner stuff than mine are! She was glad they had brought along with them the wicker basket the baby was used to sleeping in.

As soon as Sally assured him that she and the children were comfortable William resumed his work with Mr. Abeel, going every day across the bay to Amoy to distribute tracts, talk with those who asked him questions, and get acquainted with those who appeared more than once, in the room on a main street which Mr. Abeel had been able to rent from a merchant during William's absence. Sally was feeling the need of someone to help with the children and conferred with her husband about it. Already curious people were coming to the house daily to take a look at the foreign woman with—of all things —red hair! Only devils had red hair. What could she eat to make it red? Human meat? They shuddered. And the little foreign devils. They were cute, as any little child is, but so pale and washed-out looking—even their eyes. The mother must not know how to feed them. Children and men came at first, then a few of the bolder farm and fisher women drifted in. Shopkeepers' wives from down the street found they were made welcome and came during the day when they were sure the men were away. As they became accustomed to Sally's queer looks and observed that her actions were fairly normal they began to ask the questions which bothered them. Were her children born in the same way theirs were? What did she feed them to make their skin and eyes so light? Sally replied that they ate rice gruel and eggs. They looked at each other and said, "Oh, could it be the eggs? We sell ours." They looked at her feet in neat leather slippers. The general's wife who had lived in this house wore the stiltlike shoes of a Manchu and did not have the tiny bound feet of a Chinese city woman. Their own feet were not bound but encased in homemade cloth shoes and a few were barefoot, for they were country women. At last a bolder soul inquired, "Would you let us see your feet? We have heard that foreigners have only one toe. Is this true?" Sally laughingly took off her shoe and stocking, and they were satisfied that perhaps she was not as different from themselves as they had thought.

But getting a woman to consent to coming to stay and help her was a different matter. William suggested that she ask old Wong (the "old" was a title of respect and did not indicate age) if his wife would come, since he knew them better than anyone else. He replied that it would be impossible, since he was away all day and she had to look after the pigs, the potato patch, and the children. After a couple of days he came to Sally and proposed that his fifteen-year-old son, Wong Kung-chai come instead, to help her. Next morning the boy came, a tall lad dressed in baggy blue cotton trousers and knee-length Chinese jacket like his father's, a neatly braided queue hanging down his back. He had an eager, intelligent air about him, and Sally liked his appearance and his willingness to pitch in and work. She had seen him about once or twice before, but did not know he was Wong's son. He was nice with the children and was soon carrying Mary about on his back as he would have his own little sister. Sally sensed his intelligence and soon started to set aside a period each day while the children were napping to teach him mathematics and English. He was quick to learn and made good progress. William questioned him and learned that Kung-chai had attended the village school for boys, where he had studied the "Three Character Classic"; he could recite this from memory but understood little of the meaning. William decided to continue Kung-chai's Chinese education, pursuant to his belief that the church of the future should have educated and dedicated native leaders. Any boy he could help might, by God's grace, prove to be such a leader. He set aside an hour every morning before he went to the city to teach Kung-chai and heard him recite again in the evening.

Abeel and Boone had started to conduct a service each Sunday morning in their rented room in Amoy. They encountered no opposition and gradually drew a congregation of fifty or more men and boys each Sunday. It is true the congregation wandered in and out, but the missionaries had the opportunity to present each with a tract or a copy of the New Testament if they seemed really interested. Both being Chinese scholars and fluent in the dialect they had many interesting conversations with Chinese gentlemen, and William was delighted that at last he had the opportunity to preach in Chinese. They were forming friendships and felt a deep sense of satisfaction. Did not the scripture say:

For as the rain and the snow come down from heaven, and return not thither but water the earth, making it bring forth and sprout, giving seed to the sower and bread to the eater, so shall my word be that goes forth from my mouth;

it shall not return to me empty, but it shall accomplish that which I purpose, and prosper in the thing for which I sent it.

—Isaiah 55:10

They believed this and expected their sowing of the seed to bear fruit.

Sally might have been lonely except for her preoccupation with the children and her promising scholar, Kung-chai. Needing exercise and having the desire to know her neighbors, Sally and the children often went for a walk of an afternoon, Mary on Kung-chai's back and Henry running along beside his mother. Their house stood at the foot of a hill seemingly of solid rock. It was too steep to climb so they skirted around it. There were many fertile patches of earth in the hollows at the base of the great rock, each with its farmhouse. The yards were enclosed by bamboo fences and overflowed with pigs, chickens, and children. Dogs barked but never attacked as they went by. Seeing Kung-chai, children came shyly out, and Sally often stopped to chat while they exclaimed over the two strange foreign children. One day while walking along the beach Sally saw the naked body of a baby girl, washed up by the tide. She was horrified and told her husband about it that night. He said, "Honey, this is a heathen country. A girl is a liability. Parents have absolute authority over their children and when there are too many girls to find mates they are drowned at birth." Sally shuddered.

Of a Sunday afternoon Major Cowper, bringing young Walter Medhurst and a couple of the officers with him, came over for a cup of tea. The three missionaries were happy to see them and to hear the bits of news of the progress of the war and of the outside world, which they brought. They learned that after the fall of Shanghai Sir Henry had decided to press the attack and had ordered the fleet to sail up the Yangtze River. The British frigates bombarded the river port of Chingkiang at the mouth of the Grand Canal, chief waterway leading to Peking. The emperor became alarmed, for his supply of grain and other tribute from all the central and southern China provinces was now cut off and ordinary trade badly disrupted. The Chinese army, mostly made up of Manchu soldiers, had made a brave defense, but the antiquity of their weapons and methods of warfare was responsible for their defeat. On August 9, 1842, Nanking was threatened and the emperor, Tao Kuang of the Manchu dynasty of China, himself of a foreign stock, capitulated to the British. The major supposed that soon a treaty would be drawn up and peace would prevail. He hoped that there could again be peaceful intercourse between China and Great Britain—and perhaps extended to other countries as well. All were happy at the thought that there might now be a treaty and peace. Major Cowper was tired of being stuck with his ships guarding Amoy but what the missionaries saw was the opening up of the gospel to China.

Sally was never to hear of the terms of the Treaty of Nanking, which was signed on August 29. She and the children took their usual walk on the afternoon of the twenty-sixth. A woman she knew came out as they passed by and invited the little group to come in and rest. They were seated on bamboo chairs in the dooryard and offered palmleaf fans. Their hostess went into the house and returned with delicious-looking slices of watermelon on a bamboo tray. Sally, being a Southerner, loved watermelon and accepted a slice gladly. She declined for Henry, however, much to his disappointment, as he had been having some summer bowel trouble, and she thought Mary too young to indulge. The melon had been kept cool in the farmyard pond and was juicy and refreshing. They had enjoyed their little outing and returned home in happy mood. That night Sally was taken violently ill with pain, diarrhea, and vomiting. William was alarmed and treated her symptoms, which indicated Asiatic cholera, as best he could. He stayed with and nursed her all the next day and the next, but she grew steadily worse and was becoming increasingly weak. Just at dawn on August 30 she roused from what had seemed almost a coma and indicated to William that she would like to be supported. He slipped his arm under her shoulders and raised her slightly. She seemed to rally all her strength and said, "Beloved." Then, "The babies." After a pause her voice grew stronger and she said clearly, "If there is a mercy in life for which I feel thankful it is that God has called me to be a missionary." William knew that she said these words to absolve him of all blame, and it broke his heart. Her strength failed and she sank back, losing consciousness again. As the morning light grew stronger she died.

All this time Kung-chai had care of the children while the cook and Lao Wong had done all they could. Mr. Abeel took his turn nursing at night when William was worn out. In the kindness of her heart Kung-chai's mother offered to take Hen-li and sixteen-month-old Mui-li to her farm home to care for them with her younger children, but William courteously declined, saying that her eldest son was doing an excellent job.

The household was stunned at Sally's death. Mr. Abeel sent a message to Walter Medhurst and he, accompanied by the major, came over at once. The weather was hot, and they agreed that the interment must be that very evening. The cook went to the coffin shop to buy a coffin, a good supply of which was always ready. William had no woman to help him as he washed and dressed Sally in the little yellow dimity dress she had treasured. William selected a spot at the base of the rock near their house and that evening at sunset Major Cowper and Walter Medhurst returned. With them were all the officers of both ships and a guard of honor of Navy men. Mr. Abeel read the burial service while a curious but respectful group of island neighbors stood a short distance away. When the salute was fired they were alarmed and some fled in panic. Long afterwards all that Henry could remember of his mother was that he loved her and the frightening sound of the guns. Sarah Amelia Boone was the first Protestant woman missionary—the forerunner of a long line—to be buried on Chinese soil other than Macao.

William was crushed. Nothing but the claims of the children kept him going. How could this be? He knew God as just and true, but his ways were inscrutable. How could he go on without Sally? He needed her so much. Then, penetrating his numbness and tiredness, he seemed to hear the Savior's voice saying with ringing clearness, "She is not dead but sleepeth," and he knew with conviction that his Sally lived. The opening words of the burial service came to his mind though he had scarcely heard them at the graveside: "I am the resurrection and the life, saith the Lord. He that believeth in me, though he were dead, yet shall he live." For all her love, faith, and fortitude, life had been hard for Sally so far from her family. Now she was with her Lord and Savior whom she loved most of all and with her beloved parents too. The certainty comforted him. As the days went by William began to remember other promises of God and he knew that God's promises never fail. God had not and would not forget him and his little family. "Nevertheless the foundation of God standeth sure, having this seal, The Lord knoweth them that are his (2 Tim. 2:19)." These words from 2 Timothy came suddenly to his remembrance, and he felt a sense of having solid ground under his feet once more.

William wrote to the board announcing Sally's death:

It is but two short months since I came to this place with the brightest prospects of happiness and usefulness that I ever enjoyed in my life; but now it has pleased Almighty God to take out of the world my beloved wife. My house is left unto me desolate. Plead for me with our God and Savior, for I have lost as much as could be lost in the name of wife and mother. But it is the Almighty, All-wise God who has done it, and he doeth all things well. In very love and faithfulness he has afflicted us and we bow submissively to his divine and infinite wisdom. May the Lord direct my every step. I trust the Lord in sanctifying my affliction to me. I feel more determined than ever by His grace I will live and die in His service in China. I never had my heart so drawn out to love and adore Him—never felt so unshaken and firm a confidence in His mercy and goodness to me.

William had always had a close relationship with his little son, Henry, now three years old, especially so since their constant companionship in Macao before Mary was born. But he had later been so busy in the hospital there and then absent on his first trip to Amoy that he had missed much of Mary's baby days. She was now sixteen months old, and in her need reached out to him. Henry broke his heart afresh by saying, "Mama has gone on the ship to see God. When will Mama come back to us, Papa?" It was always the scripture which brought him comfort. One day as he was reading Psalm 103 he came to the verse, "Like as a father pitieth his children, so the Lord pitieth them that fear him." A rush of love for God, for Sally, and for her little ones swept into his heart and enveloped him with the sense of Sally's nearness and God's presence. From that moment he was able to raise his head again and stand erect. The children felt the tenderness of his love and care and responded to him with answering love.

In September Major Cowper received a copy of the Treaty of Nanking as drawn up in that city by Ki-ting, viceroy, by order of the emperor, and Sir Henry Pottinger. The provisions of the treaty stipulated that five ports, Canton, Amoy, Foochow, Ningpo, and Shanghai, should be open to residence and trade by British subjects. However, recognizing the hostility felt in Canton because of all the people there had suffered, it was agreed to delay the opening there a few years. The island of Hong Kong was ceded to Britain as a naval and commercial base. A large indemnity was to be paid to Great Britain in compensation to the merchants for the opium burned and to cover expenses of the expedition. This provision was particularly galling to the Chinese, who felt they had the right to control the import of opium. From the Chinese point of view opium was the sole issue causing the war, but the subject was not mentioned in the treaty other than the imposition of the indemnity! All British prisoners were to be released and an amnesty granted to Chinese who had helped the enemy. The Co-hong was abolished and trade to be regulated by "fair" tariff on exports and imports. The right was given the British to appoint at each of the treaty ports a consul empowered to treat on an equal footing with Chinese officials. The treaty was not yet ratified, and there followed a period of unrest and the outbreak of local hostilities, even on Amoy. The wedge, however, had been inserted in the crack in China's door, and it was slowly but surely being pried open to the tremendous influence of new ideas which the penetration of nationals from other lands brought with them.

William spent a good deal of his time with the children through September. As October brought chilly days he began to realize that it would be impossible to heat the house they were in, with its high rafters, dirt floors, and lack of ceilings. Nor could he be in close enough touch with the children while his work took him over to the city. When he learned that it would be possible to rent the rest of the house in town whose front room facing on the street was serving as chapel, he decided to take it. It had drawbacks, for other shop buildings adjoined it on either side, so that there were no windows except front and back in the two upstairs rooms. There was an enclosed courtyard at the rear where the children could play. By the first of November the place was ready and the family moved over. Wong Kung-chai elected to go with them and William was glad, for the children loved him and by this time he knew how to care for most of their needs. William felt that with the help of the chapel doorkeeper, who could carry water and clean the rooms, they could get along. Mr. Abeel remained in the house on Kulangsu and opened a school for the island boys there. The children were much restricted, as their father did not think it safe to take them out on the narrow and crowded stone-paved street on which the house stood.

For Henry it was a most frustrating situation. He would hear the sound of flutes and Chinese bagpipes and rush to the upstairs window to try to see the procession—perhaps a wedding or funeral—which was going by, only to be confronted by the thick opaque squares of oyster shell which took the place of glass and through which he could not see. He was an active and inquiring child and got into all the mischief he could contrive. There were tears and tantrums. He needed companionship with children his own age, instruction and amusement. Mary was a constant joy but was not at all well. The work of teaching the principles of Christianity, leading worship services, distributing Christian literature, and talking with people progressed. William held a clinic each morning and saw a growing number of patients. But he was worried about the children and began more and more to think that the continuance of his work should not be at their expense. He was afraid of losing little Mary as he had lost Sally, when the hot season should come. He finally made up his mind that the only thing to do was to ask for a leave of absence and take them home to America to his mother. He knew that his sisters, Mary and Eliza, would take pleasure in caring for and instructing them. So he wrote to the Mission Board in regard to the matter. It had been six years since he went to the Orient and he had had no furlough. His request was agreed to, and he began to make plans to leave.

When a Chinese scholar who had become William's friend heard of his decision he said. "You are right to go, though you must return. You know, of course, the story of Mencius' mother. When her son was quite young they lived near a cemetery and the boy played at digging graves and enacting funeral rites. His mother thought, 'This is not the place to bring up a son.' So she went to live in a market town. The boy was soon playing at buying and selling goods. His mother thought this too was not what she desired for her son. She moved to a dwelling next to a school. Mencius then became interested in books and reproduced in play the ceremonial rites and sacrifices that were taught the students. His mother said, 'This is the right place to bring up a son.' Go and leave your son with your revered mother."

Mr. Abeel said to William one day shortly before they left, "Why don't you ask old Wong if he would consent to his boy's going along with you? He could help you very much on the voyage and could continue his education in the United States.'' The thought had passed through William's mind before but he had put it away as unrealistic. But now that another had voiced it he decided to try. To his surprise Kung-chai's father was willing and the matter was settled, for like every Chinese parent he wanted to have an educated son. So they set about preparations for departure and in the spring of 1843, before really hot weather set in, William and the two children together with Wong Kung-chai set out on the long journey to the United States.

CHAPTER 5

A NEW BEGINNING

The sea trip down the coast to Hong Kong was a rough one on which they all found their sea legs. On arriving there they learned that ships were already taking on passengers at that port and they need not continue on to Macao. For Wong Kung-chai the trip was an initiation into many strange experiences, not the least of which was the menu. But he came of a seafaring stock and it did not take him long to become accustomed to the ship's roll. A few days out from Hong Kong, Mary celebrated her second birthday and the whole ship's company made a great fuss over her. She captivated the hearts of all, from the captain to the cabin boy. A sailing vessel was not the safest place for two small children, and Kung-chai was kept busy watching them. The voyage was long but uneventful. In the late summer they arrived off the coast of Georgia, and the captain was obliging enough to put them ashore at Savannah so their overland trip into South Carolina would be a short one. William hired a carriage and they drove the eighty miles to Walterboro, where his mother and the family were spending the summer.

Their welcome was a warm one and Mary Boone at once

took the two children to her heart. "Chai," as they called the Chinese boy, looked strange to them with his braid of long hair, but when William told the family all he had done for them they tried in every way to make him feel welcome. Chai had a fair command of English, which made it easier for him. William's youngest brother, Phillip, who was fourteen, took him under his wing and the two boys soon became fast friends. A sense of peace and well-being came gradually to William as he relaxed in the glow of family love and concern. He roamed the piney woods as he used to do as a boy, welcomed familiar places and old friends and felt that he was at home at last. But he knew it would not do to linger long. After two weeks of enjoyment William announced to the family that he must make a trip to New York to report to the Mission Board and to get his orders.

En route he stopped in Charleston to visit his grandmother, Sarah Gibbes Boone, and Sarah Amelia's brother, Henry William De Saussure, with whom he had studied law and for whom he had named his son. Both Henry and his wife, Sarah —William's aunt—were delighted to see him, though sad that their beloved sister, Sally, was not with him. William knew that their home was his and was reluctant to part with them. He preached while in Charleston at Saint Peter's Church and was eagerly listened to, for the members of this church had taken a keen interest from the start in the China venture and were eager to hear his report. At Charleston he boarded a coastal packet for the trip to New York. There the Mission Board convened a special meeting in his honor and listened sympathetically at first and then with growing enthusiasm as he told of the promise for future work in China. William indicated that he would be ready to go back as soon as his children were settled and his own health improved, for he suffered from recurrent severe pain in the spine and head. The board asked him to rest for a bit and then to make a tour of the churches as soon as he felt stronger, in order to arouse them from their flagging interest in the China mission.

William found that the people in general had an abysmal

ignorance and many wrong ideas concerning China. He had a magnetic personality and spoke with clearness, earnestness, and sincerity. Often illustrating his points with personal experiences and bits of Chinese wisdom and lore, he caught the interest of his audience and became a speaker much in demand. He told them of the vastness of China, covering as much territory as the United States or more.

"I have lived only in south China," he said, "and cannot speak from experience of the north, but travelers have told of towering snowcapped mountains and vast plains where wheat and millet are grown, constituting the chief staples of diet for the people there. In the south we eat rice, as all good Southerners do, and the moist, warm climate makes it possible to grow in addition tobacco, cotton, flax, oranges, and many other kinds of fruit strange to us here in the United States. The people of the north are taller and, I am told, more dignified and slow. The Southerners are quick-tempered and venturesome. Since I was mainly engaged in the study of Chinese for the first four years, my contacts were mostly with the scholars who were my teachers. I gained a profound respect for the Chinese classics, for China is possessed with a rich heritage of noble literature. This has been locked away from the West, just as our knowledge has been inaccessible to them. But, my friends, the day of awakening and of the exchange of friendship between our two nations has dawned. 'God moves in a mysterious way, his wonders to perform.' He has used the force of British arms to open the door which has been so tightly bolted against all of us. It is the duty of the Christian church to carry to China the very best that we know, the knowledge of the love of the one true God and of his Son our Savior, Jesus Christ. Let light, the light of truth, shine in through the crack in China's door. God forbid that we of the West add to China's darkness through greed and unfair dealing, to which we are too prone.

"For the last year of my stay in the Orient I had the privilege of living in the Chinese coastal city of Amoy and of getting in close touch with the man in the street. While the scholars of the realm, who supply officials for all government posts, worship only Confucius in the temples built in honor of his memory, offering sacrifices twice a year, the life of the common man is beset behind and before with spirits, gods, and demons, so that his life is spent in constant fear lest he offend one. As Paul found the Athenians had erected an altar to the unknown God, lest they unwittingly slight him, so everywhere one turns in Amoy, in the homes, at street corners, at the wayside, under trees one finds an altar—a niche containing an image or a tablet, incense, or a prayer flag for some spirit to be propitiated. God has created man in his own image so that man's heart, the world over, instinctively reaches out for his Father. But this swarm of man-created gods has usurped the place of the Father and the 450 million people of China live in fear and dread of them all their lives. They cry out as did Saint Paul: 'Who shall deliver [us] from the body of this death? (Rom. 7:24).' Oh, my Christian friends, if God calls you, go, and tell the heathen that Jesus is the way, the truth, and the life. God has, in his mercy, committed to us the priceless heritage of the gospel. The light of heaven has dawned upon us and he has given to us the solemn charge, 'Go ye into all the world and preach the gospel to every creature.' Can you not hear his call today: 'Whom shall I send and who will go for us?' Will you not answer, 'Here am I, Lord, send me?' "

Money began to pour in for the support of the mission and on November 14, 1843, the first recruit, Eliza J. Gillett of New York, was appointed as a missionary teacher. William's hopes soared when he heard that President Tyler had appointed Caleb Cushing, a jurist and diplomat, to go to China to try to negotiate a treaty with the United States. Early in 1844 Cushing, having failed in his desire to negotiate directly with the emperor in Peking, obtained a meeting with authorized Chinese officials in Macao. There, seated at a stone table in the courtyard of the ancient temple to the fishermen's goddess, Ah-ma, under the shade of a spreading banyan tree, he signed a treaty which extended to America the most-favored-nation policy for trade and residence. It also clarified the principle of extraterritoriality. A Chinese citizen guilty of a criminal act against an American was to be tried in a Chinese court according to Chinese law, but a United States citizen committing a crime in China against a Chinese was to be tried by the laws of the United States. This was later extended to civil cases and was, regrettably, sometimes taken advantage of and abused and became a lasting source of resentment and friction to the Chinese for many years to come. The Chinese have always regarded these as "unequal treaties" forced on them by the aggression of arms. Though they made possible the entrance of foreign missionaries into China, in reality they built up much misunderstanding as to the motives of foreign missions and retarded the spread of the gospel.

One of the churches in which William was invited to preach was historic St. Helena's in Beaufort, South Carolina, seventy miles south of Charleston. William was delighted to meet again the rector, the Rev. Joseph R. Walker, in whose church ten years before he had received the blessing that had changed the whole course of his life. Mr. Walker told him that the evangelistic meetings he had attended then had resulted in forty young men going into the ministry of the Episcopal Church. Several of them had already been consecrated as bishops, including his friends Stephen Elliott and Robert Barnwell and his seminary roommate, Charles Pinckney. William did not know that he himself was soon to join their ranks. St. Helena's Church had stood behind him in both Batavia and Amoy, and the congregation listened with interest to his report. From there he went to Savannah, Georgia, only some fifty miles away, at the invitation of the Rt. Rev. Stephen Elliott, who asked him to be his guest for a week.

There at her brother's home he met another old friend, Stephen's sister, Phoebe Caroline, who had come down from her home in Beaufort for a visit. The warmth of her personality reached out to the deep loneliness William had felt since Sally left him. The children too, especially Henry, needed a mother. William wanted to know Phoebe better.

Therefore, after he had filled a few more of his invitations to speak in southern churches, he went again to Beaufort, this time to call on Phoebe Caroline Elliott. He was received by her father, the Hon. Stephen Elliott, known throughout the South as an eminent scholar and editor. Phoebe was at home and gave her caller a heartening welcome. Phoebe, for all her blithe exterior, had a serious mind and deep piety, and she and William discovered that they had much in common. It was not long before she replied in the affirmative to William's question as to whether she could consider going to China with him, and they were engaged to be married. On September 5, 1944, the wedding took place at St. John's Church in Savannah, with the bride's brother, the Rt. Rev. Stephen Elliott, conducting the ceremony.

It proved an eventful year for William. In October the General Convention of the Episcopal Church met. Their Board of Missions had written a minute which read: "For the administration of mission work in countries beyond the United States it is expedient that there be consecrated to the episcopate those who shall act as missionary bishop in foreign lands." The General Convention received their report and passed canons for the election and consecration of missionary bishops. On October 22 the Rev. Mr. Glennie of South Carolina was elected bishop of Africa, the Rev. Southgate of Maine, bishop of Constantinople, and the Rev. William Jones Boone, M.D., "Bishop of Amoy and such other parts of China as the Board shall hereafter designate." Consecration took place on October 26, 1844, at Saint Peter's Church, Philadelphia. Bishop Chase of Illinois, the presiding bishop, officiated as the consecrator, assisted by eleven other bishops. Bishop Stephen Elliott preached the sermon from the words of the prophet Isaiah: "Enlarge the place of thy tent, and let them stretch forth the curtains of thine habitation: spare not, lengthen thy cords, and strengthen thy stakes; for thou shalt break forth on the right hand and on the left; and thy seed shall inherit the Gentiles and make the desolate cities to be inhabited (Isa. 54:2-3)." His message was to the whole church and it was stirred as it had not been before in its history in America. The new Bishop Boone and his wife, Phoebe, never forgot the challenge of their brother's words. Bishop Boone received a lengthy document, his charge, determining that he should not only implement evangelism, but also engage in educational work. The Mission Board began to receive applications from people volunteering for service in China and chose eight who should go with Bishop Boone upon his return there.

William and Phoebe Boone, together with the new appointees, began to make plans for departure. After consultation with Bishop Boone, the Mission Board decided that they had best go to Shanghai instead of Amoy, as this city had been mentioned as one of the treaty ports and was in a strategic place in central China. Phoebe agreed with William that it would be best for Henry if they took him with them, but Mary was not strong and her aunts—Eliza, who was a teacher, and Mary, who was devoted to her little namesake—begged that the little girl be left with them in her grandmother's home. Chai, of course, much to his friend Phillip's disappointment, would return with William to China. On December 14 Bishop Boone and his party sailed from New York on the ship *Horatio*. On the third day of the voyage the bishop formed a class to study Chinese, with himself and Chai as teachers. It is to be hoped that the new missionaries learned a good deal of Chinese, for the journey lasted one hundred thirty-three days!

On April 2, 1845, they reached Hong Kong, where the bishop contacted old friends. He learned that in October the French had obtained a treaty with China, similar to the one America had managed to get—only it went further, granting permission to erect Roman Catholic churches in the ports and making it possible for the Chinese to accept Roman Catholicism. Hong Kong had grown tremendously. An estimate of the population showed some four thousand Chinese and five hundred or more Europeans and Indians. The British declared it a free port and welcomed all comers to the colony.

Letters awaited William in Hong Kong. One was from Shanghai, and he was much pleased to find it was from his old friend of Batavia days, Walter Medhurst of the London Mission. He said his family had been transferred to Shanghai by their mission. To their joy their son, young Walter, had been sent to Shanghai also and was in the consular service of the British Government.

It was not long after his arrival in Shanghai that William wrote a letter to his uncle, Henry A. De Saussure, telling of their arrival:

July 6th, 1845
Shanghai

My dear Uncle;

I have been purposing a letter to you ever since my arrival in China, with a view to giving you some account of our house arrangements. But I find that these matters are as indefinite as when we arrived in Shanghai three weeks since. I therefore write at once and leave these matters for a future communication.

We left Hong Kong accompanied by Miss Morse and Miss Jones on the 24th of May and arrived at this place on the 17th of June. We all thought the journey more tedious than that from America, as our accommodations were so bad; but we arrived in good health notwithstanding.

We were delighted with the verdant banks of the Yangtze Kiang and still more with those of the Woosung River, on the banks of which Shanghai is situated. I left the ladies at the village of Woosung, twelve miles below this place, and came on in a sedan chair, which gave me a fine opportunity of seeing the country. It suited my lower country tastes, not a hill to be seen, but the richest verdure in every direction. Not an inch of uncultivated land, staples, cotton and rice, these growing side by side with only a drain between, the rice being irrigated by human labor, but I was much more interested, of course, with the people than their fields. They were everywhere civil, and I proved an object of much curiosity to them. Sometimes I saw the girls throw down their hoes and run a hundred yards or more to get a good position to see me as I passed.

You will be glad to learn that both Phoebe and I are much gratified with our field of labor. Shanghai as a missionary station surpasses, taking climate, healthiness and character of population and relative position in the Empire into account. Phoebe finds that all her expectations with respect to the accessibility of the people, their sociableness and intelligence, the freedom which the women enjoy and the ease with which she and her female associates may cultivate friendly relations with them, fell far short of reality. This you will readily understand is a matter of great moment to my feelings and I am sure will prove a matter of thankfulness to all our friends. She felt some disappointment at the physical appearance of the city—narrowness and filthiness of the streets and roughness and inconvenience of the houses. She very naturally remarked that she could not conceive how a people that make such beautiful wares, such splendid silks and satins, could live in such houses.

But even in these respects we are favored. Shanghai is by no means a dirty Chinese city, and although the houses are generally poor, there are some good ones and I have succeeded in getting one in which I think we shall be comfortable—but of this more after we have moved into it. I am heartily glad we passed by Amoy and came up here. Amoy has been sickly every year, whereas there has not been a single death as yet, of a foreigner, at this place. But Shanghai possesses still greater advantages over Amoy. It is situated in the North East, the most literary part of China, surrounded with the most delightful country, densely populated and thickly dotted with villages, among which I think we may venture to hope that not many years hence we shall see missionaries settled and quietly laboring.

We have several thousand Romanists in this district with whom we shall, no doubt, come into collision before long. The Romanish bishop, the Count de Bessi, lives just across the river from us. He travels about pretty much where he pleases. The Chinese Christians call him "Da Jen" (The big man), a title given to the Viceroy of the Province and always kneel when they come into his presence. There is in this place a temple still standing, which the people call the Temple of The Lord of heaven (Tien Ju), a phrase by which the Jesuits translate Jehovah, and a street that is called Cross Street, which are proofs of the success of the Jesuits formerly in Shanghai.

It is thought that the French Ambassador, Mr. Lagrene, will take advantage of this to demand the restoration of their Church, which is now used as a theatre. There has been a slight persecution of Chinese Christians in Nanking to induce them to inform on the Romanish priests who are now in the country in disguise. The object was, perhaps, to squeeze some money out of the Christians. It is thought that Mr. Lagrene will take advantage of this to demand greater toleration than that granted in Kic-Ying, the High Commissioner's memorial and the imperial rescript which you will have seen, no doubt, in the *Spirit of Missions* before this reaches you.

The progress of events here seems to be onward, and that at a rapid pace. I find the dialect spoken here (the Wu) is by no means as near Mandarin as I had supposed. Phoebe certainly has great tact and talent in getting hold of the colloquial and if her health continues good she will no doubt speak it fluently in a year. Henry is very much attached to her and very happy.

Miss Jones and Miss Morse are staying with Dr. Lockhart at present. We are with Mr. Medhurst. Both are missionaries of the London Missionary Society. We hope to get into our own hired house next week. We have not had a line from Carolina as yet. Letters from New York of Mar. 5th bring an account of President Polk's inaugural.

My love to Aunt and all the family. Do let me hear from you as frequently as you can. I love your full long letters.

Affectionately, as ever, my dear Uncle,

[signed] Wm. J. Boone

P.S. Henry begs me to give you his love and to Maney [Mary] five kisses. Then comes a list of love to each, too long to be written. Kiss my precious babe, Mary, for me and give my love to all at Mother's.

(The original autographed copy of the above letter has been given to Mr. Benjamin of Washington, D.C., to be incorporated in a collection of letters of the bishops of the Episcopal Church of America. The collection will become the possession of the Washington Cathedral.)

Bishop Boone was aware that Christianity had first been introduced into China very early, some thirteen hundred years ago. He knew of the nine-foot-high monument of stone discovered in north China as early as 1625. On it was carved a cross and an account of Christian teaching as carried to China from Syria or Persia by the Nestorian monk Alopen. It had been erected in 781 A.D. Alopen had come to the court of Tai Tsung of the Tang dynasty as early as 635. But reliance upon government favor is undependable, and with the accession of an emperor who was a Taoist to the throne of China, an edict proscribing Buddhist monks and the Christians was issued in 845 A.D. The missionaries were expelled, but their influence lingered. Marco Polo found a few Christian churches in existence in the late 1200's. By this time China had been invaded by the Mongols from the north, and Jenghiz Khan and his sons became the emperors of China. Along with the Mongol conquerors the Nestorians returned. But to the Chinese populace they were thus linked with the foreign invaders, an impression which has never left the Chinese mind and has done much through the centuries to retard the progress of the Christian message. ○

As Marco Polo returned to Europe after his extensive travels, the first Roman Catholic missionary, John of Montecorvino, was on his way to China, commissioned by Pope Nicholas IV. He arrived at the Mongol court at Cambaluc, as the Mongols called Peking. John sent glowing reports to the pope, who sent out Franciscan monks to join him. But again government opposition arose when the Chinese managed to overthrow the Mongols in 1368. At this period there seems to have been no effort on the part of either the Nestorians or the Roman Catholics to train and raise up Chinese leadership. This oversight was another factor setting back the spread of Christianity, for all the foreign missionaries were again driven out. There is evidence that a few Chinese Christians clung to their faith until late in the 1500's in spite of lack of leadership and persecution, but there is no record of further Christian missionaries having served in China until the sixteenth century.

During his stay in Macao William Boone had seen evidence of the intolerance of the Portuguese Catholic priests there. They showed their impatience at the presence of Protestants and, indeed, of any nationals of countries other than Portugal and were not in the least cooperative—especially toward Protestant missionaries. There was a reason for this, stemming from the time of the great explorers of the fifteenth century. Columbus, flying the Spanish flag, discovered the American continent in 1492, and in 1498 the Portuguese Vasco da Gama, sailing in the opposite direction, rounded the Cape of Good Hope. This was followed by an astounding piece of presumption. The corrupt Borgia pope Alexander VI, acting on the conviction that popes, as vicars of Christ, had authority over all mankind, in 1480 granted a monopoly in trade, colonization, and political rule over all people in non-Christian lands. In 1494 the Treaty of Tordesillas was signed in Portugal between herself and Spain, giving all of the Americas except Brazil to Spain and all discoveries in Asia to Portugal, with no voice at all given to the many countries involved. At first•their interest was mainly in trade but soon afterwards came colonization and the entrance of priests, along with the traders and armies. This explained in part the attitude of the Spanish and Portuguese abroad, who tended to think of Mexico or California, Macao or Goa as their rightful possession. Another thing which retarded the rooting of Christianity in China was the tendency of the European priests and occasionally of Protestant missionaries to identify their own civilizations with Christianity, thus marking it all the more in the eyes of Chinese citizens a "foreign religion."

Many devout Catholics felt keenly the need for cleansing within the church, and movements for reformation were set afoot, especially in the founding of groups of men who vowed to live the Christian life of purity and service to others. One such man was Ignatius Loyola, a young nobleman of high scholarship and complete dedication to Christ. In 1534 a little band of seven of his friends took vows of chastity, poverty, and obedience, and the Society of Jesus, later known as the Jesuits, was founded. They sought to raise the moral life of Christians and initiated extensive missions among non-Christians. Loyola stressed that his missionaries must first learn the language of the country to which they were sent, which had not necessarily been done before, all services having been conducted in Latin. He sent out men of learning and culture, among whom was the noted Francis Xavier who went first to India and later to Japan, where, surprisingly, he was able to live for a year. But Xavier's great desire was to go to China. The poignant story of how he had to content himself with landing on the island of Shang Chuan near Macao, having been refused permission to enter China proper, is well known. There he contracted fever and his dying words, with his face toward China, were said to have been, "Oh, rock, rock, when will you yield?"

In 1577 there arrived in Macao an Italian Jesuit, Valignano, who had been designated superior. He had with him forty-one Jesuit missionaries to serve in the Far East. He saw that for success there must be knowledge of and adaptation to national cultures. On arriving in Macao, to the scorn of the priests already there, he set new missionaries to studying Chinese. Two of them were outstanding in their influence. Ruggieri and Ricci were able to penetrate into China and, aware of the high positions held by Chinese scholars, gained permission to wear the dress of Chinese gentlemen; living quietly, they tried to conform to their ways. They became friendly with several scholars who held high positions in the government, and in 1601 Ricci was able to reach Peking. Knowing mathematics, astronomy, and geography he was soon revered as a scholar and gave not a little of his knowledge of these sciences to China. Ricci died in Peking in 1610. Several people in high positions had professed Christianity. One of his gifts to the country was the revision of the Chinese calendar.

Ricci led the way for many outstanding members of his order, among whom were Schall von Bell, Verviest, and Gerbillion, who were men of genius, became proficient in Chinese, and appreciated the ancient Chinese culture. These men were, fortunately, of several different European nationalities and so did not have political aspirations for their various countries. Too often the Franciscans and Dominicans, who also took up work in China, devoted to their faith as they were, linked Portuguese and Spanish ambitions for expansion of trade and influence to their presence in China. But the gradual decline of these two nations as world powers made these ambitions come to naught. This linking of national aspirations with religious institutions, by some, gave the Chinese a wrong impression of the real spiritual goal of missions and later proved a stumbling block to all Christian denominations working in China. The Roman Catholic Church was placed in a particularly difficult position because of the fact that its head, the pope, was an overseas foreigner, and its members were expected to give him their obedience.

With the overthrow of the Ming dynasty by the vigorous Manchus in 1644, the Catholic priests were tolerated in Peking for some time longer as teachers of music and the sciences. But in the reign of the great emperor Kang Hsi the various orders came into conflict as to which term should be used in Chinese to mean God and whether the customary rites of the Chinese in honor of their ancestors and Confucius were acceptable for Christians or not. At last the matter was placed before the pope, who decided against toleration. This view was opposed to that of the emperor, Kang Hsi, who was angered that a foreigner should attempt to enforce a decree not in accord with the imperial will. After this time there were sporadic persecutions of missionaries and their converts, of whom there were several thousand scattered in different parts of the nation. Diminished though they were, this accounted for the presence of Roman Catholic churches and adherents in Shanghai and other places in the empire when William Boone took up his residence in that city.

As he had foreseen, he came into conflict with them not long afterwards, for the French tried to obtain an imperial edict which would limit the right to propagate Christianity to the Roman Catholics. Bishop Boone heard of this and, an Anglican bishop to China not yet having been appointed, brought the matter to the attention of the British plenipotentiary, Sir John Davis, who had succeeded Sir Henry Pottinger as governor of Hong Kong. Sir John took the matter up with Peking and the same rights were extended to Protestants. The new edict read: "All those who do not make a pretext of religion to do evil are exempted from prohibition." So Protestant missions were now under the reluctant sanction of the emperor too, for the most-favored-nation policy meant that privileges granted to one nation should be extended to any other asking for the same rights.

As William had said in the letter to his uncle, the Boones stayed at first upon their arrival in Shanghai with their old friends, the Medhursts. The Rev. Walter Medhurst, D.D., was one of the pioneer missionaries in the Orient. He had come out under the London Mission to Malacca in 1817 as a printer, believing, as did his mission, that language was fundamental to the spread of the gospel and that there must of necessity be Christian literature in the native tongues. He moved about the Malay Peninsula but made his headquarters in Batavia, Java. In 1835, before going to England on furlough, he made a trip up the coast of China together with an American missionary, Mr. Stevens. As soon as China opened for residence by foreigners the Medhursts decided to remove to Shanghai and were among the very earliest of the missionaries to arrive there. This was of great advantage to all others who came during the next several years, for the elderly couple gave freely of their warm hospitality and broad experience. Dr. Medhurst was undoubtedly more extensively acquainted with the Chinese people, language, and country than any other foreigner in Shanghai. He was then working on the further translation of the scriptures into Chinese. Later he was the first chairman of the Shanghai Municipal Council. He took William under his wing and helped him to find a Chinese house just outside the wall of the old walled city of Shanghai. Narrow streets crowded with dwellings and small shops formed this suburb and ran the length of the city, ending on the muddy flats at the edge of the Whangpoo River. The house was quite large, with ten rooms and two courtyards. The two rooms which faced the street William used as his reception room and study. He hoped before long to open a school for boys in the third room. He furnished them in Chinese style, with stiff carved wooden chairs set against the walls, interspersed with tea tables, and hoped that he would soon be able to entertain Chinese guests. The second courtyard with its rooms was set aside for servants.

Phoebe had been fortunate enough, while they were in Hong Kong, to have come across a young Chinese man named Etom, born in Java, who had lived in the United States for six years, where he had been trained as a baker. He spoke good English. Etom came with them to Shanghai on the condition he would stay for at least six months (he stayed two years!). He would receive ten dollars a month and fend for himself. She selected as a cook a clean-looking boy of about nineteen. He told her he knew nothing of cooking and she replied that was just what she wanted—he could learn. Etom taught him. She found a coolie, a man of all work, named Loo-pah, a Romanist, whom William thought highly of. These five adults and Henry made up the Boone household for the present. Almost immediately they were besieged with visitors anxious to see how the foreigners lived, what they ate, and how they would be received. They were polite and left if they saw that the family was having a meal, but otherwise were present at almost any hour. They were made welcome and served the inevitable tea, and William was glad when a few of the gentlemen, finding he spoke Chinese, sat with him for awhile and inquired about the religion he came to teach.

Early in November events took place which filled William and his wife, and Henry too, with happiness. Phoebe wrote to her brother, John, of Beaufort, South Carolina, in the following words:

My dearest Brother;

There is only one obstacle in the way of my making known to these most interesting people the message of the Gospel and that is my ignorance of the language. We are daily pressing on in our efforts to acquire it and if I only enjoy health, I believe I shall be able to speak with freedom in a year or two. I can now get on with my servants and teacher, but the difficulty is not with getting hold of words in daily use, but in learning accurately words which will express faith and doctrine. The people exhibit much curiosity to hear what these doctrines are. We want to teach them and I have been requested by two of my servants to instruct them in the "doctrine of Jesus."

The other day we attended a meeting at the Medhursts' and witnessed what to us was of thrilling interest—the baptism of two Chinese. These are the first who have professed a belief in Christianity here. We had more than 20 foreigners present and ten or twelve Chinese. The missionaries went up after the service was over and shook hands with the two who were baptized and welcomed them into the Church of Christ. The whole service was in Chinese—the hymns were sung in Chinese. My dear brother, there is an immense field opening before us; but oh where are the laborers? My heart throbs with emotion when I see around me in swarming multitudes, so many creatures hurrying to eternity without ever having heard of a Savior's love for sinners and having no hope for the future. And then, when they exhibit so much kindness and cordiality towards us, we feel more anxious than ever to offer for their acceptance the blessings which are now sealed from them in the gospel. I can only say for myself that I would not change my position now for anything that the world could offer me and I am as happy as the day is long.

But the thing which has afforded me the most hope and happiness is the return of Chai to us. I wrote you of the rapid progress he made in reading when with us on the *Horatio* on his return home to China. He parted with us in Hong Kong to visit his father and mother in Amoy. Of them he used to speak in the most affectionate manner. Later Dr. Boone wrote to Dr. C. in Amoy and told him that we felt very anxious that Chai should come to Shanghai and receive education as one of our scholars, for he hoped he would be converted and become a missionary among his countrymen and requested Dr. C. to furnish the money to Chai for his passage should he decide to come up. Chai's father objected to his leaving home again and he did not come. After some time Dr. Boone called me one morning and said he had just received another letter from Dr. C. He said he had just seen Chai who had come to him for passage money to Shanghai. He had lost his Mother, Father and two brothers and there was nothing now to prevent his journeying to us and that he would be here on the same vessel which brought the letter. Dr. Boone sent out Loo-pah immediately to look for the ship but he returned saying there was no such person on board. After dinner, however, Loo-pah came to me and said, "That Fukien man is out there." I ran out and saw the shadow of Chai standing among the servants. He sprang forward and seemed quite overcome. He took my hand and said over and over he was very happy to see me again, but his voice was so tremulous and he seemed so weak that I made him come in and sit down. He said he had been walking all morning and could neither find our house nor the way back to the ship until at last he went into a little English store kept by a Jew and that the gentleman had let his servant show him the way. I asked him what was the matter, for he looked so poor and weak I could hardly keep from tears. He said, "Oh, Mrs. Boone, I have had great trouble since I came to Amoy." Then he told me that he found when he reached Amoy that his father had been sick a long time and his mother had been working to support the family. His father was so glad to see him again he got well in a day or two. He had been at home only a short while when his mother was taken sick. Chai watched her for nineteen days and all the burden of the family fell on him for all his brothers were younger.

Then his mother died and within a month his father was dead too. The day his father died a little brother, three years old, died too and a few days later another brother, aged seven. Chai said they had moved back to Koo-lang-su to the house they owned there. He said there was not a house in the place where someone was not sick. His brother of 16 was ill, but Chai went and called Dr. C. and the boy got better. I asked why he did not call Dr. C. to see his mother and father? He said he tried to persuade them but his mother said she was not used to foreigners. We found out that he had had to bear all the funeral expenses, which in China are a heavy tax upon the poor. They have such respect for parents and for the dead that they make any sacrifice rather than fail in giving them suitable coffins and observing the ceremonies considered proper on such occasions. Poor Chai had been reduced to great poverty. He seems to have parted with everything in the way of clothing except the one suit he had on. He had the fever twenty days himself. He did not say a word about having had to bear such heavy expense or make any complaint of being poor or having no clothes, but he seemed completely subdued by his trials and looked very miserable. Fung Sien-sen, our teacher, took him into the city today and bought some warm clothes. Dr. B. will pay a debt of ten dollars which I found out he owes to one of his relatives in Amoy who had assisted him in his troubles. Chai has expressed his willingness to remain with us for the purpose of being educated. He is my scholar and I shall carry on his education in English as long as I am able and he is to study Chinese with a teacher every day. Now you must help me by praying for him in your daily and family prayers. I saw a little prayer he wrote for himself and was struck by this sentence, "Let everybody pray to the Lord to give me new heart." Tomorrow I commence with him and Henry who is always ready to receive instruction. He seems delighted at the idea of having Chai again as a fellow student.

I have felt gratitude that we had Etom here at this time, for he offered Chai half of his room as soon as he arrived and they seem to get on extremely well together and have many feelings in common to bind them to each other. Both have pleasant recollections of America. Etom has a great desire to return there. They are able to exchange their views in English.

Later—Jan. 27th was Chinese New Year's Day. This whole week the stores have been closed and business suspended. Everyone is engaged in festivity, but it is quiet festivity—calling. We are pleased to find ourselves among those who have received visits. Every one who can claim acquaintance has called, not that our list of acquaintances is as yet very select. The highest class we have intercourse with is teachers. You should see them! They are dressed in furs and satins and wear black round caps covered with rich crimson silk fringe and great buttons denoting their degree on top. Scholars make up the governing class and are much respected.

Dr. B. has had three more rooms built on and the day after the festivities end we will start school. Two of the new rooms will be used as dormitories and the other the class room. The old room will be a dining hall. Dr. B. has engaged a teacher and a cook. Since Oct. Rev. and Mrs. E. W. Syle have been with us. With the other members of our mission that makes eight whites in our family and we have quite a colony of Chinese with us. The Syles will later have a house of their own. Mrs. S. is vivacious and independent and picks up the colloquial faster than her husband.

Do write often.

Affectionately,

Phoebe C. Boone

CHAPTER 6

GROWTH

In November 1842, three months after the signing of the Treaty of Nanking, Captain George Balfour had been assigned to Shanghai to act as the first British consul. He arrived on the ship, *Medusa,* charged with opening Shanghai to foreign trade and residence. The captain called at once on the governor of the city to announce his arrival and to ask where he might take up residence. Captain Balfour told William afterward that he met with a polite but cool reception. The official said he regretted that there was no house for rent that he knew of. As the British left to try another avenue of approach, a richly dressed Chinese gentleman stepped out of the dense crowd gathered at the *Yamen* (seat of government) door to watch the drama. He introduced himself as Mr. Yao, a merchant, and said he had a house which he would gladly rent to them for four hundred dollars a year. Mr. Balfour, his clerk, doctor, and interpreter followed Mr. Yao to the main street inside the walled city and found that the house in question was a mansion of fifty rooms furnished in elegant, if somewhat stiff, Chinese style. They engaged it and moved in. They found that Mr. Yao hoped to negotiate terms with them for a monopoly of the foreign trade. This they could not agree to, but gave him the promise that they would deal with him as well as other merchants.

Mr. Balfour, too, was a far-seeing man and soon asked the taotai where he might rent land for British subjects to "reside for the purpose of carrying on their mercantile pursuits without molestation or restraint," as stated in the treaty. The consul said he would prefer a site on the banks of the Whangpoo River and was shown a stretch of muddy flats. The ground was uninhabited and he was told he could rent it "in perpetuity." It afterwards became the famous Shanghai Bund.

The conservative British firms in London were a bit slow in sending their young men out to China, for the trip was a slow and expensive one. They went by ship to Egypt, overland by camel to the Red Sea—for there was no Suez Canal—and again by ship to Hong Kong and on to Shanghai. The first foreign merchants to show up in Shanghai had previously been connected with the British East India Company in Canton. Dr. Jardine and his young partner, James Matheson, were the first to arrive. They were followed by Lancelot Dent and his partner, T. C. Beale. These two firms became household words to all Shanghai dwellers throughout its history. An American, Henry Wolcott, followed. Being the first American there, Mr. Wolcott was considered the American consul for the time being.

By the end of 1842 there were only twenty-three foreigners in Shanghai. But their numbers grew rapidly. By the time the Boones settled in there were one hundred. These were the friends they met of a Sunday morning when most of the foreigners assembled at the British Consulate in the old Chinese city for worship, for there was not a church in Shanghai at that time. The missionary ministers took turns conducting the service, and it often fell to the lot of Dr. Medhurst or Bishop Boone to preach. The ladies traveled to the service in sedan chairs, while the gentlemen walked. All were busily engaged during the week at their various professions and enjoyed very much chatting together after the service. Consul Balfour was most hospitable.

On Sunday afternoon the bishop conducted an instruction class in Chinese for the students in their home, while Phoebe taught a Bible class in English for Etom, Chai, Henry, and a young man named Mr. Tien who had asked permission to join them. He was attached to the British Consulate as a translator and writer and spoke good English, having been educated in Singapore in a mission school.

Phoebe wrote to her sister in May 1845:

Chai is now in the next room with Henry and I am hearing their sage speculations about the planets. They take joy in the discoveries they make in every day matters. Henry from having only grown people to associate with really uses and understands very uncommon language for a child of his age. He is an endless talker. He is constantly asking the meaning of words that he hears, then we are sure that the next thing we will hear will be some remark made expressly for the purpose of introducing the new word! Miss Emma Jones and Miss Morse have taken on a few girls as day scholars. They meet in our second class room. The two ladies, who live with us until the day when we can erect a girls' school, are deeply interested in their scholars and have the satisfaction of seeing them improving in behavior as well as knowledge.

We have been most happy to have had with us for the past few months Dr. Boone's brother, Dr. John Boone. He came to spend the winter with us in this cold climate in search of restored health. Think of our having a visitor all the way from America as early as this! We are indebted to him for coming all this long way to see us. To our regret he must leave us soon for after June there are no more vessels going to America until October so he must get down to Hong Kong very soon or he will have to stay here all summer. In winter our temperature went down as low as 17 degrees Fahrenheit and everything froze But in summer it can feel very hot for it is damp and humid. At this time of year it is steamy and everything starts to mold. In the morning we sometimes take a pair of shoes out of the ward-robe to find them coated with velvety mold.

It took seven months for your letter to reach me. You paid ten cents and it was sent through an agent in New York, as all our letters are. It came on a merchant vessel and was transferred to a vessel coming to Shanghai, at Hong Kong. Because it is too slow to have it carried by a man, walking, the last twelve miles where the river joins the mouth of the Yangtze, along the muddy tow path at the Wangpoo River's edge, the mail is sent by galloping pony to either Jardine's or Dent's. They are so kind as to send the bag to each house and we take out the mail which belongs to us. It is a great day when the mail arrives! As we live three miles from the foreign business part of town, you may judge how convenient this is for us. The merchants out here are certainly very attentive and kind to the Missions. The other evening a gentleman called and said he had received a barrel for Dr. Boone from America and had brought it up in a little boat which was at the landing. Loo-pah soon had it in the yard and it proved to be butter from New York! It was well salted and arrived in excellent order. At the same price we would have paid in New York, too. Such a treat!

Dr. Boone, I am glad to say, is enjoying very good health now. For some time the climate or water seemed to affect him and he was beginning to look very badly and grew thin. Dr. Lockhart told him he must give up drinking water and try ale or tea. Since then he has been like a different person. The Chinese here never taste water. They think it strange that we do. They take a weak solution of tea and even the little scholars must have hot tea to drink whenever they are thirsty. The English substitute the use of beer. Though I have drunk water with impunity, I have now become convinced that it affects most people unless boiled or mixed with a little beer.

I am expecting my baby very soon now. You wrote of sending a box. Little remnants for garments, colored chintz-es. Children's wants cannot be supplied here. Little shoes and stockings, in fact any kind of articles suitable for little folks will be most acceptable. (The Chinese wear home

The water supply of the mission.

made stockings of white cotton cloth.) Cap ribbons for myself, in fact a cap or two would not be amiss. We are occasionally invited to weddings and small parties and the English are very much dressed. I might also suggest that necessity of life, some note paper in different sizes. To correspond between ourselves here—every firm or residence has a "chit book." A servant comes around with the written note, we sign for it in the book and write a reply on the spot. It is a very convenient method.

Since we have been here we have lived on very pleasant relations with the English, indeed have received much attention from them. I hope nothing will occur to interrupt this good feeling which at present exists. But the English do often ask questions about America which might provoke a saint and which betrays surprising ignorance on their part!

But I must stop. This letter is too long. We so seldom have a chance to send one that I want to tell as much as possible. My love to all our friends.

Affectionately,

Phoebe Caroline Boone

On May 17, 1845, Phoebe's first son, named William Jones Boone for his father, was born. They did not know that one day he would be consecrated a bishop too, in the footsteps of his father! The baby flourished. William temporarily took on the teaching of his wife's scholars but was glad when she could take up that duty again, as he was much occupied with the translation of the scriptures. Robert Morrison's version was in the Cantonese vernacular and the people of Shanghai said they could not understand it. Bibles were very hard to get and the mission had none to give out. A letter received by Mr. Medhurst from the British and Foreign Bible Society put all the missionaries in high spirits, for they offered to print a new edition in Chinese.

Wishing to reassure her as to Phoebe's welfare William wrote to Phoebe's sister, Mrs. Blanding:

April 17, 1846
Shanghai

My dear sister;

Phoebe has written. As I am sure however, she has said less of herself than of any other subject—which is most important to you—I will commence with her. I am sure it will be gratifying to you to hear that she is truly contented and happy. I believe she is more happy here in Shanghai than she would be if I were Rector of St. John's Church, Savannah. She feels a sincere and hearty interest in the Chinese and is conscious of an ardent desire to do them good in Christ's name—which is, my dear, the great secret for deriving happiness from those around us wherever we may be placed in the providence of God.

In this respect a residence among the Heathen population makes a strong call upon our sympathies and affections and may be made the means of much good to ourselves. Phoebe is very successful in teaching Henry and Chai, in the latter of whom she has much comfort. I think I need not fear to say he has become truly pious and his convictions and conversion are more ascribable to her instruction than to any other human means. I baptized him on Easter, which was to me the most intensely interesting service in which I have ever engaged—indeed, I could scarcely command my voice.

He is the first heathen man I have ever had the privilege of introducing into the Christian Church, and that too after seven years prayers and labors for this object. God, of his infinite mercy, grant that he may prove only the first of a long line who shall be truly consecrated to the service of the Father, Son and Holy Ghost. Our Teachers, servants and scholars and a few other Chinese were present who all seemed much impressed by the ceremony, especially Phoebe's teacher and mine. Of the former I entertain much hope.

After correspondence regarding the new translation of the Bible, missionaries on the coast were assigned portions to be translated, and it was agreed that they would all meet in Shanghai in September 1846 to correct and correlate. The bishop was also very busy translating parts of the prayer book and a catechism for the scholars. The increased knowledge of the language possessed by the present missionaries made it important to bring out, if possible, a standard edition. They would revise the translations of Morrison, Gutzlaff, and Medhurst and bring their united labors into one volume which they agreed to name *The Delegates' Version*. The committee consisted of the most eminent scholars among the missionaries: Dr. Bridgman of the American Board of Commissioners for Foreign Missions, the Rev. John Stronach of the London Missionary Society in Amoy, the Rev. Walter M. Lowrie of the American Presbyterian Mission, stationed at Ningpo, the Rev. Dr. Medhurst, and Bishop Boone.

The committee met again in Shanghai a year later. The most important question which the committee had to settle was the proper rendering of the Hebrew word *Elohim* and the Greek word *Theos* into a Chinese term which would convey the meaning of one God. Drs. Morrison and Milne had employed the Chinese word *Shen;* Dr. Medhurst, *Shang-ti.* Bishop Boone thought the latter word misleading as it meant a chief god among many gods, and advocated the word with the more spiritual meaning, *Shen*. In a land where the concept of many gods was almost universally accepted, it was almost impossible to find a term which would convey to the mind of readers a concept unfamiliar to them. Whatever term was used, clarifying instruction would have to be given.

After the committee adjourned the Boones were shocked to hear of the tragic death of the Rev. W. M. Lowrie as he was returning to his station at Ningpo. In the Chapoo Bay, just outside Shanghai, his boat was attacked by pirates. Mr. Lowrie was bound, thrown into the sea, and drowned.

The whole community, Chinese and foreign, was stirred by an incident which occurred early in 1848, almost resulting in the deaths of the well-known Dr. Medhurst, Dr. Lockhart, and Mr. Muirhead, all of the London Mission. They had taken a trip to the small town of Tsingpu, thirty miles from Shanghai. The town's people proved friendly, and they walked in the streets, distributed a few tracts, and chatted with people. They had come by boat and upon mooring it had noticed an unusual number of grain junks tied up at the jetty. They inquired why this was so and were told that an order had come that such junks, laden with tribute rice from the provinces, should not take their usual route up the Soochow Creek to the Grand Canal to discharge at Peking, but should proceed by sea. Some twelve thousand junk men, a rough lot, had protested and had been dismissed. They were spread out along the creek robbing and terrifying people. The three visitors had no sooner heard this when they were confronted by a mob of the junk men, who attacked them. They were knocked down and beaten with bamboo poles and iron chains. When it seemed they must surely be killed, the ruffians decided to haul them to a junk and hold them for ransom. But the local people had informed the patrol from the taotai's office, who rescued them in the nick of time and took them back to Shanghai.

Rutherford Alcock had recently succeeded George Balfour as British consul in Shanghai. Alcock had first been in Foochow as first British consul there and he spoke Chinese. He was refined but shrewd and had had great success in his contacts with the Chinese authorities. He took quick action, for he decided that if an outrage like this was allowed to take place, involving respected citizens of Shanghai, face and security would be lost both to the Chinese and the British. It so happened that the British sloop *Childers,* mounting two guns, came into Shanghai port just at that moment. Thinking that action must be taken quickly and that there was not time to get orders from his superior in Hong Kong, he issued an ultimatum to the taotai. If the ringleaders were not arrested within forty-eight hours fourteen hundred grain junks would be held up in the Whangpoo River. There would be a blockade of the port, and British merchantmen would not pay the customs duties on freight being unloaded until the matter was resolved. When some of the junks tried to run the blockade the *Childers* fired across their prows, and they saw that she meant business. The port was paralyzed.

Since nothing happened to clear up the situation, Alcock sent his assistant, young Harry Parkes, to Nanking to put the case before the viceroy, who sent the provincial judge down. The men were arrested and normal life restored. The people of Shanghai had been uneasy about the horde of junk men and had feared looting, so were glad to be relieved of their fears. At the suggestion of the three gentlemen who were beaten by the mob, the men arrested were put in cangues, rather than being executed. This is a square wooden collar about three feet wide with a hole in the middle to fit around the neck. The accused's crime is written on a piece of paper and pasted to the board for all to see. A chain is fastened from the board to his ankle or neck. Then the man is paraded in the streets and suffers great loss of face. He cannot reach his mouth to feed himself. It is a much dreaded punishment and does more to punish the man's spirit than his body, though it is extremely uncomfortable to the victim. He cannot lie down for the period of his punishment.

The British found, when they desired to build a consulate

and hongs for their business firms, that they had a tricky mud flat on their hands into which any ordinary building would inevitably sink. An American architect happened to come to Shanghai, a Mr. Hethrington. Some American lumber had been shipped in from Oregon, and he proposed that these logs be hammered down into the mud as piles. Standing upright, close together, they would form a platform of posts on which a house could stand. It was tried and found to work. A high platform of light bamboo was erected on which a group of coolies could stand. A heavy mallet was suspended by ropes. Each man took hold and lifted the heavy instrument, then dropped it like a sledgehammer on top of the pile and drove it into the mud. They developed a chant as they worked. The chant soon became a source of amusement to passersby, who would stop to listen to the line sung by the foreman—perhaps a jocular or ribald comment on some onlooker. Then all the men chimed in with a chorus of "Hong-ya hon-ya, ai-ya, hong-ya—hong-ya, hong-ya, hei." It amused them and helped divert them during the heavy work. In this manner Mr. Hethrington built the new British Consulate, which endured down the years. (He himself did not last as his buildings did, for he died in 1848—the first foreign man to die in Shanghai.) That city has ever since been a city literally floating on soft mud.

By 1848 the school in the Boones' home was becoming crowded, with thirty-six boys in attendance. Bishop Boone had been looking for a suitable location where he could erect both a church and a schoolhouse. In the walled city he found an available lot where he proposed to build a church seating two hundred and fifty persons, to which a day school and a Christian burial ground would be attached. The bishop had been considering another site for the boarding school, a few miles north of the Old City and beyond the British Consulate, where the Whangpoo River makes a big bend and is joined by the Soochow Creek. He had appealed to the church in the U.S. for building funds and had met with a generous response. Besides the money for the school, which the Bishop proposed to build on the Soochow Creek site, William Appleton of Boston gave funds for the erection of the church in the walled city. The latter was completed in January 1850 and given the name of Christ Church. It was the first Protestant Episcopal church to be built in China. Meanwhile, the building of the boarding school had gone on apace. Phoebe described the location in a letter to her sister which reads, in part:

> The schoolhouse is beautifully situated. We command a prospect for miles on either side and have a wide and noble river washing the front garden and offering an unbroken view for miles on each side of us. Every here and there there is a little grove of trees embowering scattered hamlets. Cows and sheep add life to the landscape while vessels of all descriptions add life to the water view. A wide creek branches from the river into which the tide flows every day. The building is 120 feet long and 100 deep to the end of the two back wings. There are upper and lower verandahs and plenty of room for everybody. It is built of brick, plastered inside and out, painted and varnished: plenty of room for everybody—and all for $5,000.

The new school did indeed have plenty of room to house their thirty-six boarders, together with the teachers, so the members of the mission decided to move there temporarily also, leaving the Chinese dwelling in the "native city" where they had been housed for the past three years. Phoebe had never complained, but housekeeping there had presented many problems, especially after the arrival of her second baby, Thomas, on May 22, 1846. There was no glass in the windows and it was a bit disconcerting to have passersby stick a finger at the oiled-paper windows, poke a hole, and apply an eye to see what the foreigners were about. They lived just outside the city wall, which was surrounded by a moat generally used as a refuse dump. It bred mosquitoes and large black rats. Even though many were caught by wire-cage traps, they kept coming. The climax was reached when one jumped onto the bishop's bed and ran across his face, waking him up!

On the whole it was a quiet city, for all wore cloth shoes which did not make a clatter on the stone paving. There was a bustle and rush in the early morning hours when farmers entered the market carrying produce in baskets slung on a pole or chickens squawking to be let out of their confining coop. Hawkers shouted their wares, sometimes musically, and occasionally the sound of a gong sharply struck was heard, announcing that a mandarin was about to pass by in his sedan chair. All must get out of the way. At night the city gates were closed and all was still, except for the barking of dogs and the resonant sound of hollow bamboo being struck by a stick as the night watchman made his rounds, letting thieves know that he was approaching and assuring the householders that they were being protected.

Further building funds came in, and the bishop purchased property adjoining the new school where he planned to build a mission residence, a church, and a girls' school. Phoebe wrote to her brother, the Rt. Rev. Stephen Elliott, about their life when they first moved to the new location.

Our life here resembles life in a large hotel at home, where different families have their own parlours. Privacy is quite unknown among us and I should be sorry to spend the rest of my days under the present arrangement. I suppose there are now at least one hundred persons on our premises and who can be quiet in such a crowd? The buildings are of course arranged with a view to the best interests of the school and those connected with it; and those who consider themselves permanently settled are much pleased with their apartments. We, being only temporary residents are the worst off, but the consideration that our stay here has made a great change in Willie's health, and Dr. Boone's freedom from the painful attacks he used to suffer from last summer, make me feel only thankful that we have been able to escape from the dreadful atmosphere we lived in for three years. We have been so long shut up between prison walls that the sun, moon, wind and other objects of the gifts of nature almost oppress our bewildered senses. The morning after my arrival I started up in great fright, thinking flames were bursting into my window when it was only the glorious beams of the rising sun shining around us!

Although so glad to escape from the filth and impurities of a Chinese city—I cannot but feel that three of the happiest years of my life were spent there. Mercies surrounded us and blessings were multiplied about us. Our children were preserved when pestilence was walking in darkness and destruction wasting at noonday. In the midst of a heathen nation no man was permitted to hurt or even to make us afraid. But the change to open country and the sight of God's creation is cheering and refreshing in the highest degree. And I am delighted at the prospect opened before us of being useful. In the city it seemed almost hopeless for us to attempt day-schools or Sunday Schools. In the ever changing throng the seed could only be scattered by the wayside. Now I hope we shall be able to go into the little quiet hamlets and make friends of our neighbors. At present we are over run with visitors. Sometimes there are heads at every window while we are taking our meals—belonging to people who have merely come to look at foreign manners, and who call out frequently that our ways are much about the same as their own. I think they flatter themselves, but no doubt they are surprised to find us sitting in a decent quiet way eating the products of their own soil and occasionally addressing them in their own tongue, when they perhaps had expected to see "foreign devils" revelling and acting in ways quite abhorrent to their prejudices and feelings.

While a house for the bishop and his family, with plenty of room for guests, was being built near the boys' school the city was affected by a flood which inundated the low-lying farmlands near the mission compound. Water crept up into the first floor of the school and lapped what would be the Boones' garden. After the flood receded the villagers found that their crops of cotton, beans, and mustard seed were a complete loss and the rice partly ruined. These small farmers had almost no reserve to depend on and soon found themselves out of food for their families. They came into the city in great numbers, pitiful groups of self-respecting people trying to find some means to tide them over until they could plant over again.

The bishop, in consultation with Mr. Syle and other members of the mission, decided to do something for these their neighbors. They decided to issue rice tickets and let the people come once a day for a nourishing meal. The people were seated around the fence which surrounded the grounds, and the bowl each person supplied was filled with hot rice, a vegetable, and a dash of fresh ginger to make it more palatable. It served to tide people over, although it was meager enough fare. When he heard that some people were criticizing the effort and saying the mission was making "rice Christians" (a term borrowed from India), the bishop's reply was, "I am not afraid of the effect of treating them with compassion in their hour of need and alleviating their temporal miseries. Did not our Lord do the same when he fed the five thousand?"

As the building of their home progressed and after the floodwaters had receded, William and Phoebe decided to plant a garden for themselves. Phoebe commented in a letter

The gardenias grow very readily and cheapness of plants with fine roots at one hundred for a dollar tempts us. Our neighbors come into Chapel now and visit us very freely. I often get a number round me when I go out to plant a tree, and they will stand and talk as long as I will. I always try to take such opportunities to make acquaintances and to explain our mission and to invite people into the chapel when the gong is sounded. It is much more pleasant to talk with the same villagers whenever you see them than it used to be to mix with a new crowd every day as it used to be in the city. The people here are much quieter and more attentive in chapel, too, than the shifting crowd in the city.

Mr. Syle has opened a "ragged school" for village boys and thinks it a great success. Dr. Boone plans to have several more opened next year under the care of native teachers.

Of course there will be no English taught but the Chinese classics with the addition of figures and the scriptures. Several of the other missions are now convinced that this is a good method and are opening the same kind of schools. Some of the mission families have taken two or three children to live with them. The mission stations have all voted that the translating committee must go on and translate the Old Testament now that the New is finished all except for the insertion of the terms for "God" and "Spirit." There has been a great deal of controversy and excitement over these two terms. Dr. Bridgman was again selected delegate from Canton. This will oblige him to remain in Shanghai several years longer. Mrs. Bridgman says she will open a day school for girls immediately.

Canton, as you know, by the agreement made with the British two years ago, was to be opened to foreigners on the 6th of April, 1849. For some time past people have been speculating as to what the result would be, as the Chinese continue to manifest hostile feelings and seem determined to resist the fulfilment of the treaty. But the news when it came was very different from anything we had anticipated. An Imperial Rescript had been received by the Chinese authorities at Canton forbidding the opening of the gates at all, and John Bull was left in an awkward position! The Queen has given her orders that no warlike steps are to be taken out here by the English without directions from home. The English Governor could only say he would represent the matter to his Government and beat a retreat. We feel sorry the British took the first step. Everybody says it is not necessary for trade that Canton should be opened. I don't believe it could be done without bloodshed.

The foreign community was glad to welcome the Rev. Mr. Lowder of the Anglican Church, who came to take up duties as rector to the English-speaking residents. His wife and five children came with him, and Phoebe was interested to see that the little boys were dressed in kilts, for that is how she had dressed Henry. She had no way of keeping up with changing styles except as someone came out from England or

America. Bishop Boone had felt for some time the need of a church building to house those who now met at the British Consulate. He and Mr. Lowder worked on plans together. The congregation contributed handsomely to a building fund. A lot was secured on Shantung Road. When the building actually began to rise Bishop Boone was able to contribute a great deal of practical knowledge, since he had just built Christ Church in the native city. Slowly the new edifice grew and became known as Trinity Cathedral, Shanghai's most beautiful church building. About the same time two of the other missions built churches for their Chinese congregations, so there were now four Protestant churches in Shanghai as well as the Roman Catholic churches. There were several Buddhist and Taoist temples which had been there for years, the best-known being a large one inside the walled city and the very famous one at the "Bubbling Well," as well as several other smaller "joss houses," as the British merchants called them. All, great or small, had the graceful curved roofs, lacquered pillars, and beautiful gates guarded by fierce warrior gods, examples of the unique and beautiful Chinese architecture. Ten miles out from Shanghai there was a set of dusty temple buildings clustered around the famous Lung Wa Pagoda—the "Leaning Tower" of China. Family groups, both Chinese and foreign, found a boat trip out to the pagoda made a pleasant excursion.

The middle of May 1849 a gala event occurred quite unexpectedly. Phoebe described it animatedly in a letter to her cousin:

I will tell you how our heads have been turned this week. One morning we rushed out to the verandah to see the stars and stripes sailing by! It was not long until the ship anchored and Captain Glynn came over to our landing to make us a call. He stayed a long time with us, went over the school and said he had a number of friends in New Haven who were interested in our Mission and he wanted to see everything. He gave us an account of his recent visit to

Japan. He went there to rescue some American sailors who had deserted a whaler and wandered to Japan where they were put into cages (where they could neither stand upright nor lie down at full length), forced to trample on the Cross and treated in the most inhumane manner. They had been caged for six months—one or more had died and the rest were brought here in a miserable condition. The Captain had not been allowed to land at Japan and was surrounded by armed boats. The sailors were, however, all given up.

The very day the *Plymouth* arrived we had another visit, from Mr. Beal and Captain Wilcox of the *Fury*. They invited Dr. Boone and others aboard to see their very first steamboat. Dr. Boone came home excited and described the whole ship's company as charming people—so we agreed forthwith to give our beloved countrymen a party. I wrote to them all from the Commodore to the Clerks to invite them for the next evening and then wrote to most of the Americans here and several American merchants and a few select English friends. A party with us is a rare event now-a-days and we had to have a contribution of furniture from all our parlours, also a joint stock company to furnish cups etc. We made "the best cake ever eaten in Shanghai" and I had my mocha coffee parched—but all this time we had not heard who would come. We found there was to be a dinner party at the British Consulate for the Diplomatic Corps and several little private parties of two or three friends. However, the Commodore sent an excuse to the Consulate and accepted our invitation—bless his American heart, I say! As many of the officers as could leave the ship came also and a very nice set of young men they proved—from the best families of Virginia, Maryland and Philadelphia. We had a roomful in spite of the other parties and we did enjoy ourselves particularly.

Later the Commodore invited every American lady to go on Board. The Tao Tai and the Military Colonel were to pay him their visit of ceremony then, and he wished to introduce them to his countrywomen! We shouted, we clapped our hands and did everything to assure the Commodore we would be charmed to meet the Chinese officers—'twas the thing we had never expected to accomplish. By eleven two large American boats with banners flying were ready to convey us on board and the Chinese looked on in astonishment at our doings at the idea that we were going to see the Tao Tai. The steps were covered at the sides with flags and we took possession of the ship as if it were something that belonged to us. It was soon announced that the Tao Tai was coming. As soon as the small boat reached the ship the Commodore and all the Officers drew up to receive him. But instead of there being any great form or ceremony, as I had expected, the Tao Tai rushed up in the most affectionate manner and held out his hand to the Commodore saying, "How de doo," and then went round shaking hands with all the officers. Upon being introduced he went round and shook hands with all the ladies. Then we took our seats, ladies and gentlemen all together. I got seated next to the Colonel. We sat still while three guns were fired loud enough to upset me for quite a little while. The Tao Tai's daughter was with him. She had been out quite a little in foreign society and has got quite used to being waited on by foreign gentlemen and promises to be a spoiled piece before she gets through with her education. Her father is proud to show off his few words of English and pulled off his appendages to show us his fan, pouches and beads and so on. The Colonel could not speak English at all so I made bold to turn around and tried my "Eartha Chinese" on him. He was a local man and could understand me quite well. He was kind enough to initiate me a little in the court dialect. At last the Colonel said to me, "You are acquainted with the Wong family?" (The ones Mrs. Syle and I called on at Chinese New Year time.) I said, "Yes." "They came this morning early to visit the steamer," he replied. "Mr. Syle escorted the gentlemen and ladies of the Wong family on board." He continued, "The Wongs are my relations." So it seemed, as with acquaintance in common elsewhere, to me a sort of letter of introduction.

When they played, "Yankee Doodle," Mrs. Syle burst into a flood of tears and was quite overcome. "Bless the woman," the sailors said. I suppose it has been mentioned in all the papers at home! In the afternoon Captain Glynn, who is very infirm, rowed over in his boat and wanted to know if

Mrs. Syle had gotten over "Yankee Doodle" yet? Dr. Boone preached on board in the morning. Commodore and all went to the ship instead of to Trinity Church. Today Captain Glynn is here to dine with us. As he is too infirm to go into the city and wants to buy some Chinese things, I have ordered a perfect show of things to be brought here for him to see. They say they were disgusted with Canton and this has been a great treat for them.

When the bell rang for chapel this morning, the American sailors at the landing said to Miss Morse that they would like to go in to the service if the Commodore had no objections. He said, "None at all," so she ushered them in from the boats, about twenty men. Dr. Boone spoke to the boys in Chinese and then turned to the sailors and said, "What I was saying to these boys was —— etc." He took the opportunity of giving them a very plain application of the subject as applied to their own lives. That afternoon at four o'clock, being Ascension Day, Dr. Boone held a confirmation service for the woman and A-voo, baptized on Easter Sunday last. Several persons and three Officers were present to witness the administration of the rite and one of them said it was the most beautiful sight he had seen since he came East. All seemed interested and pleased by it, but he particularly came again next day and said in the course of conversation, "Bishop, I shall never forget the scene I witnessed yesterday." The seamen notice the children a great deal. They made a suit of sailor clothes for Henry Syle and Henry Boone, to their great delight. I feel as if my gratitude ought to be unbounded to the giver of all these blessings. Among my mercies I ought to mention the arrival in Shanghai of an excellent dentist. It seems as if he had just come in time to save my teeth.

In 1850 the community had another blessing in the arrival on a visit of the newly elevated bishop, George Smith of the Anglican Church. Through the influence of the Anglican Missionary Societies in London, Queen Victoria had, by letter patent, created the office of "bishop of Victoria" and the Rev. George Smith, who had been a missionary to China, was nominated for the post. His jurisdiction was extended to include all five treaty ports. When he visited Shanghai, as part of his charge, Bishop Boone welcomed him and they formulated a practical working plan with no friction at all. The two bishops entertained great respect for each other and later, when Bishop Smith was on a visit to the United States, he spoke publicly of his high regard for Bishop Boone's zeal and ability.

There was a great deal of sickness in Shanghai through 1849 and on into the summer of 1850. Two epidemics, which Dr. Lockhart diagnosed as black measles and cholera, took the lives of very many in Shanghai and its environs. Among them were several who had been friends and neighbors of the Boones when they lived outside the walled city. In the city the sound of flutes and bagpipes and the wails of the mourners were common occurrences as a funeral procession with its banners, Taoist and Buddhist priests, and men staggering under the weight of the heavy wooden coffin with its red draperies passed by. The missionaries escaped these two particular diseases except for Mrs. Syle, who was suddenly stricken with cholera but managed to pull through. However, almost everyone suffered from attacks of malaria, especially Henry. The weakening attacks of chills and fever occurred very frequently, much to the worry of his parents.

There were several deaths among the foreign community from other causes. A frightening number of wrecks along the coast caused a heavy loss of life. One of those lost was a beloved member of Bishop Boone's staff, the Rev. Phineas Spalding. He had shown marked aptitude for the language and was especially loved by the boys in the school, where he taught. He was in charge of the school chapel and had shown great taste in the beauty of its appointments. It was a great sorrow to him that, having developed consumption, he was advised to leave the damp climate of Shanghai for a season. His co-workers were equally sorry to see him leave on the ship *Coquette* in August 1849 and hoped he would soon recover and be able to return. But the ship foundered in the China

Sea during a terrible gale and was never heard of again. The news was a great blow to his friends.

William Boone, too, was not at all well for he suffered from agonizing spinal pain and seems to have suffered a heart attack which laid him low. He was advised not to preach for a while, but he still carried a heavy load with administrative work, overseeing the building operations, and his duties at the boys' school. He daily conducted both morning and evening prayers in the chapel, at which there was an average attendance by this time of about seventy. The bishop believed in the regular, daily catechetical mode of instruction and met with the boys of the school each Sunday afternoon to teach them. At Easter Bishop Boone had the privilege of baptizing a teacher, Koo Sien-sen, Tho Chung, the matron in charge of the girls at Miss Morse's school, a child, and four of the school boys in the upper class, one of them Chai's younger brother.

Phoebe wrote to her sister, Harriett, on February 9, 1850:

The [Chinese] New Year ought to come on the 12th of February, but it has just been discovered at Peking that there will be an eclipse on that day. A proclamation has gone out throughout the Empire ordering the eleventh to be observed as the first day of the year. Should an eclipse take place on New Year's Day all sorts of calamities might be expected to ensue as a consequence, particularly affecting the Emperor. We intend to make a New Year's call on some of the Chinese ladies, according to custom. I received a clandestine call from unmarried girls of the rich Loo family, in top Chinese society. The girls were too frightened and shy to speak. It was evidently a great adventure for them to go to see the foreigners.

Wong Kung-Chai has just been betrothed. He was getting anxious to make some matrimonial alliance and we were quite as anxious to further his wishes, but the trouble was to know where to find a suitable wife for our candidate for the ministry. He was ordained as a Deacon some months ago. We finally selected a girl of suitable age who is the niece of Toh Chung, our Matron. We went through the usual ceremonies customary for a betrothment and the girl was delivered to us, as Chai's guardians. Our present plan is that she should remain under our care for two years previous to her marriage and be regularly and daily instructed during that time. We must pray that she may become a child of Grace before she assumes her responsibility as a married woman. Miss Jones and Miss Morse now have four girls who are boarders at the school but all are young and are under the care of Toh Chung as far as their food, clothes, etc. are concerned. I mean to consider her niece my charge, even if she does live over at the school house, and quite agree 'twould be better for her to go there, for unless she is kept very secluded with us, she would be liable to meet Chai continually downstairs and thus violate all Chinese custom and propriety. At the other house the girls can have a large airy apartment opening onto the front verandah where the boys never go and where they can have fresh air and exercise and be far happier. Dr. Boone has advanced the money for the dowry, $40.00, but Chai is to refund it from his monthly allowance. This we all think best as he will value his wife more and will have to learn habits of economy before his marriage.

Dr. B. has been very unwell lately. The translation of the scriptures is very difficult work. But he is the most wonderfully and uniformly cheerful person I ever saw. He thinks it a positive duty to "rejoice evermore" and is often the liveliest of our circle at times when we know he is suffering most particularly.

His parents felt that they were doing an injustice to Henry, now ten years old. They were not only worried about his health but felt he lacked normal companionship. His two brothers were still babies and though he loved them dearly, they could not play with him. Miss Jones, who had taken over the supervision of the boys' school because of the bishop's ill health, was disturbed because the boys, coming from cultured families, were far too dignified to play! They would stand by and watch men fly huge kites in the form of butterflies, centipedes, and other ornate forms, or spin humming tops, but they would not do it themselves. They were all friendly with Henry and he was often over at the school-house, but he had to study alone with his mother as teacher, for all his studies were in English. His parents felt he needed normal companionship and competition in study, and they also wished him to know his many relatives. Miss Jones observed that the girls played a game of hitting a shuttlecock dexterously with their heels, but this was a girl's game beneath the dignity of boys. Miss Jones introduced the game of "dance rope" and found they had some life in them. But Henry needed playmates.

An unexpected opportunity to send him to the United States came in October 1849. Miss Morse had for some time been having trouble with her throat. Frequently she lost her voice completely. Dr. Lockhart strongly advised that she return to the states and have it attended to. She was loath to go but finally consented and booked passage for Hong Kong, where she would transship to the *Vancouver*. The Boones thought the opportunity to send Henry along in her care too good to miss, and there ensued a great scurry to get him ready. Almost before Henry realized what was happening he and Miss Morse and Chung Ling, a schoolboy going along for the trip (Miss Morse having every intention of returning within the year), together with a group of friends going as far as Woosung to see them off, were boarding a junk heading for the mouth of the river where the ship lay at anchor. They all boarded the *Vancouver,* and the boys were excited as they investigated everything with curiosity and interest. But soon farewells had to be said and William held his son in a last embrace, speaking encouragingly to him though he thought his heart was breaking. Henry was too excited to realize that this was a real parting. But Phoebe and the little brothers were not there, and he suddenly realized he would not see them for a long time. Chai was there, standing on the muddy Woosung dock, and Henry waved to him, wondering how he could get along without the big brother he had known all his life. The excitement drained out of him and Henry looked little and lonely as he stood there at the rail, his curly red hair glinting in the sun. William, looking across at him, thought how like his mother his little son looked. He could not bear this separation. He could only place the child in God's hands and pray for his safety and guidance. As soon as he reached home from seeing Henry off he wrote to Henry De Saussure, sending the letter via England.

Shanghai
Nov. 14, 1849

My dear Uncle:

I have been obliged to send my beloved son, Henry, away from the parental roof and I write to commend him to your care. When we parted you were kind enough to draw up my will for me and to consent to become the testamentary guardian of my two children by your dear sister, Sarah Amelia. This emboldens me to send the lad to you. . . . It is a sad duty for a living man to perform—the giving over of the most precious part of his treasures and responsibilities to his Executors. In my sore grief and trouble in sending my first born so far away from me, my heart and judgement both turn to you, my dear Uncle. I therefore make the request that you look after my dear boy, become his guardian, let him find in your parental control and fatherly admonition restraint and counsel. I know how much I am asking, but it is because I have so much to ask that I turn to you. Take then, I beseech you, my dear Uncle, oversight of my precious child and do with him and for him whatever you shall judge best for his moral, intellectual and physical well being. God in his infinite mercy grant him grace to walk in the way of righteousness and peace.

He went on to tell of Henry's health, his need for formal schooling and for companions his own age. At Phoebe's suggestion he recommended Mr. Fielding's fine school in Beaufort, where Henry would be near his Elliott and De Saussure relatives. They did not think there was any good school near the farm of his grandmother, Mary Jones Boone. But he left the decision as to where Henry should study entirely up to his uncle, Henry William De Saussure, for whom Henry had been named. He spoke of provision for expenses and continued:

Phoebe is of a most magnificent size. If our prospects bear any proportion thereto, there is no telling what the number of our family may be after the middle of next month. She enjoys very good health. Willie's cheeks are like roses and he is a very strong, active, lively, brisk child. Our dear little Thomas is a tender plant. A most precious little fellow he is.

My own health was much better last summer than it has been any time since my attack and it was supposed winter would set me up and quite restore me. But the first appearance of cold has had a contrary effect, irritating my spine and causing sudden dreadful pains in my heart, but I have been better for the past two weeks. Miss Morse's departure throws some school duty on me daily. Our mission is sadly depressed by the loss of Mr. Spalding also. Of his return we have no hope; indeed it is most probable he has already passed away from this life. In Miss Morse's case we think a few weeks at sea will quite restore her to health and she may return to us.

It is time to bring my long letter to a close. Give my warmest love to my dear Aunt and all my cousins. And for yourself, my dear Uncle, accept the assurance of the sincere affection and gratitude of your Nephew,

[signed] Wm. J. Boone

P.S. I am enclosing a letter to my Brother John and a copy of this letter for my Mother. I would send it to them direct except that the overland postage is so very high. Please will you forward it to them.

It was unfortunate that the above letter was delayed and William's uncle did not receive it until after Henry had arrived in New York.

Bishop Boone, his second wife, Phoebe Elliott Boone,
and their son, William J. Boone, Shanghai, 1846.

CHAPTER 7

WHERE
IS HOME?

Miss Morse together with the two boys need not have rushed off in such a hurry, for the *Vancouver* made very good time and reached Hong Kong in five days. The little party went to the new European Hotel and there they stayed for over a month. When on December 1 they boarded the large ship *The Great Britain* to cross the Pacific, they found that there were quite a large number of passengers. Among them were a number of ladies whom Miss Morse had known in Boston, accompanied by their physician. Word had reached China of the discovery of gold in California and there was quite a crowd of Chinese men on board going to *Kam Shan* or "Gold Mountain," as they called San Francisco, to seek their fortunes. Their passage cost them $125—but what was that when they were going to come home rich men! The presence of her friends made the voyage a pleasant one for Miss Morse but, schoolteacher that she was, she saw to it that Henry and Ling had two hours of instruction every morning. The rest of the time they were free and found plenty to amuse themselves with, for the American consul's wife from Hong Kong was on board with her children, and for the first time Henry had American children about his own age to play with. The voyage passed quickly for all of them.

As they sailed into the Narrows and across the beautiful land-locked upper bay to New York harbor Henry was immensely excited. He had always been told that America was "home" but he could remember it only faintly and felt a bit apprehensive. When he thought of home, that meant Shanghai. Well, anyway his Uncle Henry would be there to meet him and perhaps even sister Mary and he would be whisked off to South Carolina and maybe that would seem a little like home. But when they actually docked there was no one there to meet Henry. Miss Morse's brother from Boston was there and was anxious to take his sister and Chung Ling home with him. What to do with Henry? The problem was speedily resolved with the coming aboard of Mr. Fred Winston, an agent of the shipping company. Miss Morse told him of her dilemma, and he at once said that he knew and had high regard for Bishop Boone and was in correspondence with him in regard to the forwarding of packages and mail. He had known Henry was on board but had supposed he would be met. He offered to take Henry home with him and inform other friends of the bishop's, particularly Mrs. Ennis (who had gone by her maiden name of Haines since she returned from Java), as he knew she was expecting Henry.

All this talk went on over Henry's head, but he was an interested listener and felt great relief that someone was going to take him home. Mr. Winston had matters to attend to on board so Henry was asked to wait. He felt a sharp pang of homesickness as he said good-bye to Miss Morse and Ling and saw them disappear on shore as they followed Mr. Morse, impatient to be on the way back to Boston. While waiting Henry amused himself by watching the activity on the dock. Passengers he knew were being ushered away by their friends —the ladies elegant in tight-waisted dresses and long full skirts. Henry giggled as he saw one lady in brown and yellow whom he thought looked exactly like a wasp. Her escort wore a coat pinched in at the waist too and a shiny tall hat. They did not look like the gentlemen and ladies he knew in Shanghai or Hong Kong either! What struck him most was the sight of American men handling luggage, wheeling away boxes and trunks and working in various ways on the wharf. Where were the coolies? It looked queer to see Americans doing these things.

While he was still absorbed in watching the unfamiliar sights of an American dock, Mr. Winston came up behind Henry and laid a friendly hand on his shoulder. The boy looked up into the kind face of a man about his father's age who said, "Well, young man, I think we can go home now." They gathered up Henry's valise; he put on his round straw hat and carrying carefully his prized Chinese kite which Chai had given Henry as a parting gift, they went across the wharf to Mr. Winston's waiting carriage. Henry was told his trunk could be sent for later when they found out where he would stay in New York. The coachman flourished his whip, the horses made a delightful clatter as they sped over the cobblestones, and Henry was enchanted. As they turned in to Broadway a bell clanged urgently and two great white horses dashed by pulling a red fire engine, a string of small boys racing along behind. It turned off into Twenty-fifth Street. Henry had scarcely recovered his breath when they turned into Madison Square. Children played on the grass and elegant carriages dashed by, liveried men in tall hats driving them and beautifully dressed ladies sitting inside. Before Henry could ask what the name of this enchanting spot was, the carriage drew up before a neat brownstone house with yellow window frames. The carriage had scarcely stopped when the front door burst open and three children rushed down the steps and besieged their father as Mr. Winston stepped out. He stretched out his hand to Henry, saying, "This is where I live and these are my vagabonds," with a flourish of his other hand toward the children. "Children, this is our friend Henry Boone and he has come all the way from China on one of our ships." The children looked at Henry curiously for a moment and then young Fred, remembering his manners, came forward and took Henry's hand. His sister, not wanting to be outdone, took his other hand and they went laughing up the steps and into the house where Mrs. Winston was waiting to greet them.

There ensued for Henry a series of enchanted days. The Winston children were not unused to having visitors from abroad and were delighted that this one was so near their own ages. Besides, he was the cause of many extra treats for them! Since the ship was in, their father had some free time and took the children on several delightful excursions. He also took Henry to call on some of his father's friends, the Rev. F. Irving, Dr. Grey, the Rev. Stephen Tyng, rector of Saint George's Church, and others. This Henry endured and tried to be polite, but he did not enjoy it. However, they all made much of him, treating him like a young man, so that he felt quite flattered. Word was sent of his arrival to Miss Haines, who was in Batavia when Henry was born and had been a dear friend of his mother's. She came over to the Winstons' to see him immediately and invited Henry to move over to her school at once. But the Winstons prevailed upon her to leave him with them for a few days.

Upon returning home that day Miss Haines wrote to Henry's uncle, Henry William De Saussure, to inform him of his nephew's arrival.

New York
March 8, 1850

My dear Sir:

Per last steamer we had letters from Bishop Boone announcing his determination to send Henry home by Miss Morse who was returning to the United States because of ill health. Today we have had the pleasure of welcoming them. Henry is much improved in health, but looks feeble. Mr. F. J. Winston and I think it would be advisable for him to prolong his stay in the North until he is quite recovered.

I write, therefore, to intercede with you, to allow me the privilege of having him, for a few months if not 'til next

Fall. May I not urge my claim as an old friend of your Sister's and as Henry's Godmother? You will perhaps remember I was with your sister at Henry's birth and that the two first months of his life he was entirely in my charge. During that overwhelming sorrow which finally caused my return to America, he was my solace and delight, and your dear sister's tender sympathy and unfailing kindess to me—all conspire to render me very anxious to have the charge of Henry.

My circumstances are these. I am engaged in teaching in a school in this city. My Mother, an old lady of seventy-eight, resides with me. My school is prosperous and I am accustomed to the management of children and of boys. My school closes in July and I shall go into the country with four children who are orphans and left to my sole care. We propose going to a quiet mountainous region in Connecticut where the children can have fine pure air and range of beautiful country with country pleasures. I usually take a riding pony. Would it be asking *too much* to ask you to entrust Henry to me till next Fall? What would you think of his attending school in the North?

I enclose one of my circulars.

With sentiments of the highest consideration, Respectfully

Your Obedient Servant,

Henrietta B. Haines

My address is 10 Gramercy Park, New York.

The circular stated under the caption, Miss Haines' Young Ladies School, No. 10 Gramercy Park, East Twentieth St., New York:

The course of study is thorough and comprehensive; conducted on those plans which from experience have been found best adapted to develop the various powers of the mind, inspiring scholars with a true love of learning, forming habits of attention and application, at the same time strengthening their reasoning powers. Young ladies who may wish private instruction or who would like to pursue some particular branch of instruction, such as History, English or Classical Literature, or any of the Modern Languages, will be received at a moderate charge. Able masters are employed in the extra branches and lecture in the natural sciences and in an extended and scientific English education. Spanish, Italian and German languages are also taught.

Terms for boarding students.

	Per annum
Board and tuition in Latin, French and English	$300.00
Fuel for the season	3.00
Stationery	4.00
Seat in Church	6.00

Miss Haines can accommodate comfortably in her family twenty young ladies. Day pupils are also accepted.

There followed a long list of testimonials headed by Theodore Frelinghuysen, LL.D., chancellor of the New York University.

Mr. Henry De Saussure replied promptly upon receiving the letter from Miss Haines.

Charleston
March 20, 1850

Miss Haines,
Dear Madam;

Your favor of 9th inst. was the first intimation I had of the safe arrival at New York of Miss Morse and our dear little Henry Boone, the son of my lamented and beloved Sister. Some time previously by overland mail I had received a very interesting letter from his father, Bishop Boone (who had himself lived with me many years as a son and studied law in my office), consigning my nephew to me for paternal care, nurture and education.

This movement was the result of a plan arranged between the Bishop and myself prior to his return to China. It was then decided that he should not carry his daughter Mary back with him and that, if the climate did not agree with Henry he should be sent back to me. The ill health of Henry has now forced the Bishop to the self-denial and sacrifice of a painful separation from his first-born child. His letter to me indicates the agonizing conflict in his mind between the course of duty and parental feeling and his final acquiescence and submission to what he deems the Divine will. My promise to the Bishop is sacred and must be inviolate; and duty blended with affection conspire to make Henry a great object of solicitude to me. From these facts and circumstances you will appreciate my motive in desiring to have Henry early domesticated with my wife (his father's Aunt) and myself.

I am aware, dear Madam, of the overwhelming sorrow which finally caused you to return to America and of the endearing relation which existed between you and my lamented sister and her husband, and I can readily sympathize with the motives and refined feelings which induce you to desire the domestication of Henry with you for some time. I am not insensible to your generous intimation about his education. But as his father has decided upon the plan which he prefers I feel bound to carry it into effect. I will therefore be greatly obliged if you will add to the obligation already imposed on us by your kind attention to him in New York, if you will have him placed on board one of the steamers between New York and Charleston under proper protection about the middle of the month.

With high personal respect, Dear Madam, and esteem

Your obliged,

Henry W. De Saussure

It was several days before Henry's round of being feted was over and Miss Haines was at liberty to fetch him home to her Young Ladies School. It was recreation hour and the young ladies were gathered in little groups in the large parlor awaiting the arrival of this unusual creature, a boy, who was to be a member of their household for a while. They had heard a great deal about him from Miss Haines and were anxious to set eyes on him. When he entered the room all eyes were upon him and Henry heard a suppressed giggle. He was

formally introduced to each pupil and felt acutely embar-
rassed. Amelia, Susanna, Charity, Aurelia, Jane—the names
were a blur and he was sure he wouldn't remember any of
them. His experience with girls was exceedingly limited and
he had an uneasy feeling that they were all looking at his legs!
His relief was great when Miss Haines finally said she would
take him across the hall to her own private parlor to meet her
mother. The girls were about to start out on their afternoon
promenade, two by two, with their teacher. He would see
them again at the supper table. Henry learned that he was
to sleep on the couch in the little parlor-office adjoining the
downstairs bedroom of Miss Haines and her white-haired
mother, with whom Henry felt at ease with the first greeting.

When the gong sounded for supper his elderly friend invited him to accompany her to the dining room. As they
crossed the hall a small bevy of girls was coming down the
wide staircase. Henry caught a sentence or two of what they
were saying. "Is he trying to look like a girl too, wearing those
kilts? And those curls? He looks like a tall baby. Nobody over
six wears them." Henry turned scarlet and wanted to run. He
had never given his legs a thought until now. He tried to slide
onto his chair next to Miss Haines as quickly as possible and
hide the offending legs under the table. When he dared look
up from his plate he met the eyes of the girl across from him
and was aware that she looked like a friendly human being.
Miss Haines and her mother were most kind and maybe it
wasn't going to be so bad after all. If only he could get
his godmother to buy him some long checked trousers, which
he realized now most of the boys his age wore. But when he
timidly approached Miss Haines on the subject she replied
that since he was so soon going to his uncle, she thought it
wise to let him decide on Henry's wardrobe.

The young ladies under twelve were permitted to play in
Gramercy Park in the center of the square instead of going for
a walk after school, and Henry begged to be allowed to play
with them. The little girls had wooden hoops which they
enjoyed chasing around the square, guiding and impelling

them with a slim iron rod. There was no traffic to fear as they rolled their hoops, for if a carriage did approach they could hear the sound of the horses' hoofs some distance away and guide their hoops onto the grass. The attractive miniature park was not enclosed by a fence. After the first time or two Henry got out his beautiful kite in the form of a butterfly, slightly battered by its long journey. His young companions vied for the honor of holding and letting out the string while Henry raced with the kite the length of the park, trying to give it the impetus to be airborne. Sometimes it fell to the ground with a plop, but once in a while it caught an air current and sailed above the little trees which bordered the grass. Then what a thrill it was to feel the string tug at his hands as the kite soared higher and higher, its two ribbonlike tails streaming out beyond the gaily colored wings!

It was six weeks before Miss Haines found a suitable escort with whom her charge could travel down the coast to Charleston. She wrote Mr. De Saussure when to expect Henry saying:

I have engaged Henry's passage on the 20th of April and he has a very good escort to you. He is with us now and I esteem it a gt. privilege to have had him only these few weeks. He is a fine manly boy and promises to reward amply careful culture. He is looking forward with great pleasure to the time of his departure and begs me to enclose a little note he has penned to you.

Mr. Frederick Winston, a warm friend of Bishop Boone's, went to the vessel and received Henry and he remained in his family, receiving the tenderest care, 'til he came to me. In fact all of the Bishop's friends have been so kind to Henry that I have had serious fears that the flattering attentions would spoil him and rob him of the simplicity which is now one of his greatest charms.

Henry's letter, written in a round childish hand, read as follows:

Dear Uncle.

Miss Haines has just got that letter from you she has been very kind to me. I have been to the City Hall and over to Elizabethtown and Huntington gallery of art, Highbridge, which is a very pleasant place and we ran about and threw snowballs and played nicely.

Your Affectionate Nephew

H. W. Boone

If only William Boone had known that his beloved son, Henry, had arrived safely in Charleston and was comfortably housed with his esteemed aunt and uncle. Seven months after Henry's departure—mails were so uncertain—he had had no word as to his son's arrival. He was afraid his letter committing Henry to his uncle's care had never been delivered and pictured his uncle's amazement at seeing Henry walk in with no arrangements having been made. To add to his confusion a letter from Miss Haines was finally received by Phoebe. Her friend stated that Henry had arrived in New York and that she had asked Mr. H. W. De Saussure to let her keep and educate the boy at her school. Then William was sure his uncle had not received his letter. He wrote Mr. De Saussure urging him never to send a letter directly by ship but to send it to Mr. Irving in New York, asking him to forward it by the overland route from England, as being more reliable. Such were the inconveniences of having no postal service. In this letter to his uncle, William told of the birth, about six weeks after Henry left home, of Phoebe's third little boy. He was named Stephen Elliott after Phoebe's brother. It did not turn out to be twins after all!

Dr. John Boone's year spent at sea and in visiting his brother-in-law, Henry De Saussure, had not restored his health to the degree he had hoped. His mother, Mary Boone, was seriously concerned about him upon his return to Charleston where she was living in the old Boone "town house"—so named when the family lived on the old plantation at Boone Hall. She proposed that they sell the house and buy a farm in the hill country somewhere so that John might try an out-door life instead of going back to his medical practice. John finally came to the reluctant conclusion that this would be a wise move and went off to see if he could locate a farm. He found a small one in the northwest corner of the state near a town named Pendleton. He thought he would like to try raising livestock rather than going in for a lot of planting. Shortly before Henry's arrival in Charleston his grand-mother had left that city and, with her daughters Eliza and Mary and their younger brother, Philip-Smith, had moved to the farm, taking Henry's sister, little Maney, with them. The farm lay at an elevation of some two thousand feet in the foothills of the Blue Ridge Mountains, and they named it most fittingly: "Rocky Retreat." John had erected a comfort-able farmhouse to which they added a carriage house, barns, and smoke house. Mary brought up some of the old furniture and fireplace equipment from Charleston. They had long since dispensed with all but a few of the old house servants, and John built small houses for them and their families. John bought a couple of milk cows, two horses, and a few pigs and chickens to start with. It was a drastic change in the pattern of living but all agreed that, in spite of the rocks, the clear mountain air and wooded hills were enough compensation for the change.

The Boones found that although some of their neighbors were honest but rough farm people there were others with whom they could enjoy social contacts. John's mother wrote Henry De Saussure:

My Dear Friend,

My son, George Fraser, has been visiting me but he and Mary leave for Charleston on Monday. Fradge being with me has enabled me to return all the visits of my neighbors. I had the pleasure of dining with Senator John Calhoun and took wine with him and was handed to the carriage by him. Mrs. John C. has been quite marked in her attentions to us. I dined out three days running. I went with Fraser as John don't like to go out and we have no one to drive us but

John. I took the opportunity to pay off all my calls. While I drive with Fraser the girls go on horseback. John's health is as usual.

As soon as his grandmother heard that Henry had arrived she and all the rest of the family wrote to greet him and to ask his uncle to permit Henry to come up to the farm for the summer. In one of these letters to Mr. De Saussure, Henry's grandmother said:

Eliza bought herself a carryall—holds four persons. Everyone who has seen it says it is the neatest they ever saw up here. The price $100.00. Liz gave all the directions herself, chose the colors of the lining, binding, painting, had the door to open in the back, steps fixed her way. Ordered it fixed to draw with one or two horses and when it was finished he told several persons he would not build another like it for $100. again. It has a neat appearance. She then bought herself a gentle, quiet horse, Mary and herself can drive. Mary drove me to Colonel Pickens, about five miles. They never could get the farm horses—always ploughing or hauling rails or going to the mill—something or another. And now they are quite independent to go out whenever they like. A very gentle quiet beast for $50. Des. advised Liz to ride as often as she could.

I enclose you William's letter [the one regarding the care of Henry, which had arrived at long last], and thank you for sending it to me. William was truly distressed when he wrote that letter! I sincerely feel for him but Henry can't be on kinder hands than you and my sister and I know your children will be kind to him. All unite in most affectionate love to you, my sister and all your children,

Your truly attached friend and sister,

M. J. Boone

It was very near the end of the school term when Henry arrived at the tall, narrow De Saussure home on Meeting Street. He found a warm welcome there and felt most grateful to his Aunt Susan when one of her first acts in his behalf was to take him out to the barber and to the tailor's to be measured for long trousers, full at the top, of beautiful checked material, short jackets, and white ruffled shirts, which were then in style. The weather was already warm and it was pleasant to sit with the family on the wide open galleries which ran the length of the house or to play in the large garden at the back, among a riot of blossoms—wisteria, azaleas, honeysuckle, and roses, and the last of the camellias. But there was no one to play with. Henry was beginning to be bored and was glad when, after ten days or so, his uncle announced that there was a chance to send him up to Pendleton in care of a friend and Henry had better go up to visit his grandmother and sister, Mary (whom they all called Maney), since they were all so anxious to see him. The plan was for him to stay a month, but Charleston was so afflicted that summer with an outbreak of breakbone fever (dengue), which affected almost everyone, that as it turned out Henry stayed all summer at Rocky Retreat. Mary Jones Boone wrote to thank her sister-in-law for sending him, giving a charming picture of the meeting between Henry and his sister, Maney. She wrote:

> I wish you could have seen the dear children when they met. The girls had been out and did not return before candlelight. We did not tell them Henry had arrived—wanted to see if they would know Henry. Maney looked at him, he went up and took her hand and said, "Howdye." Maney said, "Who is this?" I said, "Henry." She hugged him and kissed his face, cheek, forehead. I told her she would devour him with kisses. She can't bear him out of her sight—holds his hand as if she is afraid to lose him. Dear children, I hope God's blessing will be upon them. Miss Haines must be a warm friend to the children.

Almost everything was new to Henry and he reveled in it all. Best of all was to be surrounded by warmly loving relations who made much of him and to have his little sister, Maney, nine years old now, to play with. He loved riding the horses and helping to feed the animals. In July he wrote to his Charleston family telling some of the delights of country life:

The Rocky Retreat
July 16th, 1850

My Dear Uncle;

    I had a very pleasant ride yesterday afternoon to Pickins'. Uncle John went to call there. Many and I went with him and we both rode Uncle Dessy's horse which Many has called after me, it is a very tame horse. Many sat on the saddle I sat behind it. I often ride on horseback and I like it very much. I like this place very much. Many and myself are allowed all the fence corners of the garden to plant in and we have some peas and corn growing very well. Many has just got from her garden an ear of corn which is the earliest in the neighborhood. We were all sorry to learn from Aunt Glover's letter that Aunt Susan and yourself have had falls and hurt yourselves. I hope you are quite well by this. Many says I must give her love to Aunt Susan and yourself and tell you she is trying to dry some apples to send to you. She has never dried any before but hopes to succeed well enough for you to be able to eat some of them.

    I congratulate you on the birth of your grand daughter. Do give my love to Aunt Susan and all of my cousins.

I am your affectionate Nephew,

H. W. Boone

Two people on the farm who took a special interest in Henry and Maney were old Aunt Malby and her son, Benji. Aunt Malby had been in the family for three generations and had many stories to tell of Master Willie when he was a boy and of his father, Master Tom, back when they lived at Boone Hall plantation. Henry loved a good story, and he and his sister often went over to Aunt Malby's house and sat on the porch on either side of her while she told them stories of the early days. Aunt Malby did not work anymore, for she was stiff with rheumatism, but her son, Benji, was John's righthand man. Uncle Benji had a son about Henry's age and desired that he should grow up with Henry just as he himself had grown up as the friend and companion of Master Willie. It was told that when Cindy, Benji's wife, took the baby to be baptized the minister said to her at the appropriate time in the service, "Name this child."

She replied, "Ah names him Beelzebub."

The minister looked at her in astonishment and said, "But Cindy, Beelzebub means the devil."

"Fo' Lawd's sake," she exclaimed in a horrified voice, and then, as quick as a flash, "Name him Trumpeter for to praise the Lord." So Trumpeter was Henry's companion on the farm as Benji had been William's.

The summer passed all too quickly, and Uncle Henry sent for his nephew to return to Charleston to be ready to enroll when school opened. The parting with Maney and Trumpeter and his grandmother was hard but there was no good school for him to attend in the area of Pendleton. Their Aunt Eliza had been teaching Maney and proposed doing so for one more year and then applying for a teaching job in some school, hoping to take Maney along with her. Henry entered school in Charleston and soon became popular among the other boys. Having lived abroad he had an aura of romance about him and already showed promise of becoming the accomplished raconteur which he afterwards became. He soon was popular with them as a storyteller. They loved particularly his tales of the sea, and he made them salty enough by weaving into them the yarns sailors on shipboard had recounted to Henry and the other children aboard on their long trip from China. Henry was also a born mimic and caused much laughter by impersonating his teachers behind their backs. This accomplishment brought him trouble after he had been in Charleston about a year. His uncle was put up for some office by his admirers, who organized a campaign parade. Henry W. De Saussure did not march in the parade, such an act being beneath his dignity. But Henry did! He managed to sneak his uncle's tall silk hat and walking cane out of the house and, holding a placard on which was written "The Hon H. W. De S. for Senator," imitated his straight-backed uncle to the vast amusement of the crowd. He had meant no harm but when Henry William learned of it he was anything but pleased. Henry was told that to mimic was not the way a young gentleman should act and felt the strap.

In school he did well in some subjects and poorly in others. He had read anything he could lay his hands on and had absorbed those things which interested him and which he understood and dismissed the others. Consequently, he had poor habits of study, tending to shy away from anything which seemed dry or uninteresting. Latin was one of the subjects he deemed dry. His father had started him in Latin and Greek when he was only six. He detested them, but Latin especially was a must for all educated people. His teacher complained to his uncle-guardian that Henry was not handing in his Latin assignments. Mr. De Saussure decided it was time Henry learned that there were some things he must do whether he liked them or not. The boy was led to a room and told he would stay there on only bread and water until he completed all his back assignments and handed them in in perfect form. It became a battle royal between Henry's stubbornness and his uncle's determination. The contest lasted for two days and then Henry had the translations ready, as he had been capable of all along. But he never came to love Latin. This became the pattern of young Henry's life for the next few years—the school terms in Charleston, the summers at Rocky Retreat.

While life was flowing evenly for Henry in America, it was not going as well for his parents in Shanghai. China was in a period of turmoil. The emperor, whose reign name was Tao Kuang, was not the strong leader that the early rulers of the Ching dynasty, Kang Hsi and Chien Lung, had been. During the first one hundred and fifty years of the Manchu or Ching dynasty China's borders had expanded, internal order had been maintained in spite of a growing population, and the arts and learning had been advanced. But as with most imperial houses, the leadership deteriorated. It was a long dynasty, lasting from 1644 A.D. to 1912. The early emperors had had dealings with the foreigners but had held them in their proper place, as outsiders, guests. Tao Kuang had not been able to preserve his country from defeat at the hands of Great Britain. The land was troubled with unrest and revolts. In 1850 he died and was succeeded by his son, Hsien Feng. When Phoebe heard of the death of the emperor she said to one of the servants that she was sorry to hear of it. He replied that it didn't matter for the nation had suffered so many calamities during his reign that he must have been a bad man. Floods, famine, war, and pestilence could not have occurred had he been a man of virtue.

Up to this time Phoebe had had excellent health but now her health as well as the bishop's seemed to be failing. He kept having attacks of the spine and heart trouble. The treatment was to apply plasters until blisters appeared and was most uncomfortable, although it seemed to supply some relief through counterirritation.

But there was some progress in the work to cheer them. A version of the Gospel of Matthew in the Shanghai or Wu dialect had been completed through the joint efforts of the bishop and Mr. Syle. Twelve candidates had been baptized during the year 1850, making twenty-two in all, and there were nine others who were candidates. The boys' school had increased in enrollment, and at last a school building for the girls and a church for the compound were to be built. Mr. Syle contrived a novel plan for the distribution of the newly translated Gospel. He had a woodcut made of the church and beneath it in Chinese the words: "Whoever reads this book and does not understand its meaning, at any hour may come to Christ Church and personally receive explanation. The church is in Shanghai at the south side of the Hong Bridge. Every worship day (Sunday) at 9 and 3 o'clock the Religion is preached."

Drawing of the Church of Our Saviour, bishop's residence,
and Girls' Boarding School, Hongkew, Shanghai, 1853.

Also to lighten their load Miss Morse was returning, improved in health, and was bringing with her a new missionary, Miss Lydia Fay, who soon won the hearts of everyone. The bishop wrote to his uncle:

> We are in daily expectation of Miss Morse and Miss Fay in the "Horatio." They will bring very seasonable relief to some members of the Mission, to myself in particular, as I shall be able to give up my class in the school which occupies me now three hours a day. It is a great mercy that we can get self-denying women to come out to join the Mission, deserted as we are by the male sex. I assure you these ladies are doing good work and a most important work for the

spread of the Gospel here in China. The American Board of Commissioners had tried it in their Mission and had come to the conclusion not to send out any more single females unless they went to reside with a brother or sister.

The late lamented Walter Lowrie who was a Presbyterian missionary at Ningpo, after he had been staying in my family a few weeks [in connection with the Bible translation] said to me, "I now see why it is you can employ single female missionaries in your mission with success. It is owing to your having a Bishop and the respect that is felt for that office by these ladies. We could not have them in our mission in Ningpo." If any number of Presbyters—if nothing short of a Bishop can keep single ladies in order, shall I not have my hands full when the Horatio arrives and we have four of these unmanageable creatures in the mission? Let the matter be accounted for as it may, our school has been remarkably blessed and the success that has been vouchsafed I ascribe, under God, mainly to the excellent influence of the ladies who have charge of the boys. It is a woman's gift to win upon the hearts of the young as men can never do and it is this faculty which opens for them so wide a field of usefulness in heathen lands.

William and Phoebe had a terrible blow in August 1851: their youngest son, Stephen Elliott, was taken ill suddenly and died. On August 30 Phoebe wrote a heartbroken letter to her sister, Hetty:

My bright and merry and beautiful little Elliott has been called away to join the other happy spirits around the throne of God, cut down oh so suddenly. We could hardly realize he was sick before he was gone. He was nineteen months and twenty-three days old. From his birth he had developed rapidly in all physical qualities. I never saw a happier, prettier specimen of rosy childhood. He never had any sickness worth mentioning and so never was fretful. I have been able to say and to feel throughout this trial, "Thy will be done." Before my darling babe had breathed his last, grace was given me to feel that God's decision would be my choice.

People at a distance in Christian lands where the blessings of Christianity and civilization are enjoyed are apt to think that there must be so many trials incident to a life in a heathen land and consequent on it, that missionaries must of necessity feel more weaned from earth than other Christians and that they must certainly realize, if any do, the fact that they are pilgrims and strangers there. This is not the experience of those who are living in *China*. We are beset with the same temptations, exposed to more evil influences and have the same sinful natures than those we have left behind are subject to. We need the lessons to be learned from affliction quite as much as those do who seem to have more of earth born pleasures and cares to bind their hearts to the passing world than we have. I feel that it is the case with me. I often feel I am too much like Martha, careful and troubled about household matters when it would be more profitable to be sitting like Mary at my Saviour's feet. May God grant this trial He has lately sent upon me may prove a blessing to my soul, and while I mourn for my precious boy, oh pray that I may seek more earnestly than I have ever done the things which are at God's right hand.

Willie has an excellent understanding and a simple faith. He came in one day when I was feeling very much distressed and without asking any question came up to me and said, "Mamma, you ought not to cry so much. I don't cry—and 'tisn't that I did not love Ellie. I loved him very much, and I think about him a great deal, but God took him and he has gone to such a nice place that I don't cry about it, and you ought not to cry either."

Tomorrow will be the seventh anniversary of my marriage and leaving home. Since the 6th anniversary I have had two dear little infants, [she had recently lost a stillborn] committed to their graves. They lie side by side in a strange land far from the dwelling place of their forefathers. But God has promised to gather his own out of every land.

Soon after the death of the little boy an event occurred

which brought joy to the Boone family. Wong Kung-chai, whom they considered as their son, was ordained as catechist on September 7 in Christ Church, Shanghai. At the same time another young man, Soo Long, was ordained a deacon. From the beginning of his missionary work Bishop Boone had envisaged a church in which the leadership would be Chinese. He saw in these two young men and in one of the other students, Yen Yung-kiung, the first three stones on which the living church would be built. Nor did they disappoint him. The first two became outstanding church leaders and Mr. Yen was for many years a professor in Saint John's University, which grew out of the little boys' school all three had attended. Wong Kung-chai was made happy when the girl he was engaged to asked to be prepared for baptism. She had profited exceedingly by her residence at the girls' school and promised to make an excellent wife for Chai. She was loved by her teachers, Miss Jones and Miss Morse, and admired by the other girls, who were all younger than herself.

In the first year of the reign of the new emperor, Hsien Feng, the Mission Board of the Episcopal Church in New York began to have applicants for China other than the doughty females the bishop found not too unmanageable. The Rev. and Mrs. R. Nelson were the leaders of a promising group of new recruits who reached Shanghai on the 400-ton bark the *Oriental,* under Captain Dale, 145 days out from Boston. With them were the Rev. Cleveland Keith and a teacher, Mr. J. T. Points. They were met at the Chinese customshouse landing and taken directly to the Boones', where Christmas dinner awaited them. The Rev. and Mrs. McClatchie of the English Church Mission joined them. Everyone was in a festive mood and it was a gay occasion. Mr. Keith was immediately captivated by the vivacious Miss Caroline Tenney sitting across the table, who had come out the year before. It was not many months before the two were engaged to be married.

Some time later Mr. Nelson, recollecting those early weeks in Shanghai, wrote:

We were introduced to the members of the various other Protestant Missions then living at this port. These together with our own body of missionaries in Shanghai made 46 in all. Of all the missionaries in Shanghai in 1851 Dr. and Mrs. Medhurst were much the oldest. I know he considered the "Delegates Version" of the Scriptures in Chinese the great work of his life. I felt a reverential regard for him, but he was not at all pleased when I said to him in all sincerity, "I suppose we must look on you, Dr. Medhurst, as the grandfather of all missionaries." But the word "controversy," over which term should be used in the "Delegates Version" to mean *God*, was rife at the time and he was not flattered to my allusion to a family likeness! Mrs. Medhurst's kindly hospitality, however, was a cordial to all newcomers. Dr. Lockhart, there when we arrived, was another ruling spirit of the London Mission. As a medical man I have never known one more prompt in coming or more careful in attending to his patients. And as a surgeon I have never seen one operate with more ease and skill. Dr. Bridgman of the American Board [Congregational Church] was supposed at that time to be far gone with consumption. But soon after our arrival he took a voyage around the world and the year at sea gave him an additional ten years of life in China. Transparent simplicity and godly sincerity marked his life. After his death Mrs. Bridgman named her girls' school the "Bridgman Memorial School."

Outside the missionary circle we met many interesting people. Of course at that time there were no diplomatic Ministers resident at Peking, nor in China .The Governor of Hong Kong, Sir George Bonham, was Her British Majesty's Representative at Hong Kong, having communication with Peking only through the Viceroy at Canton. Mr. [later Sir] Rutherford Alcock was the British Consul here. He showed great ability at the time of the outrage done to Dr. Medhurst, Mr. Muirhead and Dr. Lockhart. Mrs. Alcock was a true Dame of Grace and had by nature the refining attractions which titles alone cannot give. Young Mr. Walter Medhurst, afterwards knighted, was interpreter at the Consulate, having for a time acted as Consul pro tem. Mr. [later Sir] Harry Parkes had not yet won his spurs. As there was no U.S. Consul at Shanghai, Mr. Ed. Cunningham of the house of Russell & Co., did the duty of a Consul, and signed himself "U.S. Acting Vice-Consul"—a man of whom I would say had no superior in capacity, grasp and largeness of view among his contemporaries whom I have met in China. France had a Consul, M. Montigny, who like the British Consul was not connected with any mercantile firm. The consul for Portugal was Mr. T. C. Beale, head of the house of "Dent, Beale and Co."—a man of ability and also of great good taste as is evident from his residence and surroundings on the Bund, unequalled to this day for simple elegance. It is sad to see its beauty gradually becoming marred for the accommodation of brick and mortar. In proof of the esteem in which Mr. Beale was held by the Chinese, I may mention at his funeral, as his body was lowered to the grave, I saw a Chinaman, who had some business connection with him, come up to the grave and pay him just such worship as he would have paid his father.

There are few places in the world, I suppose, which have changed as rapidly as Shanghai. When my wife and I arrived in 1851 all the space from the North Gate of the Walled City and the creek which later marked the foreign settlement boundary line [the Yang-king-pang] was a Chinese suburb in the midst of which M. Montigny, the French Consul, had his residence. Near the present bridge—there was no bridge then—stood a few foreign houses, chief of which was a jewelry and variety store of Messrs. Renni Schmidt and Co. Very few foreigners lived on that side of the creek, only the Yates and Shucks of the American Baptist Mission and the Taylors and Jenkins of the Methodist Mission, all from the Southern States. The American Presbyterians have since 1845 maintained a Mission Station at Ningpo, manned by Mr. Culbertson and others, but in 1850 he was transferred to Shanghai and appointed to take the place of Mr. Lowrie—killed by pirates—on the Committee for translating the Old Testament. Thus he was closely associated with Bishop Boone. Mr. Culbertson was joined in July 1850 by Mr. and Mrs. J. K. Wright, and the Presbyterians first lived in a house outside the Native city, at Yang-king-pang. That is where

I first met them, but they were already planning to build a mission house and hopefully a school inside the city at the South Gate. These, together with the men, predominantly British, of the several export and import firms and a few shipping companies and the Captains and crews of the many ships which came and went, comprised our foreign community in 1851.

Those of you who came to Shanghai on or before that date have but to look around you to be aware of the tremendous physical changes which are taking place in the city. We may yet see a cosmopolitan metropolis here: And old China, too, has begun to change—from the lower levels upward, instead of from the government downward. There is coming up a ground swell from this sea of human elements which will act on all above it. To change the figure, there are entering wedges in the lower strata, through trade, emigration, contacts with those from the outside and treaties signed between China and other nations, showing already signs of an upheaval which will gradually influence every upper layer until it reaches the very top. But the motive power producing these results is not any eagerness of the Chinese Government to follow foreign ways. Far from it—it will be the growing number of skills acquired by Chinese artisans, the increasing trade in foreign goods of many kinds, the wealth of new knowledge in geography and the sciences to be added to Chinese ancient classical wisdom, the growing acquaintance with the English language which will open up much world literature to the people, indeed, the translation of the finest literature— above all the Bible—into their own language, and finally the extending influence of Christian Missions who have ever been pioneers of good will which will gradually effect the change which we now see in its beginning. "Knowledge," said Lord Bacon, "is power"—and this increasing knowledge in many of the lower class of the Chinese, especially along the seaboard, must be accepted by the literati and the Government or they must give away before it.

Mr. Nelson was a far-seeing man!

CHAPTER 8

THE TAIPING
REBELLION

Mr. Nelson's prophecy was already beginning to come true. Old China was indeed starting a slow change, beginning at the level of the peasant and the artisan—a change which has been gradually taking place ever since and is reshaping the face of the nation. But news traveled exceedingly slowly in Nelson's day. Shanghai did not yet boast of its *North China Daily News*. There were no news media at all, other than the erratic mails. Thomas Edison was a small child with the uses of electricity still coiled up in his head. So Shanghai had no means of knowing that in the south China province of Kwangsi, a place of peppery, short-statured men, revolution was brewing,. It was led by a man named Hung Hsiu-chuan. He was a native of Kwantung and had been a scholar of promise, but when he went up for the provincial examinations in Canton (which, if passed, would assure him a government post) he failed. Hung tried three times with the same result. While in Canton he was handed a Christian tract with the title *Good Words to Exhort the Age*. It both intrigued and puzzled him. It spoke of the true God, "Shang-ti." He already knew that Shang-ti was a God over the other gods and that it was a part of the office of the emperor in Peking to sacrifice to him once a year on behalf of the people at the famed temple and altar of heaven.

About this time Hung fell ill and in his delirium had a vision. He seemed to be in a luminous place where an old man cleansed him and ordered him to cleanse the country of its demons. When he recovered, this dream stayed in his mind and he decided the old man he had seen must be Shang-ti and the devils, idols. He went over into the neighboring province of Kwangsi and gathered a group of young men about him. They organized an "Association to Worship God," which was at first just that. But uninstructed in Christian doctrine, they formulated a hodgepodge of superstition and Christian belief. Some able men joined the movement but they were more politically minded than Hung was at first, and some of them suggested that the devils were the Manchus and that they were the ones who should be driven out. The idea took hold among the hotheads and those who felt themselves oppressed. A "Triad," a secret revolutionary society which aimed at restoring the Ming dynasty, joined them. But most of the rebels had the aim of destroying the Manchus and establishing their own dynasty, to be called Taiping or Great Peace. The movement was limited to the far south until 1852, when their army began a march northward into the buffer province of Hunan, traveling by way of the sizable Hsiang River. It was an army of the dispossessed with a grudge against not only the Manchus but also the rich and landed classes. Hung declared himself the son of God, Shang-ti; but could not control his hordes and they increasingly pillaged and burned wherever they went. Early in 1853 they captured Nanking and there they established their capital. Uneasy rumors began to drift in to Shanghai.

Things had been going well with the Episcopal Mission stationed at Shanghai. The schools were prospering and new day schools were opened in various parts of the city under the supervision of Wong Kung-chai and some of the new missionaries—with Chinese teachers, of course. One thing worried Bishop Boone. Phoebe Boone's health had declined steadily ever since the birth of her last baby. William thought a sea voyage might do her good, and since she had taken no furlough since coming out in 1845, she was finally persuaded of the wisdom of going to the United States first and taking the two little boys, with the promise that William would follow her when he felt he could leave. He wanted to see to it that the new members of the staff, the Nelsons, Mr. Keith, Mr. Points, and Miss Fay, should have uninterrupted time for language study and planned to offer them evening classes in Chinese customs and culture. In February 1852 Phoebe and the little boys, Willie, aged six, and Tommy, five, together with their beloved amah, Bo Bo—"Old Lady"—said their farewells. Bo Bo was a widow with one son who had been acting in a way that was childish for his years. He depended on her for everything and she was tired of it. His mother thought she would see what would happen if he had to depend on his own efforts for a while. Besides, the old lady had a streak of the adventurer in her and already savored the fine tales she would have to tell her neighbors when she came home. And she was truly fond of Willie and Tommy. So they set sail, though for Phoebe it was hard to leave William, unwell as he was. William was relieved when at long last he received a letter saying they had arrived safely in New York on the fifteenth of June.

The little party of four did not linger long in New York, for Phoebe was eager to be reunited with her dear relatives and friends and to show them her fine little boys. In spite of the heat in Beaufort, South Carolina, and in Savannah, Georgia, where they stayed for some time with Phoebe's brother, Stephen Elliott, they had a wonderful time. But they were glad to accept the invitation of old friends of both William and Phoebe's, the Barnwells, to stay at their summer home at Bay Point, where it was much cooler. The children especially enjoyed the beach. One day not long after they got there Phoebe went down to the beach and found Bo Bo digging determinedly. "Why, Bo Bo," she said, "why are you doing that?"

The old lady astonished her by bursting into tears. "I don't know what my son is doing," she sobbed. "Tommy told me we are standing right over China on the other side of the world and if I dug I could make a tunnel and go through." Phoebe tried to comfort her by telling her the bishop would surely come before long and they would all go back home to China together.

The bishop did come, but not until January 1853. He had appointed a committee composed of Messrs. Syle, Keith, and Nelson to look after the affairs of the mission during his absence. When he left, everything was in good order and Shanghai temporarily at peace. Upon arrival in New York he appeared before the Mission Board. They were shocked by his gaunt appearance and advised that he go to a quiet spot and forget all duties for a while until he regained his strength. They vetoed any effort to speak in behalf of China until he was a great deal better—a great concession on their part and a disappointment to the bishop, who wished he had the strength to tell about the great need and opportunity there was to present the word of God in populous China. The bishop had with him a young man, Tong Chu-kiung, who was already a candidate for the ministry. The board members took him under their wing and suggested that he stay in the north while the bishop went home to the south.

So William departed, going first to Beaufort for reunion with Phoebe and the boys and Bo Bo and then going with them to the home of his beloved aunt and uncle in Charleston. They arrived at the De Saussure home, where William had spent so many of his scholastic days as a youth, on a Saturday. Henry was out playing shin ball with his friends but was soon sent for. He came in hurriedly, hot from the exercise, his curly auburn hair in disarray. He advanced cautiously with his eyes solely on his father and put out his hand, but his eyes were shining. William took his son in his arms and the flame of love and understanding between them glowed again, never to be extinguished. Phoebe stood waiting, and Henry turned to her—remembrance of her love and care as his mother and teacher flooding his mind and heart. He had seen her and the boys several times during the past few months and it always brought him joy. He gave Willie a pat on the back and chunky Tommy a chuck under the chin. The family was reunited at last, except for Mary Eliza (Maney) in Pendleton with her grandmother, Uncle John, and Aunt Eliza. Aunt Mary had recently married their neighbor, J. C. Pickens, and young Phillip-Smith was away at medical school.

William and the family stayed for a week in Charleston, but there were so many invitations from old friends, which could not be denied, that William found it heartwarming but by no means restful. He looked forward to a period of quiet inactivity at his brother John's farm, and the family, except Henry, departed for Rocky Retreat. It was a pity that the Christmas holidays were so recently over and school had commenced, for Henry had to stick at his books. He bid them a reluctant farewell, his father promising that he should join them during the coming summer.

William could not help holding the image of a two-year-old little girl which lingered in his mind when he thought of his daughter, Mary Eliza. When a tall eleven-year-old young lady in full skirts and ruffled pantaloons rushed out of the house, as at long last their carriage stopped in front of Rocky Retreat farmhouse and threw herself into her father's arms, her father couldn't believe his senses. They went quickly into the house and were warmly greeted by the rest of the family. William saw that his mother had aged considerably and noted with a professional eye that his brother John did not look as well as when he had visited them in Shanghai. Eliza was her same efficient, schoolmarmish self. She told him that old Aunt Malby could not wait to see him, so he went almost immediately over to her little house. She held out her arms to him from her rocking chair and said over and over, "My little Marse Willie done come back to his mammy." Benji came in while William was there, a warm glow of affection in his eyes and smile. The years and responsibilities slipped off William's shoulders and he felt that they two were boys again roaming the woods of Walterboro. Benji called in his son.

Trumpeter, and told William that he had given him to Master Henry to be his boy, just as he himself had been Master William's boy in those happy days. So William relaxed in the healing glow of family love and attention. He had not realized how exhausted he was. The boys were enchanted by the new experience of riding the horses and helping to milk the cows, and Bo Bo took upon herself the care of the chickens and felt more at home than she had since coming to this strange land.

It was a treat to William to have a daily paper to read. His mother subscribed both to the Walterboro *Courier* and the *Mercury*. He perused them eagerly in an attempt to catch up on the news. Franklin Pierce of New Hampshire had just been elected to the presidency, a man of good education who was considered a hero because of his record during the Mexican War. He was with General Scott in the advance toward Mexico City and had been promoted to brigadier general. But after Pierce's inauguration William read with a deepening concern reports of the debates going on in both the Senate and the House of Representatives in regard to repealing the Missouri Compromise, passed in 1820. There were those in the South who wished to see the territories opened to the importation of slaves so they might obtain control over them. The Missouri Compromise, which had restored peace to the country at a time when the issue of slavery might have imperiled the Union, was again in peril. It stipulated that states and territories lying above the parallel 36° 30′ north latitude should exclude slavery. Its repeal would open the territories of Missouri, Kansas, and Nebraska to slavery. The controversy again made a direct issue of slavery as against freedom—a controversy which had been quiet for over thirty years. President Pierce, not wishing to anger the friends who had helped elect him, was conciliatory toward the exponents of slavery, and in May 1854 the law of 1820 which established the compromise was repealed. Thus the rift between the North and the South was widened, and William could see that grave consequences might arise.

By spring William felt physically much better and wrote the board that he felt well enough to undertake a speaking tour. In May 1853 the family left Rocky Retreat and journeyed to Georgia, where William left Phoebe and the boys with Bishop Elliott in Savannah; here he spoke in several of the churches before going on. He met with a good response, for many of his listeners were already deeply interested in the China Mission. Two ladies, Miss Wray of Georgia and Miss Conover of Philadelphia, applied and were appointed to go out with Bishop Boone when he should return. Mr. Points had come home from Shanghai on a short furlough and was now ready to return. In October 1853 they, together with the Boone family, Bo Bo, and Tong Chu-kiung, sailed for Shanghai. It proved a pleasant trip, if a bit long, and Tong proved valuable to them all in their study of Chinese while on board. They arrived in Shanghai on April 14, 1854.

A few months before Bishop Boone had left Shanghai on his furlough a significant change had started to take place in Japan. That country had been determinedly closed to foreign influences for a hundred years or so. During the sixteenth century there had been trade with the Dutch, Chinese, Portuguese, Spanish, and English. Former relations with China had deteriorated, though Japan owed her much as teacher and spiritual guide in the introduction of writing, the arts, Buddhism, and the Confucian ethic. She viewed the European nations with distrust because of their rivalry and vilification of each other. Japan had noted with alarm the acts of piracy by the Portuguese on the China coast, the taking over of the Philippines by Spain, England's activities in India, and the Dutch exploits in the East Indies. Who could blame her for thinking the only safe course was to close her doors? Christianity was proscribed too and Christians persecuted, because it had been introduced by European Jesuit missionaries who owed their allegiance to the pope in Rome and, it was suspected, not to the emperor of Japan. Edicts were issued prohibiting any Japanese citizen from going abroad, trading with foreigners and building ships capable of carrying on foreign trade. Thus they had sealed their doors.

After that seamen of other countries wrecked or forced ashore on the coast of Japan were treated with utmost cruelty and as often as not killed. Distrust of the foreigner was implanted in the minds of all. But by 1852 the government in Washington, under President Fillmore, began to realize that intercourse with Japan would be of great advantage to America. Steamships were beginning to appear, and if the United States was to develop direct communication with China across the Pacific by their use, it was essential that there be coaling stations along the way. Commodore Perry was instructed to sail for Japan with three main objectives: protection for American shipwrecked sailors, the opening of ports to American vessels to refit and obtain coal, and the opening of ports for trade. He sailed from Norfolk, Virginia, in November 1852 and entered Yokohama Bay in July 1853, to the great consternation of the people on shore. No one had ever seen a steam vessel before and wild reports were sent to the capital at Yedo (Tokyo) throwing that city of over a million people into panic. The country was being attacked by a foreign fleet!

Perry had determined to take a strong stand while at the same time emphasizing the peaceful intentions of the United States. He refused to negotiate with any but a high official and succeeded in receiving a dignified reception and in delivering the president's letter for transmission to the emperor. He told the official that time would be given for the reply and he sailed away to the China coast, saying he would be back in the spring. In February 1854 he returned, was well received, and succeeded in negotiating a treaty. Nagasaki and two other ports would be open to the coaling and refitting of American vessels; the right to appoint a consul to reside in Shimoda was agreed to; protection was guaranteed to shipwrecked sailors; and most-favored-nation treatment endorsed. Advantage was taken of the last clause and of the success of his mission by other nations, and soon England, Holland, and Russia also drew up treaties with Japan.

Even before the Boones' party set foot on Shanghai soil in April 1854 two big pieces of news were told them by the Chinese pilot they engaged to guide their boat past the mouth of the Yangtze and up the Whangpoo River the twelve miles of tricky sandbars to Shanghai. He replied to their questions in regard to Perry's mission in Japan, which they had heard was in progress, with little enthusiasm and then launched into the dreadful news that Shanghai had been captured by the Taiping rebels, who were even now in occupation of the walled native city. He told horrifying tales of burning, looting, and slaughter. Phoebe and the two new ladies were frightened, and all hoped it wasn't true. But when they drew near Shanghai they saw that the usually busy harbor was silent and empty and the town had a dead look.

Very soon after getting back to the mission compound William wrote to his brother-in-law Major John De Saussure to tell him of their safe arrival and also to thank him for having taken William's daughter, Mary, in as a member of his family in Camden, South Carolina, where she could attend school with John's own children, her cousins. He told of the trip and went on to say:

The state of things we met upon our arrival was most sad. The town outside of the walls, that contained when I went away many tens of thousands of inhabitants, is all burned up. The river, which was crowded with native junks for two and a half miles along the shore moored thirty deep in a tier, was bare without one single junk at the wharves. The house where I formerly lived and where our two little boys were born is burned up and with it all that quarter of the town. The city within the walls is in possession of a set of miscreants who are called by the Chinese "Hong Tur," red heads or red caps [red republicans?] who exercise the most despotic rule over the wretched inhabitants—robbing, plundering them and committing the most frightful outrages upon their women and children. The misery which is now experienced throughout the length and breadth of the land is beyond what the human mind can compass in its conception. It is a fearful thing to throw such an Empire as this into anarchy and confusion. Truly "rebellion is as the sin of witchcraft," and Tai Ping Wong [king] has incurred an awful responsibility to both God and man for the misery into which he has thrown myriads of his fellow creatures and the torrents of blood he has shed and is still causing to flow. When people contend for some ennobling principle, a nation may be the gainer tho' much precious blood is shed, but here I fear ('tho it is not the common sentiment) that if Tai Ping Wong succeeds we shall only have a young hothead, with intolerant enthusiasm instead of an old effete don't-care polytheism. How much the cause of truth will be the immediate gainer by the present disturbances, no one can now say; that in the end God will over-rule for the advancement of His cause, I cannot for a moment doubt. I think it too late in the "last days" for the wheels of His providence to roll back the advancing tide of Christianity in China. I think too, we must accept the wonderful opening of Japan, without the shedding of a drop of blood (a thing that has amazed me and indeed all here in the East, and which I think can only be ascribed to His hand) as an earnest of what he is preparing for the Far East. I take courage to press on with new force. I believe that our generation has never before seen any crisis calling for so much prayer and energy in the conduct of missions in this field. We may have to send away our women and children, but my mind is, God giving me health and strength, to stand by the work with all the *men* that will cling to me, let what may come. The Gospel is sent to bind up the broken in heart. It is when men are in affliction and despair of any good in this world that they listen with most interest to the Gospel message, and so we think it is now. I have received several applications for baptism since my return. And if distress can drive this people to the Gospel we may expect to see them come "as doves to their window." It is really heart rending to hear the sad stories they are coming to me with every day. They bring their children in great numbers to our schools and refuse to take them away when we, sorrowing, are obliged to decline them. There is no saying when the present state of anarchy will be over. The last news from the North is that Tai Ping Wong has met with a repulse.

The time has come for closing the mail. We are all on tiptoe for European news to hear whether it is war or peace with Russia. Our friends need have no anxiety as to our safety as we can fly to the ships in the case of an emergency.

I am sincerely and affectionately

Your obliged friend and brother,

Wm. J. Boone

Three weeks later the bishop took time to write his uncle on family matters, knowing that the relatives would all be anxious for news.

Shanghai
May 30, 1854

My dear Uncle:

I found myself upon our first arrival immersed in a sea of business so that I could only send Hal [Henry] a hurried account of matters. We had a house to set in order from which the Missus had been absent for two years. Two weddings at which we had to act the Papa and all the native members to look after and an endless variety of small details. [Two engaged couples had been waiting impatiently for the bishop's return, wanting him and no one else to perform the wedding ceremony—Wong Kung-chai and his bride, and Mr. Keith and Miss Tenney.] Phoebe has been overworked getting her house in order and preparing for the weddings. This has caused so much standing as to bring some swelling to her feet and ankles again. In other respects she is quite well. Willie's hearing was good all through the passage but he is quite deaf just now from a cold he has taken. Poor Tommy seems to have no taste for books. He yawns and becomes sleepy if he has kept at them for five minutes. We exceedingly need a school for them where they would feel the stimulus of other children, pursuing the same studies.

At Chai's wedding Tong, who visited you in Charleston, contributed a band of seven or eight musicians to play three days and parts of nights at an expense of U.S. $2.00 for the whole time: Don't you wish you could get such cheap music in Charleston? What a pleasant diversion for one's friends—a fine band to play while you are taking your tea! But music is eminently a thing about which tastes differ. This band I thought produced the most harsh, brassy unpleasant sounds I have ever heard, even in China. This induced me to ask Tong's opinion about which was best—foreign or Chinese music? He blushed a good deal as if he was going to give an opinion that would not be concurred in and said, "I think, Sir, the Chinese music is the prettiest." Tong's trip to the United States has greatly enlarged his mind and I do not think he will suffer any permanent injury from it but it is evident that he will find it hard to come down contentedly to his five dollars a month for food, clothing and all expenses after the free use of money in the United States. We must not in our vanity, however, suppose that he considers all he heard and saw in the United States superior to what is to be had here in China. When he was first back he went for a visit to his mother in Soochow. He says his mind is fixed and settled to study for the ministry and he has behaved with great propriety ever since he became a candidate.

Old Bo Bo has been a woman of great consequence since her return. The wages paid on our arrival was U.S. $105.00 —the largest sum, perhaps, she has ever had in her hands at once. On the strength of this sum she determined to pull down her old house and build a greater on the site thereof. This has been accomplished and we were invited to the feast of dedication. She put on her silver spectacles, a large cracker bonnet and a crimson calico shawl with white flowers all over it and came to invite us. Thus habited she was the greatest figure of fair that has ever been seen in these parts and the Chinese collected to gaze at her. She boasts very much that she did not suffer the most insignificant heathen ceremony to be used while the house was building. When she first arrived they feasted her up so much that we could seldom get a sight of her and all we could get out of her when we did see her was that she was "Ka weh sah tsay"—"I am rejoiced to death." But poor old soul, she has been made to realize, as millions of others have, how fleeting our joys are here below. Two days ago she came to me with a sad countenance to say that her son was not good. He did nothing but smoke and gamble. This is the son for whose marriage she was making patchwork quilts and saving her money so carefully that she only drew five dollars the whole time she was absent. The graceless chap got married before she got back and resisted her when she was flogging him for gambling. She is quite pressing in her request for baptism but her mind seems like the sand on the seashore. Every impression made on it is soon gone. It would be most gratifying to our feelings if the dear old creature could be truly enlightened. Your old friend, Wong Kung-Chai, our Deacon, has not only taken himself a wife but has built himself a two story house for $370. He is doing very well indeed.

In regard to the revolution he wrote:

The state of things here is most deplorable. The people are downtrodden both by the insurgents and imperialists and the acts of cold-blooded cruelty that are narrated are enough to make the hair stand on end. A regular price is set on heads by each party and there is a set of inhuman wretches here who will deliberately kill an innocent country man and take off his head to get this price of $100. and I am exceedingly sorry to say that there are some renegade foreigners here who exceed even the Chinese in barbarity. The English Chaplain, Mr. Hobson, told me last evening that there is a Dr. Martyn in the city who actually practices "revolver shooting" upon a gang of prisoners, killing and wounding them merely to test his skill in the use of that weapon and this man, I am told, is an American!

You may judge in some measure from the above what a state of terror and confusion reigns around us. The Imperialists have an array of fifteen or twenty thousand troops besieging the city which has been here now for eight months and ought to be able to take the city at any moment. But they are such cowards that when they make breaches in the walls, which they have done on several occasions, they are afraid to enter and on the contrary have allowed the rebels to sally forth at the breaches made by themselves and chase them all around the neighboring fields. We are most anxious that an end should be put to this fighting and bloodshed. We hear the booming of cannon day and night, a sound that made my poor Phoebe and Miss Conover very nervous at first—and indeed it is very unpleasant music to go to sleep by.

The news from the northern camp is not very important. Our only source of information is the Peking Gazette, published by Imperial command, and it is not very reliable. According to this paper the rebels have met with a repulse —the general impression here is, however, that the rebels may soon take Peking. The rebel chief, Hung Hsiu-Chuan has taken the title Tai Ping Wong—Prince of Peace. I am still persuaded he is a religious imposter who is using the name of God and of Jesus for his own private ends and is seeking to use the story of Moses and Joshua as a foundation to induce his followers to believe in his own divine mission. It is impossible to conjecture what the course of events will be. The most probable seems that the country will be thrown into a complete state of anarchy for want of any sufficient government.

The climate, I am sorry to say, affects both spine and heart as it did before and I have suffered much since my arrival. This, however, is the worst part of the year for me. Phoebe joins me in warmest love to my dear Aunt and all the household, also to all the outdoor members of the family. His Mother and brothers send much love to Henry and his father begs him to write and prays God to keep him.

Ever your affectionate nephew,

Wm. J. Boone

Amid all this tragedy and unrest the bishop's letters in the year 1855 reflect his discouragement for the first time.

Henry was engrossed with his adolescent interests and was careless about writing to his father. His father complains to Henry De Saussure:

> Can't you persuade Hal to write to me sometimes? He is a sad boy about writing. If he knew how his father's heart hones and yearns after his first-born he would write oftener and more regularly. Will you please get Henry to have his daguerreotype taken for me and send it to Mr. Irving to be forwarded. I would like to have one taken annually. I have requested Mary to have hers taken and sent to you to come with Henry's.
>
> Our work is progressing slowly—and so the work of converting men goes on everywhere. It is a long time since Augustine and his monks went to England and yet all England is not yet converted—but we are expected to get on faster with the Chinese! We have had no changes of importance since I last wrote except the betrothal of our young friend Tong to Miss Seur Yun, a young lady of nineteen of Miss Jones' school whom I baptized two Sundays ago.
>
> The high rate of exchange has been so much against us and the Foreign Committee have been so unsuccessful in our collections that our mission has got deeply into debt so that besides what we owe to the Bible and Tract Society, I have been obliged to borrow on my own personal credit, for which I have given my promissory note of the sum of $1550 to keep us afloat. The disturbed state of things has made articles for housekeeping, sugar, flour, soap, etc. so dear that I wrote last autumn to New York for a year's supply and I shall have to write both New York and to England for articles for our use. This makes it necessary to call on my funds in the United States as I must pay for these orders in advance—but my salary is only paid month by month.

It was not an easy period.

Had Hung possessed any real powers of leadership and had he possessed a plan for the betterment of the country, the Taipings might have succeeded in overthrowing the weak Manchu regime. But they ruthlessly destroyed the very poor whom they professed a desire to help and their cruelty turned the conservative elements of society against them. The rebellion had arisen because of the pressures of overpopulation and inadequate economic stability. Religion had very little to do with it. The weakening Ching dynasty was distraught by the humiliation of defeat at the hands of Great Britain. The current emperor, Hsien Feng, was an incapable man and much more interested in personal pleasure than in the affairs of the nation. There were rebellions in other parts of the empire in widely separated places, causing his armies, none too strong in the first place, to be scattered. If it had not been for a courageous scholar-statesman from Changsha, Hunan, Tzeng Kuo-fan—who, though not trained in military matters, raised an army of militia with fighting qualities which surpassed those of the regular army and went after the Taipings with determination—they might have succeeded in toppling the dynasty. A rebellion was not a new way of getting rid of a dynasty which had failed in the "mandate of heaven" bestowed upon each emperor, vesting him not only with autocratic power but with the definite responsibility of maintaining peace, order, and a degree of prosperity among the people he served. Confucius stated, "In a political state the people are the most important, institutions come next, the monarch is the least important."

The Taiping Rebellion lasted a long time: from 1850 until 1865, when the last of the rebels were driven out. They early captured Nanking and made it their capital, and were able to hold it for ten years while they made sorties in all directions, once getting as far north as Tientsin. To understand the hold Hung and his lieutenants had on his adherents, one must realize the general hostility to the Manchus, the incompetence and oppression of much of the local government during the years of the Ching dynasty's weakness and decline, and China's history of rising up to overthrow a dynasty whenever it showed weakness. Religious fanaticism was only one element in the revolt and not a major one. It showed discontent with existing conditions by the peasants, poor gentry, artisans, burden carriers, and boatmen. Some went into it for the love of adventure and a chance to plunder, while others thought of themselves as true patriots. They were in and out of Shanghai on several occasions after they had finally been driven out of the walled part of the city.

When the Boones returned to Shanghai in 1854 after their furlough they found changes which affected them directly. Refugees from the part of the city which had been burned and from nearby towns and villages captured and sacked by the rebels were pouring into Shanghai to take shelter in the foreign settlement, which had so far been immune to attack. Those who could, came with what capital or goods they possessed, but the majority were destitute, having lost all they had. They squatted in the British concession along the Da Mo Lu (called by the British Park Lane and later Nanking Road) but particularly across the Soochow Creek in the area of small farms, the area chosen by the bishop as the location of the Episcopal Mission. The American consul had built the Consulate on a narrow strip of land between the creek which ran in front of the mission compound and the Whangpoo River. Along it was the towpath used by farmers taking their produce into Shanghai and by the galloping mail pony.

Another quite different set of people were also invading the get-rich-quick city of Shanghai. Adventurous young men had come from the eastern part of the United States to California, lured by the Gold Rush of 1849. Many of them were disillusioned or had become scapegoats who needed to get far away. They heard from seamen in San Francisco and Monterey of the way Englishmen were piling up fortunes in Shanghai and of the revolution which might offer adventure. It was easy to obtain a passage as a seaman before the mast, and many took advantage of it. They dribbled into Shanghai, a motley lot indeed. There was also a rash of men of other nations: French, Spanish, Portuguese, and Filipino, mostly seamen who jumped ship, trickling into Shanghai in search of fortunes and excitement.

One such was Frederick Ward from Salem, Massachusetts, the master of a small bark. He was only a lad of twenty but was already a leader of men. The lure of the Taiping Rebellion brought him ashore. In the taverns which had begun to spring up on the waterfront near the American Consulate in the area known as Hongkew (Mouth of the Rainbow) Ward hatched a dream. He began to enlist men for his own personal army to "kick the rebels out of Shanghai and chase them into the countryside, picking up the booty." The British Navy was aghast at the number of desertions and the American consul by the endangering of his country's neutrality. Ward was brought before the consul and told to desist. But Ward was not taking orders from anybody. He said he had become a Chinese citizen and was not responsible to the consul! His army grew by leaps and bounds and, including Chinese as well as foreigners, was said to have reached the number of four thousand men. They were well disciplined and courageous and sallied far into the interior, winning so many battles against the Taipings that even the emperor in Peking took notice of them and named them "The Ever-Victorious Army."

When Ward was wounded and died in battle another American, Henry Burgevine, assumed the leadership but proved himself utterly incapable. He quarreled with the Chinese authorities and at one point marched into Shanghai and took by force the funds he considered due his army. The Ever-Victorious Army was becoming a threat rather than a protection to Shanghai, and the British decided discipline must be reestablished. They appointed a British officer, Major Gordon, later known throughout the world as "Chinese Gordon," to take command. Gordon, by his organizational powers and personal courage, soon won the admiration and allegiance of his men and led them into victories far into the interior. He did not permit looting of the towns he captured from the rebels, but instead helped the starving people as far as he was able. The rich silk-weaving city of Soochow was one of the rebel strongholds he set free, with General Tzeng Kuo-fan and the able General Li Hung-chang pushing the rebels out of the Yangtze Valley and finally out of Nanking, and Gordon harassing them from the south, the Taiping army at long last capitulated. Hung was reported to have committed suicide. Gordon disbanded his army. The emperor conferred on him the highest decoration in the empire: the peacock feather and yellow jacket, and he left China to serve Great Britain in other parts of the world.

There was peace again, but it took China many long years to recover only partly from the destruction and bloodshed which had been perpetrated. The rich Yangtze Valley had been laid waste, historic libraries and *shu yuan* or centers of learning were burnt, never to be replaced. The violence retarded the progress of China as she entered a new era, for it caused many intelligent Chinese to recoil from change in the established order. At the collapse of their cause, however, some of the leaders of the Taiping escaped abroad, and there kept alive the idea of the need for political reform in China. The historian Kenneth Scott Latourette suggests that Sun Yat-sen, revolutionary leader of the twentieth century, seems in his youth to have had close contact with groups of Taiping origin. The Taiping Rebellion was no small affair. It was estimated that twenty million people lost their lives as a direct result of it.

Not all of the young men who drifted into Shanghai from the outside went into the Ever-Victorious Army. Some of them with a more commercial turn of mind saw, together with Shanghai merchants both Chinese and foreign, that there was a great need of housing for the refugees, some of whom had wealth. The Americans were particularly enterprising, for they did not already have lucrative businesses as the English did. They centered on Hongkew and bought up or made land. What was the use of having a creek inland so near the edge of the Whangpoo River? They bought up the small farms whose owners had been the Boones' neighbors and friends and, in the name of progress, decided to fill in the creek— along which small flatboats and sampans, "three-boards," meandered—and make a road out of it, which they quickly named "Broadway" in memory of the main street of their hometowns in America. The scholars at the boys' and girls' schools at the Episcopal Mission no longer looked out at the

Rice as cultivated by the mission's neighbors, Hongkew, Shanghai.

pleasant little creek but across a muddy street at a row of cheaply built shops and dwellings, into which refugee families soon crowded. The graceful new chapel, The Church of Our Saviour, no longer stood in the country but on a busy street.

The quiet life turned into one beset by clamor and competition. In the early morning there was the clatter of shop front shutters being removed, instead of the crowing of roosters. The clang of a little gong announced the traveling restaurant man selling a breakfast of twisted fried bread and *tien chiu tsao*—the refreshing sweet rice malt. A barber stood at the corner with his brass basin over a charcoal fire. When a customer appeared he opened the tiny drawers under the bench he had provided, took out his instruments, bade his customer be seated, and proceeded to tidy up his queue for the day. A farmer plopped down with his baskets of vegetables at the side of the road and a housewife emerged and began to bargain in loud tones for what she wanted. Neighbors called to each other good-naturedly. The day of busy sounds had begun. The bishop wished more than ever that he had a larger staff, for there were constant calls for advice and help and the mission might have served many more people if it had had the men to open more day schools and enter into new avenues of service. More people than before dropped in to the services at the Church of Our Saviour. But over all hung an aura of uncertainty and impermanence, for these people were refugees from their homes and desired above all things for peace so that they might return from whence they came.

Dr. H. W. Boone.
Surgeon – U. S. Coast Survey

Henry W. Boone, M.D., as a young surgeon in San Francisco.

CHAPTER 9

HENRY

Henry's first year in the United States, between 1850 and 1851, had been a difficult one. The household of which he was to be a member was exceedingly dignified and proper. His great-aunt, Susan Boone De Saussure, welcomed him warmly but her husband, Henry De Saussure, felt so heavily the responsibility of bringing up this lad in the way he should go as proxy for his father that he seemed to Henry too strict and unbending. His cousins, Susan, Richard, and Frances, were all older than himself and seemed grown-up to the eleven-year-old boy. Henry had longed to attend a real school and to have companions his own age. Now he was in school. When the boys taunted him on the playground for his bookish manner of speech and scant knowledge of the games they played, it did not take him long to win their admiration by his wit, agility, and daring. Slight and quick, he could outwit and outdare them, and his mischievous pranks soon earned him the nickname of "Whirlwind" by his most intimate circle of friends. His practical jokes were not always acceptable to his teachers and family, however, and he often found himself in disgrace. By the time Henry entered high school at the age of twelve, he had as classmates a circle of admiring friends, which made life enjoyable outside the classroom at least. In his second year of high school the death of his grandmother, Mary Jones Boone, sobered him, for he loved his grandmother dearly. He was far advanced in Latin and

Greek, for his father had insisted on that, and being so widely read gave him a good comprehension of literature and geography; but he was somewhat behind in history and mathematics. He soon caught up and at the age of almost sixteen graduated from high school near the top of his class.

Everyone took it for granted Henry would go on to college. Since the College of Charleston, the oldest municipal college in the United States, founded in 1785—the pride of its citizens—was just up the street from the De Saussure home, Henry was enrolled there. In September 1855 he crossed the grass shaded by oak trees and entered the dignified red brick building, with its tall Corinthian pillars, and commenced his short career in college. He was a slight boy with curly red hair and keen blue eyes, with a puckish face and disarming smile. Henry had always been a bit small for his age but was now beginning to stretch out, and his slim arms and legs protruded too far from the sleeves of his Eton jacket and the legs of his long pantaloons. But so did those of most of his classmates. They were looked upon with scorn by the sophomores, elegant in frock coats, and with pity by the seniors, who enjoyed being regarded with awe as they flapped about the campus in scholastic gowns.

At first Henry entered into college life with enthusiasm. But he was severely disappointed when he discovered that there were the same old subjects of Latin, Greek, and mathematics to hold his nose to the grindstone. But it refused to be held there. He took sidelong glances and discovered that he thought his professors for the most part too pompous, the assignments too long, and the compulsory chapel services, held daily, boring. He enjoyed being with his friends after classes, but the time between the afternoon session and supper at home, where it was required that he be punctual, was all too short. On Saturdays he was free for delightful excursions on the bay with his best friends and on a Sunday he attended Saint Philip's Episcopal Church in deference to his father, while the Henry De Saussure family attended the Presbyterian church a short distance away, where the head of the house was a ruling elder. The straw which broke the back of Henry's discontent came in March of his first year in college.

A classmate was suspended by the faculty for the misdemeanor of setting off fireworks, which Henry considered too trivial a crime for such a punishment. In defiance next day he took with him to the chapel a large firecracker with which to challenge the authorities. Just at the close of the service he touched a match to it in the back of the chapel. It caused a louder explosion than even Henry had expected and everyone was startled. All knew who had done it and Henry was soon called on the carpet to defend himself. This he would not do and soon found to his dismay that he too was suspended. The same day, February 21, 1856, Mr. Henry De Saussure received the following communication from Mr. Finley, president of the College of Charleston, in regard to his ward:

Mr. Boone was summoned to appear before the Faculty on a charge of exploding a torpedo in the Chapel this morning at the close of the Chapel exercises. He admitted the truth of the charge and offered no palliation of the Offence.

The Faculty having suspended one of his classmates yesterday for a similar offence, and regarding this case as an act of open defiance of their authority, Resolved that Mr. Boone be therefore suspended from participation in College exercises until Friday, 2nd May next, when he will be required to undergo a satisfactory examination on the studies of his class, and that during the term of his suspension, he be not allowed to come upon the College premises.

Henry De Saussure was stunned. His wife, William's Aunt Susan, wrote to William about his son at once:

My dear William,

It is an exceedingly painful subject to my husband and myself to communicate unpleasant intelligence respecting Henry, but duty and affection both call upon us to do so, and it is with the sincere hope that your affectionate admonitions will cause him to see and feel the value of study that I have taken upon myself to write to you. I have talked a great deal with Henry, not only now but in times past, strongly remonstrating with him that God has, in the excellent mind and quick observation he has given him, committed to him talents which he ought not to throw away, and will be accountable for hereafter. But I am grieved to say that though he hears me with respect and attention, it has made no difference in his studies. French is not taught at the College and Henry took some lessons with Charles's children in private. I wished him much to pursue it at home and both of his cousins would have assisted him in the study but he says French will be of no use to him. With regard to his present position in College he tells me that he wishes only to return and take a dismissal that he may get a situation on the Bay and that his letter to you is to that effect. I asked him if he did not think that Education would be of importance there—that if he looked around he would find all men that rose to important stations and filled them were men of Education and industry. His reply was that he did not desire to attain Eminence and that he knew many young men on the Bay with much less education than himself. His character now is very light and trifling. The least pleasure turns his mind from things useful. These are grievous things to us, dear William, but Henry is young and I cannot but hope that he may be brought to see things in a better light. As he looks away from us to you for direction it is but right that you should have a better knowledge of his Character and views that you may the better direct him. I was sorry to learn through your last letter of your continued indisposition and hope you will soon be better.

Your affectionate,

Aunt Susan De Saussure

A few months before receiving this depressing news William had written to his son to announce the birth of Henry's youngest brother, Robert Habersham Boone, on January 27, 1856. When Robbie was three months old he had the distinction of having tried out twelve wet nurses, none of whom lasted more than a week or so. A supplement of buffalo milk enabled him not only to survive but to flourish, which his parents considered quite a feat. His older brother, Willie, was ten years old when Robbie was born and Tommy nine. His father realized that Willie, who was quite a serious student, must soon be sent to the United States to school and dreaded to see that day of separation arrive. In one of his letters he wrote:

> We are jogging along in our family, the boys growing and crying out for better educational privileges than we can give them here. This is one of the sad features of missionary life to me. It robs the missionary of nine tenths of the comfort of his children for he is either suffering the privation of their society or looking forward to a separation from them from the time they are out of the nurse's arms. Poor little Rob, I even see it marked on him that he must go.

It was not until May that his father received Henry's and his aunt's letters telling of Henry's suspension from college. He wrote at once, an affectionate letter of advice and encouragement pointing out that education was preparation for life's work, whatever that might turn out to be, and reminding Henry that he would most likely have a wife and children to think of at some future date.

Henry hunted for a job on the waterfront without success. In March a letter arrived from his Aunt Mary at Pendleton which said that since Henry was not in school it would be a real help to his Uncle John if he could come for the summer to Rocky Retreat. John was in poor health and very much needed more help. Henry snapped at the invitation for he knew what he really wanted was not a job but time to think. His uncle and aunt concurred in his desire to go up to the farm, for they knew that Charleston was not a healthy place in the summer and thought a little manual labor would not hurt Henry at this stage. In a few days Henry took the train for Pendleton and was met there by his Aunt Mary in Aunt Eliza's beautiful carryall, driven by Trumpeter. There was an undercurrent of sadness in the affectionate welcome he received from his aunt, for not long before the news of her sister Eliza's death had been received. After taking Henry's sister, Maney, to Camden to become a part of her Uncle John De Saussure's family, Eliza had decided to look for a teaching position. She found one at Dr. Savage's Female Academy near New Orleans. An exceptionally cold winter was experienced that year and in February Eliza contracted pneumonia. She was carried to her brother Fraser's home in Mobile, Alabama, but died on the first of March.

The farm seemed strangely silent without his grandmother, sister Maney, and Aunt Eliza there, but there were still Uncle John, Mammy Malby, Uncle Nick, who used to be the coachman at Boone Hall, ancient and warped with rheumatism now—together with Uncle Benji and Aunt Cindy and his own companion, Trumpeter. They were of his family, people he had heard about, all his life, and Henry felt a close bond of fellowship between them all. He scarcely remembered his own mother, but these were the household members of his own deeply loved father, and he felt he belonged to them. In the restlessness and upheaval which had marked the past weeks it was with a sense of relief and deep comfort that Henry relaxed into the quiet and love which surrounded him.

But there was work to be done. Henry could see at once that his Uncle John really did need help. He and Benji were ploughing and it was all too evident that it was too much for Uncle John, for the exertion brought on serious fits of coughing. Henry offered to take his place and it was agreed that since he was not used to the work, he and Trump would take turns at the plough. Henry found that he was glad enough for Trump to take over when his turn came, for the plow handles blistered his hands and the horse nearly pulled him off his feet as he stumbled over the rocky ground. There was satisfaction, though, in reaching the end of a long furrow and knowing that he was doing work really needed by his family. The sky above was blue, a mockingbird poured out his joy from a bare branch high above, daisies and buttercups flourished in the fence corners, and Henry shouted and sang. At the end of his stint he loved to drop by at old Mammy Malby's house, where she regaled him with refreshing buttermilk and hot johnnycakes. Uncle Nick loved nothing better than telling tales of the old days when the family lived at Boone Hall. He saw himself as young again, dressed in his maroon uniform with silver buttons, high on the coachman's seat behind the matched bays, cracking his whip as he drove Henry's grandmother and old Miss Sarah home up the long driveway to the mansion. That was when Master John was a little bitty baby! Henry enjoyed it more when he told tales of animals and "haunts" and sang plaintive old songs.

If it had not been for these visits to his friends Henry would have been lonely. He missed the presence of his grandmother, of energetic Aunt Eliza, and gay little Maney. Aunt Cindy was the only woman about their house as she cared for the daily needs of Uncle John and Henry. More and more as time went on Uncle John was forced to stay in bed. Henry took to riding over to Aunt Mary's place quite often. He enjoyed his aunt, for she was a woman both imaginative and ingenious. Her husband, Major Pickens, often had to be absent, for he had become a Methodist circuit rider. His little son, Andy, amused Henry.

Henry's restlessness began to return as he felt an increasing urge to go to see his parents in China. He did not speak of it but finally wrote to his Uncle Henry asking him to inquire about ships sailing for the Orient and how much the passage would cost. His uncle replied that this was not the time of year for vessels to cross the ocean and that Henry had better wait until spring before making plans for sailing. At first the boy resented the delay but afterwards was glad that he had not rushed away, for Uncle John's illness became alarmingly worse. Henry found that he had to take over many of his uncle's duties, including all the bookkeeping and buying of supplies. It was good training for him and he began to develop a sense of responsibility. Aunt Cindy nursed John untiringly and, since there was little outdoor work to do in winter, Benji helped in many ways. The doctor came often to see John but finally advised that he be moved to the hospital in Anderson. There he died on January 1, 1857.

It was a great blow to everyone in the household, but particularly to Henry. If it had not been for Pastor Pickens, who took charge of all arrangements, Henry would not have known what to do. It seemed to him that the whole house and farm had fallen about his ears. He would have been alone in the house if Aunt Mary had not come forward at once and urged him to move over to their place, which he did most gratefully. His Uncle John had long disliked the institution of slavery and after his mother died had deeded the house where old Nick lived at Rocky Retreat and a plot of ground surrounding it to Benji and his family. When John bought the farm at Rocky Retreat he had drawn up emancipation papers for old Uncle Nick's whole family, the only slaves they had retained from the many who had been owned by their ancestors at Boone Hall. When that property had been sold to Mr. Horlbeck the slaves had gone with it, except for the house servants. Nick and his family had chosen to move to Rocky Retreat with the Boones, for they felt them to be "family." Now they would stay on and do their own farming.

Finally in March 1857 Henry wrote again to his uncle:

Dear Uncle;

The letter which I wrote to Aunt informing her of Aunt Mary's having a little daughter has no doubt reached you before this. She is still quite well and we hope that she will be able soon to resume her place among us.

If you please let me come down to the city I will be very much obliged to you. It cannot be very long before some ship will be starting for China for this is the time of the year when most of them start. If you cannot let me come please send me some pantaloons or cloth to make some for I have worn out all that I had except the pair I am now wearing and these are very much patched and will not last much longer. And please send me some money to buy a pair of shoes as the boots I have are nearly worn out—the ploughing and working in the fields is so hard that they do not last long.

Please give my love to Aunt and to Cousins Sue and Fan and Cousin John and all my friends, and believe me your attached,

Nephew Henry Boone

The reply came promptly:

Charleston
April 5th, 1857

Dear Henry,

I received your letter of the 27th of March requesting permission to come to the city. I acquiesce in your wishes. I now enclose you fifteen dollars to pay your expenses down. You had better come down to Columbia where you will arrive by three o'clock in the day, and take the cars at four o'clock for a night ride to Charleston. From circumstances which will be communicated to you on your arrival here, it is very doubtful whether you can go to China immediately. Therefore it will be unnecessary for you to go to Camden at present to take leave of your sister. We will however communicate more fully on the subject hereafter. Tell Aunt Mary I will write her shortly, fully.

Your affectionate uncle,

H. De Saussure

Henry was completely mystified by his uncle's letter. Henry De Saussure had written previously that he had made inquiries about engaging passage to China on a sailing vessel and had even named one, *The Celestial,* on which passage might be obtained. Why should he not say farewell to Maney? But he would just have to hold his horses and find the answers when he got down to the city. Aunt Mary helped him wash and press the few clothes Henry had, and he took leave of her and the children and went to Charleston. There he found out that the reason behind his uncle's letter was that he had received a letter from William Boone in China saying that his health was so impaired that he was afraid the only thing to do was to come to the United States and try to regain it. Plans were not at all firm and if he improved he would try to stay. But he had always found the summers in Shanghai most trying to his health.

Henry and his aunt and uncle conferred at length as to which was the best course for Henry to take. He very much wanted to go to China if his father would still be there. But there was the risky chance that they might be "ships that pass in the night" if he and his father both set out from opposite directions. At length it was decided that Henry would go to New York, book passage a month or two in advance, and await further word from his father. He could cancel the passage if he heard that his father was coming. Henry felt exceedingly shabby in his worn country work clothes and was relieved when the new clothes ordered from the tailor were ready.

It was an exuberant moment for Henry when he stood on the deck of the vessel which was to carry him up the coast to New York. Dressed in his natty new suit with its vest and bow tie he felt able to tackle the world. Now at least he was off on his own with no aunts and uncles to tell him what to do. And best of all, by hook or by crook, he was going to see his father. He had pleasant memories of New York and knew he was expected by his old friends the Winstons. It felt good to be on the deck of a ship again. In fact, everything felt tops! Sure enough, Mr. Fred Winston met him when the ship docked, just as he had when Henry was ten years old. Being a ship's agent he had access to passenger lists and assured the boy that he would watch to see if his father was aboard any ship.

Henry dropped his uncle a note to let him know of his safe arrival. It was not long before an exciting epistle arrived from Charleston. Henry tore it open and read the following:

Charleston
June 22, 1857

My dear Henry:

By last evening's mail a letter was received from your father, directed to you and your sister, Mary. She received and opened it. It was dated April 5th last, Shanghai. He stated that his health was so much impaired he was advised by Dr. Lockhart to return to America and remain for three years to restore his health and that he had taken his passage on the ship, "Golden West," to sail on 15th of May. He had not heard of the death of your Uncle John for he requested you to write to your Uncles, John, Thomas and Fraser and Aunt Mary informing them of his intended return, nor could he have received any letter from you referring to your going to China. Of course all your arrangements must be altered and you also must return home to await his directions.

But Henry did not return home. He was having too good a time in New York and decided to wait there and meet his family when the ship arrived. The time went quickly and toward the end of August Henry had the supreme joy of meeting the *Golden West* and being reunited with his family. His parents did not look at all well. The boys had grown beyond recognition—Willie was now twelve and Tommy eleven. The baby, Robbie, Henry had not seen before. Henry compared him at once with the only baby he had had much contact with—Aunt Mary's baby, Mary—and Robbie came out on top. They all went to the home of the bishop's old friend Mrs. Doremus, where Henry had been staying for some time. The bishop was of the opinion that he had best avoid hot weather as much as possible and decided not to go south for the present. After looking about he found a house in Orange, New Jersey, and the family moved in. Except for visits to the South it turned out that they stayed there for nearly two years.

This period in close companionship with his father and mother meant much to Henry. His father adhered to the old custom of leading family prayers each evening after supper and, although his eldest son sometimes appeared not to be paying too much attention, words that he read from the Bible, the beautiful prayers from the prayer book and comments made by the bishop stayed in his mind. He always remembered his father's words, "It is a wise person who asks guidance from God before he pursues a certain course and does not wait until he is launched upon it and has doubts and regrets. God has a plan for each of our lives and we do right and avoid many a heartache if we ask him to show us the way"; and, "Life is a tapestry woven of the many threads of individual lives into the beautiful pattern of the whole. Each of us is a part of the whole social design of the world. If we refuse to let the Master Weaver place us where we contribute to the perfect design or take on a dark tone where he had intended a light, we mar the whole. I think that is what Jesus meant when he talked about 'the kingdom of heaven.' When each man trusts God to lay the thread of his life in the right context and position the 'kingdom of God' will have come and the perfect pattern be complete."

Before he came north the birth of his Aunt Mary's baby and the long illness of Uncle John had made a deep impression on Henry. He thought deeply about what he should do with his life and came to the decision that he, as his father and three uncles had done, would like to study medicine. Upon discussing the idea with his parents it was decided that he should try for the entrance exams at the College of Medicine of the College of the City of New York. His thorough grounding in Latin stood him in good stead. He passed and in October moved to a boardinghouse in the city to enter upon the two-year course.

Bishop and Mrs. Boone watched the news with keen interest, for the peace supposedly made between the Chinese and the British by the signing of the Treaty of Peking in 1842 and by the American Treaty in 1844 had been in reality no more than a truce. China thought the foreigners had asked too much, the outside nations involved thought they had obtained too little. Several incidents had taken place to disrupt what peace there was, especially around Canton where the foreigner was hated—and not without cause. The spark which ignited further conflagration was a minor incident in 1856. A small vessel, the *Arrow*, Chinese-owned and manned by a Chinese crew, but having a British captain, registered out of Hong Kong, was boarded near Canton by Chinese officers; the crew was arrested on the charge of having engaged in piracy and the British flag hauled down. Two strong men, Viceroy Yeh Ming-shen of Canton and Sir Harry Parkes, British consul at that city, were both uncompromising. The British started hostilities by once again capturing the forts guarding Canton and firing on the viceroy's yamen. China declared war. France joined Great Britain giving as an excuse that a French priest, Chapdelaine, had been killed in Kwangsi. The United States was invited to join the fray but she declined to do so. Russia, having so recently suffered defeat in the Crimean War, was in no position to fight but was eager to take advantage of any power gained by the other foreign nations.

It had been understood that the earlier treaties were to be reviewed after a period of twelve years had elapsed, and Britain, America, and France felt that the time had now come when that should be done. Canton was taken and the unfortunate Viceroy Yeh sent as a prisoner to Calcutta. The four powers mentioned above now sent demands to Peking. Deeming the reply unsatisfactory, the combined fleets of Britain and France proceeded northward to be nearer Peking and captured the Taku forts guarding Tientsin. Alarmed at Peking's being so closely approached, the emperor yielded and the Treaty of Tientsin was drawn up and signed in 1858. Russia and the United States joined Britain and France in signing the treaty. The treaty extended foreign trade by opening up ten new ports, three of them in the north and four up the Yangtze River, including the river port of Hankow. Two were actually on Formosa and one in the south, Chaochow or Swatow. Others were added later. Foreign goods channeled through these entrepôts could flow throughout China. It was specified that ministers and ambassadors with their staffs were to be permitted to reside in the sacrosanct city of Peking and were to be treated as envoys on an equal footing with China. Foreigners were to be allowed to travel throughout China, provided they had proper passports. Both Chinese and foreign Christians were allowed to propagate their faith and were to be protected in the practice of their faith. Sometimes this later led to abuses as Chinese appealed to missionaries to protect them from persecution.

In the negotiation of the American Treaty the United States minister, the Hon. W. B. Reed, successfully contended for the admission of the gospel. The bishop of Victoria, the Rt. Rev. Dr. Smith, said of him at the time, "It is right that the friends of Christian Missions on both sides of the Atlantic should know how pre-eminently they are indebted for the Christian element, in the wording of the treaties, to the hearty zeal, sympathy and co-operation of his Excellency W. B. Reed."

The French Treaty further gave the Catholic Church—the Tien Chu Chao or "Lord of Heaven Church"—the privilege of renting and purchasing land anywhere in China and of erecting buildings. It also restored to them their buildings which had been confiscated or destroyed. These provisions assisted the Roman Catholic Church in spreading their faith very widely over China. It was about this same time that Sir Harry Parkes secured for the British in perpetual lease a part of the Kowloon or Chiu Lung, "Seven Dragons," Peninsula opposite Hong Kong and the Portuguese gained a firmer hold on Macao. A clause which affected all the nations involved was the elaboration of the rules for extraterritoriality, making the foreign concessions which developed in several of the treaty ports possible and freeing foreigners and some of the Chinese citizens whom they protected from Chinese law, notably in Shanghai.

Through these concessions granted in the treaties and by using an occasional show of force later, foreigners were enabled to obtain many privileges in China which the Chinese resented all down the years. Bishop Boone foresaw this and wrote to his brother-in-law, the Rt. Rev. Stephen Elliott, in 1860; "This aggression is one of our greatest difficulties in the way of extending our intercourse among the semi-civilized nations—the overbearing and violent conduct of our own people. The Lord himself sees the necessity to restrain the too rapid spread of dominion of the white race." Through the impetus given to trade and through the contact made possible between Chinese citizens and persons from abroad, through foreigners living in China, and through travel, work, and study abroad by Chinese citizens new ideas percolated into China.

The spread of Western ideas can be attributed to the missionary rather than to the businessman or diplomat. The missionary came committed to life service and at once started to study the language as a prerequisite to any success. There were exceptions, but the businessman usually did not think he had time to bother with the difficult study and had to conduct all his dealings with the Chinese through an interpreter or compradore (agent) or by the use of pidgin English. The missionary was often called upon to act as an interpreter and in this way exerted considerable influence. All those who did study Chinese in the early days had to rely on the dictionary and Bible translated by Morrison and Milne. Later there were other translations. Many of the first missionaries brought with them their own printing presses, and literary work was one of their earliest contributions. Very early the British and Foreign Bible Society, soon joined by the American Bible Society and aided by the Religious Tract Society, printed and distributed religious literature which grew into a volume of millions of copies over the years. The Christian Literature Society added much by translating and publishing many valuable works, as did the YMCA and other organizations. But all that grew up gradually over the years.

An early venture into service by missions in China was through medical service. Dr. Peter Parker of Yale University was the first with his ophthalmic hospital in Canton. He would have been amazed if he could have seen the many mission hospitals, small and great, medical schools, specialized schools for the blind, deaf, and maimed, colonies for leprosy patients, orphanages, famine and disaster relief work, and all the many forms of service to people in need which were started and maintained by missions.

Bishop Boone was interested in education and did what many early missionaries and some later ones did: he took a Chinese child or several into the home to grow up with his own children. Many were given the chance to study abroad. Boarding schools and day schools were a part of early missionary effort. Bishop Boone could not even dream that the start made in his time in Christian education would grow by the year 1949 into the establishment of thirteen Christian universities with an enrollment of nine thousand students and that one of them, Saint John's University in Shanghai, with its medical school, would grow out of the boys' school he started in Shanghai.

Missions supported 220 middle and primary schools serving 175,000 children, and there were countless kindergartens, day nurseries, literacy campaigns, and special educational projects of various kinds. Libraries, reading rooms, and recreation centers were opened and campaigns launched to rectify such abuses as foot binding and slavery. In Shanghai the Door of Hope was opened and became a refuge for many a girl trapped by prostitution. Deeds of mercy are far beyond counting, but embracing and motivating them all was the belief that Jesus saves and that faith in God's love shown through the redeeming power of Christ is of more value than all else in life. The church used many methods of preaching and demonstrating that redeeming power, available to all men. Missionaries carried out their commission to share their Lord and Savior through preaching and teaching at the grass roots as the China Inland Mission did, by the establishment of theological seminaries and Bible schools, by Bible classes, and women's and children's meetings, and by the many ways mentioned above.

The Treaty of Nanking in 1858 opened up the interior to

travel and residence by foreigners and sparked enthusiasm for missions in many countries. Most of the Roman Catholic missionaries of that period were French; the Protestants, British or American. The French missionaries were protégés of their government and sometimes used this position to obtain special privileges in buying land or in extracting reparation for damage done their property or converts. They were therefore subject to more suspicion by the Chinese government than were the Protestants. The two churches largely avoided each other. But the mass of the population could not distinguish between the two. Some had heard of the "Lord of Heaven Church" and the "Jesus Church" but what was the difference? If they both believed in the same God why didn't they get together? Most people, especially in the country districts, had never heard of either.

As missionary personnel multiplied they came in all shapes and sizes. A few were intolerant and bigoted, tending to seriously offend by insisting that idols be violently thrown down and age-old customs, such as reverence for the dead and the worship of ancestors, be rooted out. They did not know how deep the roots of Chinese culture went or in what pride the Chinese held their heritage. But most realized that it took time and instruction and a willingness to seek God before he could be found. The church in China developed along lines and rituals and institutions familiar to the West, it is true, but what other model did it have to go by until such time as Chinese Christian leaders arose to lead the Chinese church into a pattern compatible with its own culture, as it was surely doing in the several decades before 1950. No wonder a favorite hymn in the Chinese Hymnbook, No. 232, was so often sung: "Church of China Arise and Stand." And it was set to a Chinese tune.

There were other black marks chalked up against the missionary. He always looked so queer with his pale skin, big nose and feet, and ugly hair and strange clothing—much like the Chinese conception of a devil. He usually insisted on building large residences, churches, and schools quite out of keeping with Chinese architecture. He spoke Chinese haltingly and made absurd mistakes with tones which gave words meanings he didn't intend.

One unfortunate young bachelor missionary grew tired of the monotonous fare his cook set before him. One day he said, or meant to say, "Please buy me a chicken today." The cook's eyes widened but he replied, "I will do my best but it may take me some time to find one and it will be expensive." The young American wondered why and the cook departed. It was afternoon before the cook returned piloting a strange-looking chicken indeed. She was an awkward young girl of about sixteen, looking very reluctant and frightened.

The pious young preacher was astonished and indignant. "What is the meaning of this?" he shouted. The servant remonstrated that he had done the best he could and it was only because the father was so poor that he at last consented to let his eldest daughter go. There were so many children in the family! The distraught young man woke up to the fact that he had aspired where he shouldn't have and had said *ch'i tz* instead of *gi tz,* "wife" instead of "chicken." The delighted father received both his daughter and the price agreed on that same day.

The foreigner did not know the proper and courteous way to conduct a business contract. He wanted everything written down in black and white as if he did not trust the other party. The Chinese business system was built on credit. Cooperation and confidence took the place of cash over the counter. It worked. A "squeeze" or commission on the transaction involved was taken for granted, but the foreigners called it stealing. Foreigners did not know how to be guests, how to comply with their hosts' manners. They thought only their own ideas and practices were right. How could it be right to eat with a set of spikes that would injure the lining of the mouth instead of graceful and slender chopsticks? When a person was hurt the witness to the accident laughed to show his commiseration and the hope that it wasn't serious. But even a foreign child would howl with rage and say you had laughed at him. It was incomprehensible. And foreigners were always in a hurry! The motive of the merchant the Chinese could understand. They were there to make money, of course. But why the missionary? It was quite plain that they were not making money and were not able to live in anything like the style of the merchants. Why had they left home and come to China? Their deeds were often benevolent, a stance which the Chinese well understood—did not one gain merit with the gods by doing good deeds? But they might have done that at home. Their interest in education was commendable, but China had many schools. Were they trying to infuse the minds of Chinese youth with foreign ideas so they could make them "the running dogs of the foreign nations?" Plainly an international struggle was going on for the control of China. How were the missionaries involved in this? Could they be spies probing into the interior of China for her secrets? The growth of the Chinese church in a period of ruthless imperial expansion made it suspect even though it was producing many things of real value to China.

Bishop Boone was dimly aware of some of this, but his own relations with the Chinese with whom he had come in contact had been cordial. He was a friendly and outgoing man, qualities shared by his wife, and they had had friendly relations with their neighbors both close to the wall of the Old City of Shanghai and, after they moved, with the neighboring farm people. He was firm in his conviction that God had laid his hand on him and had commissioned him to carry the word of God to the heathen of China. Through many discouragements he reminded himself of the words of hope and encouragement spoken by the prophet Isaiah:

> For as the rain and the snow come down from heaven,
>   and return not thither but water the earth,
> making it bring forth and sprout, giving seed to the
>   sower and bread to the eater,
> so shall my word be that goes forth from my mouth;

it shall not return to me empty,
but it shall accomplish that which I purpose,
and prosper in the thing for which I sent it.

—Isaiah 55:10-11

He believed that God's word, with its message of reconciliation, forgiveness, and redemption, was for all men—but how should they hear or know without a preacher?

Now he set his heart and mind upon getting well so that he might go back to China. This would mean another great wrench for himself and Phoebe, for it would mean separation from the children. He was not worried about Henry for he was well launched on an honorable path, but he and Phoebe decided that they ought to leave Willie and Tommy in America so that they might attend a real school. Willie had been a good student even alone, but it was only after he attended school with children of his own age here in New Jersey that Tommy had shown the slightest interest in learning. Tommy was now nearly twelve and it would be selfish to take him back with them. Only little Robbie would go with them.

By early January 1859 the bishop felt strong enough again to undertake filling his numerous invitations to speak in the churches. One of these was at the church of his one-time colleague in Batavia, Java—the Rev. Henry Lockwood at Christ Church in Pittsford, New York. The bishop had never before had such an enthusiastic reception as he met this time in the American churches. Not only was twenty thousand dollars subscribed for the work in Shanghai but an additional sum was raised to open a new station in the interior. Many candidates to go out with the bishop were received by the Foreign Committee and twelve were chosen—eight men, four of them with wives. The bishop had the pleasure of ordaining four of them to the diaconate: Messrs. Purden, Smith, Thomson, and Schereschewsky, whom he later admitted to the priesthood in Shanghai. Mr. Parker was also ordained. The whole party gathered at the Church of the Ascension in New York on the evening of July 10 and were given an affectionate farewell.

CHAPTER 10

TRAGEDY

The voyage on the clipper ship *Golden Rule* proved to be the longest the bishop had yet experienced, for they were becalmed for a month in the southern seas. However, this afforded them all the more time for language study. Not far from home they met another ship, which, according to sea courtesy, stopped to take mail back to America. The passengers of the *Golden Rule* only had time to write brief notes. the bishop's read: "We are all, by God's blessing, well. We commenced with full class the study of Chinese this morning and our prospects are fair in every respect. Ship well found, Captain and Officers as obliging as they can be."

One of their little party astonished them all by the rapidity with which he learned Chinese. He boasted the jaw-breaking name of Samuel Isaac Joseph Schereschewsky (pronounced Sherri-sheff-ski) but soon came to be affectionately called "Sherry" by his shipmates. He had a most unusual background for a Christian missionary to China, for his parents were Russian-Lithuanian Jews. Both his parents died when he was quite young and he grew up in the home of a brother in Krazi, where he attended the rabbinical school, as his relatives intended that he should become a rabbi. From there he went on to the large Jewish center of Zhitomir, where he entered the higher rabbinical school. Here he obtained a Hebrew translation of the New Testament which had been sent from London. The young student was intensely interested in what he read. He did not at that time make an open confession of his belief in Christ, but going on to enter a university in Germany he came under further Christian influences. In 1854 Schereschewsky made up his mind to emigrate to America and was given a letter of introduction to a Christian Jew. This gave him entrance to a circle of Christian Jewish friends, one of whom was pastor of a Presbyterian church in New York. These friends were in the habit of celebrating the Passover, and in the spring of 1855 invited young Samuel to join them. They observed the customary Jewish rites but at the close of the meal each man was asked to rise and tell what his faith in Christ meant to him. Samuel was profoundly moved. When all were finished he arose and said in a quiet voice, "I can no longer deny my Lord. I will follow him without the camp." He applied for baptism and decided that he wanted to enter a theological seminary. He tried a Presbyterian seminary but found it too rigid in its views and transferred to the General Seminary of the Episcopal Church in New York. It was while there that he had heard Bishop Boone make an appeal for men for the China Mission and at once offered his services. With his background in Hebrew and rabbinical law he hoped to be useful in translating the scriptures into Chinese. This he later did in an outstanding way.

The ship touched at Shanghai on December 21, 1859, after a voyage of twenty-three weeks. When he stepped ashore Schereschewsky astounded the natives by being able to write in Chinese characters what he wanted to communicate. The mission staff which had been carrying on during the bishop's absence greeted Bishop and Mrs. Boone and Robbie and the new reinforcements with joy. They had enjoyed a fair degree of peace during the past two years, interrupted by forays on the part of the rebels, until August 1859. The ratification of the new treaties with the French and English had sparked keen resentment among the Chinese. The animosity had spread throughout the whole country. It reached Shanghai in the summer and serious riots occurred there. Foreigners did not dare to go out in the streets. A mob had attacked Christ Church in the walled city and had wrecked its interior. It would have been utterly destroyed but for the interference of the Chinese officials. A new station had been opened at Dzang Zok, a town near Shanghai, under the leadership of the Rev. Wong Kung-chai, who was also in charge of Christ Church. He went there on one occasion with Rev. John Liggins but they were attacked and both severely beaten. Mr. Liggins' injuries were so severe that Dr. Lockhart had advised him to go over to Nagasaki, Japan—now open to foreigners—to recuperate. He left for that city on April 23, 1858, and was soon joined by the Rev. Channing Williams, who had come out the year before the bishop left on furlough. They were the first Protestant missionaries to visit Japan. Unknown to them at that time, the Foreign Committee in New York had decided in February to establish a mission in Japan, and had designated Nagasaki to be its first station. They had already mailed a letter to these same two gentlemen, Liggins and Williams, saying that they were appointed to Nagasaki for mission work. So when the bishop returned he was glad that he had replacements for these two valuable men.

Attempts at new work had been undertaken in his absence. Mr. Nelson and Mr. Williams had ventured on a visit to the famous silk-weaving city of Soochow, capital of the province of Kiang-su. They had been able to preach in a temple and distribute tracts there without opposition. Mr. Syle had established an industrial school for the blind in Shanghai and had been able to raise an endowment for it locally. He had also set up a printing press and a book shop for the sale of the scriptures. The three ladies, Miss Emma Jones, Miss Fay, and Miss Conover, had had good success in the two boarding schools. The bishop was well pleased with these indications of some advance. Darker days for the mission were to follow, but mercifully they did not know it then. It was a disappointment when the Rev. Tong Chu-kiung requested to be deposed from the ministry, giving as reasons for his resignation his want of success in the work and insufficient means to support his family.

Having been enjoined by the church in the United States to open a new station when he returned to China, Bishop Boone looked into the possibilities and decided on the newly opened treaty port of Chefoo, on the north coast in the province of Shantung. He asked two of the young couples who had lately come out with him, the Parkers and the Smiths, to go there. They were not hospitably received and found some difficulty in finding a place to live but were able to settle at the village of Chookie, near the city. Dr. John L. Nevius, noted advocate of self-supporting missions, of the American Presbyterian Mission, had come early to Chefoo and Mr. Holmes of the American Baptist Mission had also come to Chefoo to work. After the Parkers and Smiths had been there for six months the city was threatened by the Taiping rebels, with their uncombed flowing hair and fierce appearance. As they approached the city they burned the villages and slaughtered the people. A delegation of Chinese merchants came to the home of the missionaries asking them, since they believed in God as the rebels professed to do, to plead with them to spare the lives of the people of Chefoo. Mr. Parker volunteered to go and was accompanied by Mr. Holmes, while Mr. Smith stayed behind to protect his wife, Mrs. Parker and the mission house. The two missionaries set out on their errand of mercy and encountered the rebels, who paid no attention to their pleas; the two young foreigners were executed on the spot. The Smiths remained at their post but Mrs. Parker sailed shortly for home. Mr. Smith too was to suffer bereavement, for in July of the next summer Mrs. Smith was stricken with cholera and died. On the advice of the bishop Mr. Smith took his infant daughter to Shanghai where she was cared for by one of the staff, but he himself returned to Chefoo. The mission suffered another loss in the death of Mrs. Syle.

When they had first arrived in Shanghai young Elliot Thomson and Samuel Schereschewsky lived with Bishop and Mrs. Boone at the bishop's house in Hongkew. But in order to give their whole time to study, early in 1860 they moved to Christ Church in the Old City and settled into rooms there. Mr. Schereschewsky was determined to learn not only the Wu dialect of Shanghai but also the Mandarin, so widely used over a great part of China, as well as the classical or Wen-li Chinese of literature. A Presbyterian missionary, Dr. W. A. P. Martin, later to be known for his scholarly attainments, arrived in Shanghai shortly after the above-mentioned two young Episcopalians. He came to Christ Church to call on them and found Mr. Schereschewsky busily engaged in reading the famous Chinese historical novel *The Three Kingdoms*. Upon questioning him he learned that the engrossed student had not been out of the house for a week and had been absorbed by the book night and day.

Schereschewsky himself wrote the board:

> A missionary without a respectable knowledge of the book language of China could not expect to have any access to the educated Chinese. Besides, the Chinese literary language is the embodiment of the Chinese mind. There are some fifty or sixty thousand characters in the whole range of Chinese literature. It is true that one-fourth or one-fifth of this number will be quite sufficient to answer all practical purposes—but think of even eight or ten thousand different characters to be committed to memory! It really looks very formidable. However, many have acquired a good knowledge of the Chinese written language and, so far as I can judge, it can be acquired by persons of ordinary capacity, but extraordinary diligence. Great patience and perseverance are most necessary. A missionary who has gone out or wants to go out to China must fully make up his mind to be engaged the first five years at least in very laborious study. It is very hard work but it must be done.

This young Schereschewsky set out to do.

Not long after Bishop Boone's return to Shanghai he confirmed twenty-seven persons at the school chapel and eight at Christ Church in the city. One boy of the graduating class was received as a candidate for holy orders. In October 1860 he admitted Messrs. Schereschewsky, Thomson, and Smith to the priesthood. In November thirteen more persons were confirmed in Christ Church, so regular congregations were slowly building up to bring joy and hope to the mission workers.

Disturbing accounts began to drift in from America early in 1861 as to the unrest and sharp divisions of opinion between the states in the North and those in the South. Since nearly all the missionaries of the Episcopal Church were from the southern states, particularly Virginia, they were all much worried to hear of Lincoln's inauguration and not long afterwards of the seceding of South Carolina. They did not know what this might mean. No one really believed it would end in a war between the states. It was well that they could not foresee the disastrous effect it would have upon the mission and upon their personal lives.

But there were a few bright spots on the dark horizon. The Chinese student who had gone from the boys' school for study in the United States, Yen Yung-kiung, graduated from Kenyon College with honors and returned to Shanghai in January 1862. Upon his request, he was accepted by Bishop Boone for holy orders and became a candidate. Yen became a great Christian leader and educator, serving as a professor in Saint John's College, which grew out of the boys' school where Miss Jones, Miss Conover, and Miss Fay labored so faithfully. It was said long afterwards that the rare quality of the first Chinese Christian priests of the Episcopal Church in China was an indication of Bishop Boone's wise emphasis on Christian education.

Another heavy blow to the mission was the loss of both Mr. and Mrs. Keith. It had been nine years since Cleveland Keith had fallen in love with Miss Caroline Tenney across the

Christmas dinner table a few days after his arrival in Shanghai. In February 1862 Mrs. Keith was in failing health, and the couple sailed for Japan in the hope that a change of climate would restore her to health. But she grew worse, so they decided that there was nothing for it but to return to the United States for medical attention. Upon arrival in San Francisco the Keiths were kindly received into the home of Bishop Kip, but a few days later Mrs. Keith died. After two weeks Mr. Keith embarked on the new steamer *Golden Gate*. Off the coast of California she caught fire, and Mr. Keith was among those who lost their lives. He had done a great deal of translation work and had aided Bishop Boone in the translations of the New Testament and prayer book into the Shanghai dialect. He had also translated school textbooks into Chinese and had just completed a dictionary in the Wu dialect, the manuscript of which was lost at sea with him.

During that spring and summer, following ravages by the Taiping rebels on the towns and villages, epidemic diseases rampaged. Smallpox, typhus, typhoid, and cholera swept away thousands of Chinese and foreigners. Mercifully, none of the much reduced band of missionaries in the Episcopal compound fell victim to these diseases.

During this spring the Taipings again attacked Shanghai. The residents of the Old City had again to flee to the settlements for safety, Schereschewsky, Wong, and Thomson among them. Three members of the American Presbyterian Mission who lived inside the city lingered too long—Mr. and Mrs. Farnham and Mr. Mills. Mr. Farnham told of their escape:

> While we were at the table taking our noon meal the cry so often heard, "The rebels are coming!" was changed to the shriek, "The rebels have come!" We had heard so much of their wanton cruelty, and had so often seen faces blanch with fear while listening to stories of those who had escaped from them, that we had caught the contagion and rushed into the street to make our escape. They were already at our gate and we at once found ourselves surrounded by long haired rebels and entirely at their mercy. They were a horrid

set of fellows, clad in a variety of costumes and some had scarcely any costume at all. They were armed with a great variety of weapons, rifles, and smooth bores, double barrelled pistols and revolvers. Those who had no gun carried some kind of sword or long knife.

The leader was mounted upon a fine horse—a well dressed, good looking young man. "Whither away?" he exclaimed as we sprang into the street to make our escape. Knowing that the rebels worshipped God and destroyed all idols we replied, "We worship God and wish to go to a place of safety." "I too worship God," he replied, "Remain where you are; you are safe. My followers will not meddle with any foreigner." He leapt off his horse, went into the house and dashed off a proclamation to put on our church door forbidding his followers to injure our person or property. We thanked him but asked his permission to go beyond the city. He agreed.

About that time came the booming of cannon and the crash of brick and window glass as the ball, passing over our heads, entered our house. The British soldiers were on the city wall and had commenced firing on the rebels. We heard the rattle of the rifles as they poured a deadly volley into the city. If we attempted to pass through the gate perhaps the rifles of half a dozen sharp-shooters would be aimed at us. What should we do? The Lord had protected us from the rebels but we were in imminent danger of being shot by those who would protect us. I determined to throw open the gate and stand in full view hoping the soldiers would not mistake me for a rebel. It seemed the only thing to do and I flung wide the gate, calling to Captain Budd, "Please don't fire this way till we can leave." "All right," was the reply, "but the drawbridge is up and you will have to go round to the East."

We skirted the south-eastern wall, coming to the gate guarded by Captain MacGilvary. He, too, had opened fire on the rebels and his bullets were flying across our path and towards our mission houses. Again we hailed, "Captain MacGilvary, please hold up till we get past." "Certainly," he replied and called to his men, "Stop firing." We now left the city wall and entered the streets of the great eastern suburb.

225

During the delay the rebels had preceded us, and we fell in with them at different points along the streets. But they were the only persons to be seen. The inhabitants had fled. Whenever we came across a party of rebels we called out, "We worship God." They responded, "We worship God," and let us pass. After such a narrow escape we were grateful to reach a place of comparative safety. All day Sunday the smoke could be seen ascending from burning houses at the South Gate and we supposed that our mission premises, with all our earthly possessions, were gone. The rebels retreated a few miles into the country. On returning to our home we found that the neighbors' houses had all been destroyed, but the mission premises had not been touched.

Understandably, with the news from home worsening, Bishop and Mrs. Boone were anxious about their children in the United States. All three were at school in the North and as the dreadful news of the declaration of war between the North and the eleven southern states which had followed South Carolina's lead and had seceded reached them, they envisaged the children cut off from their guardian, Henry De Saussure in Charleston and unable to receive funds from him. Henry was in medical school in New York and may have graduated by this time but the two younger boys, Willie and Tommy, were still in boarding school in New Jersey.

To make matters worse, in February 1861 the bishop received instructions from his Mission Board that all possible retrenchments in mission expenses must be made. Contributions from the churches in the South had been cut off and donations from the North were declining sharply because of the war. It turned out that for three out of four years of the Civil War the mission received no funds at all from the Mission Board. Drastic economies had to be resorted to. If it had not been for the generosity of anonymous Chinese friends the mission would have had a still harder time. An event occurred which remained a mystery to the bishop to his dying day. He was invited one day to go to the Oriental Bank and was ushered into the office of the manager. Here he was informed that the sum of ten thousand taels had been deposited to his credit. This was a large sum, amounting to some thirty thousand dollars in U.S. currency. The bishop did find out that two Chinese gentlemen had visited some of the business houses in his behalf and had received a generous response. This sum tided the mission over.

Across the ocean Henry, attending medical college, had also been practicing economy. Tuition for the year was forty dollars but for the first year he was granted a "beneficiary ticket," which enabled him to pay a fee and attend private lectures also. This kept him busy day and night but he enjoyed the work and came to the conclusion that he had made a right choice. His board cost four dollars a week and he set aside four dollars for pocket money, which allowed him to spend Saturday evenings with fellow students over a mug of beer and to drop something in the collection plate of Trinity Church, which he attended in deference to his father.

During his second year Henry had his clinical experience at Bellevue Hospital. This he found somewhat distressing, for the hospital was crowded with the poor and the treatment given them was often slipshod and unsanitary. Henry decided that he would try to make up for it by keeping himself immaculate, and he scrubbed his hands so thoroughly that the attendants vowed he would scrub the skin off.

At last the grueling course was over, and on March 9, 1860, Henry wrote proudly to his uncle:

Dear Uncle;
   It is with much pleasure that I am able to inform you that I have succeeded in obtaining my diploma. About two weeks ago I stood my examinations and night before last the degree of Dr. of Medicine was conferred on me.
   Yesterday I was examined at the Brooklyn City Hospital for the position of House Physician and although there were several other candidates, one of whom had obtained two of the prizes given by the College, I was fortunate enough to obtain the appointment. This is the best post in the house, being considered higher than that of House Surgeon. I am

to go on duty on the 20th of April and to remain one year. I will have about fifty patients under my charge all the time with the advantage of seeing the practice of the visiting physicians and I will have my room, board and washing furnished me free of charge during that time. I am doubly glad of all this as it was what my Father wished me to do and the situation is an advantageous one.

Willie and Tommy came down to the city and I was glad to see them. Willie is a good student at school, for his age, and Tommy is improving. Tommy looked rather thin as he has recently had the whooping cough.

With much love to Aunt and my Cousins. Believe me your

attached Nephew,

Henry W. Boone

When he wrote the above letter Henry was just three months short of being twenty-one years old. He did not mention that, though the youngest in his class, he had graduated at its top. When this good news eventually reached Bishop and Mrs. Boone it put their hearts somewhat at rest about the children. They placed them in God's hands, trusting his love.

At the close of 1861 Bishop Boone wrote the board: "I have never had so sad a heart to undertake my annual report." Of the twelve volunteers who had arrived in December 1859, only two—Thomson and Schereschewsky—remained. Mr. Parker and Mrs. Smith had died in Chefoo. Eight of the original number had returned to the United States, including Mr. Smith, who eventually went home because of his infant daughter. Mr. Syle had taken his motherless children to the United States, and the Nelsons and Miss Conover had been detained on furlough. Miss Fay was on short leave of absence and Miss Emma Jones, who had given long years of service to the boys' school, had retired and was residing in Wiesbaden, Germany. If it had not been for the bishop's associates, Wong Kung-chai, Yen Yung-kiung, and Wong Vong-fee, and other Chinese teachers and workers it would have been impossible to carry on the work of preaching, teaching, administering the school for the blind, manning the outstations, and going on with the literary program.

Funds were not sufficient and something drastic had to be done. It was regretfully decided to ask Miss Fay, when she returned, to transfer twenty of her boys over to the school of the English Church Missionary Society, at their generous invitation. The boys' school building on the Episcopal mission compound was sold and several of the other buildings rented. In Hongkew only the Church of Our Saviour and the bishop's residence, together with some of the smaller buildings, were held back. Of course the churches and chapels were kept open, as were the several day schools.

Other missions had also suffered losses. A friend in Shanghai whom Bishop Boone had known back in the Macao days, the Rev. Dr. Bridgman, of the Congregational Church, died. His wife had been in charge of their girls' school but at his death decided to return to America. She turned the school over to the American Presbyterian Mission, with Mrs. Farnham in charge. Many of the girls from the Episcopal Mission girls' school were sent there. Thus was ecumenicity practiced on the mission field, and in many other ways as well, though the term was not then in common use.

About this time there arose a remarkable opportunity for Mr. Schereschewsky to make a trip far up the Yangtze River as an interpreter. The British vice admiral, Sir James Hope, planned to explore the river and on February 11, 1861, he and his party—composed of Major Sarel, Captain Blakiston, Dr. Barton, the Rev. Schereschewsky with his Chinese teacher, three Chinese servants, and four Sikhs, members of the sepoys of the 11th Punjab Infantry—set sail on the H.M.S. *Attalante*. In Nanking they visited the camp of the Taiping rebel army. This produced a very bad opinion of the rebels. Schereschewsky noted:

I have now a decidedly bad opinion of the Taiping insurgents. Since I have seen them with my own eyes I have come to the conclusion that they are utterly unworthy of any Christian sympathy. The spurious Christianity which they pretend to profess, besides its horrid blasphemies, does not seem to have produced in them the slightest moral effect for the better. All the regions they have overrun are perfect deserts. It is impossible to form an idea of the ruinous condition of the places held by them, if not personally seen. No trade, no agriculture, nor any other element to be met with in any well-organized heathen society, is in the places occupied by these pseudo-Christian insurgents. It is positively preposterous to call them, as some do, "the regenerators of China."

The type of junk on which Joseph Schereschewsky and party explored the upper Yangtze River.

They went on to Hankow, Hanyang, and Wuchang—which they found in ruins. Wuchang was the best of the three "triple cities," and they were impressed by its comparatively clean and broad streets. Here they transferred to an eighty-foot junk and went on up the Yangtze to the Tungting Lake, stopping at the town of Yochow, Hunan, at its entrance. They were now 750 miles from Shanghai and realized that they were farther up the river than any foreigners had before penetrated, with the possible exception of French Jesuit priests, who always wore Chinese clothes and shaved their heads in front and wore queues in the Chinese fashion of the Manchu dynasty (the queue being a sign of servitude imposed upon the Chinese by their conquerors). At this point the admiral turned back but the four explorers with the Chinese teacher, the sepoys, and the servants hired two smaller junks and went on. They stopped at Ichang, Hupeh, and then were hauled up the treacherous gorges by rope and tracker into the vast province of Szechwan, far in the depth of west China. Here they had constant warnings of fierce and cruel bandits who infested the area. They were surprised to frequently meet Roman Catholic Christians, and at a small river port called Hulin they came across a whole village of them. Word of their approach had preceded them and the foreigners were astonished to see people lining the river's edge to greet them. They were carried in sedan chairs to the village, a deafening din of firecrackers preceding them in welcome. The Christians came bowing and asking a blessing, though Schereschewsky remonstrated and told them they were not Roman Catholics but Protestants. This they had never heard of and said it made no difference. They told that their church had recently been destroyed by bandits and begged the travelers to report their plight to the mandarin in Chungking. This they promised to do.

But at Chungking the explorers were threatened by the local militia. A French Catholic missionary sent them a warning that these soldiers planned to murder them and take their boats if they came ashore. The two British military men and

Schereschewsky determined to chance it and called at the yamen and at the French Mission. The Frenchmen made them welcome but marveled that they had dared to come to the interior dressed in Western costume. Schereschewsky said afterwards that he felt much gratified to be the first Protestant to go to west China. He felt that the Church of Rome had been much more zealous than the Protestants in furthering the mission cause and regretted that so much of her teaching had become mixed with superstition. Their junks continued up the Min River to Pingshan, eighteen hundred miles from Shanghai. They had been on the way for nearly four months. They had hoped to travel overland from there to Tibet but were warned of the many bandits they would surely meet on the way and gave up the idea. Going downriver was much swifter than coming up because of the current. Leaving Pingshan on May 30 they arrived in Shanghai on July 9, 1861. It had been a glorious adventure and Schereschewsky had added much knowledge of the extent of China and of the Chinese customs and language.

The intrusion of foreign powers upon the China scene necessitated some drastic changes in the handling of affairs by the Chinese government. Much in the provinces had been administered by local authorities, directed only at long range from Peking and possessing a great degree of autonomy. Now foreign ambassadors refused to deal with representatives, such as had been the custom up to the time of the Treaty of Tientsin in 1858, and wanted direct access to the emperor in Peking. Foreign ministers were ready to take advantage of the treaty clause which granted them the privilege of residing with their staffs in Peking. Some machinery had to be set up to deal with such matters and a new body, the Tsungli Yamen, was formed in 1861 to deal with foreign affairs, whereupon English and French legations were established in Peking. As yet other foreigners were not permitted to reside there, only those connected in some way with the legation. But the French held a government protectorate over her missionaries, a privilege the other nations never claimed, and there were French Catholics working in Peking.

In 1861 the British ambassador, Sir Rutherford Alcock, invited Dr. William Lockhart of the London Mission in Shanghai to become medical officer for the legation at Peking. A short time later the Rev. John S. Burdon came there as chaplain to the legation in addition to being a representative of the Church Missionary Society. When an opportunity came in the summer of 1862 for Samuel Schereschewsky to go to Peking as interpreter to the new American minister, the Hon. Anson Burlingame, Bishop Boone was heartily in favor of his going. Peking was not only the seat of government, but was the cultural capital of China. There Schereschewsky would have a chance to come in contact with Chinese literary men. His going would also temporarily provide for his financial support. Dr. S. Wells Williams, eminent student of Chinese, went with Burlingame as secretary to the legation. The party spent several days in Tientsin en route and there Schereschewsky met the Rev. Henry Blodget of the American Congregational Mission, who moved not long afterwards to Peking; there the two men were associated in the work of translation and became lifelong friends.

The little band of Episcopalian missionaries in Shanghai was thus further reduced in numbers by the departure of Mr. Schereschewsky. Miss Lydia Fay and Elliot Thomson both hailed from Virginia, William and Phoebe Boone from South Carolina. They did not know for a long time that one reason they received no mail from home was because, after the northern troops under Major Anderson had been ousted from Fort Sumter in the first battle of the war, all southern ports had been blockaded in retaliation. Only such ships as could evade the blockade and slip out gave the southern states any contact with the outside world. Their trade and the procurement of needed supplies was seriously interfered with. The last letter William Boone received from his son Henry was written in July 1861. It had managed to get through the blockade and was postmarked the West Indies. It did not reach his father until nearly Christmas.

Knowing they would be anxious to hear it, Henry told first of family news. The most exciting bit was that his sister, Maney, was engaged to be married—to Albert Rhett Walker, the son of her father's honored friend, the Rev. Joseph Walker of Saint Helena's, Beaufort. Albert had been studying for the ministry at Columbia, South Carolina, under Bishop Davis, but as soon as the war broke out in April he had enlisted. The bishop, however, had persuaded him to return to his studies, since he was so soon to graduate, and prepare to enter the army as a chaplain. It was at the bishop's home as a guest that Maney had met Albert. They planned to be married as soon as Albert completed his theological course. Henry had recently seen Uncle Henry and Aunt Susan. His uncle had aged considerably and Aunt Susan was not at all well. Both sons had enlisted as officers in the army. Henry had not seen Willie and Tommy since he left New York in April but they were both well and busy at school then, though Tommy looked a bit thin for he had just gotten over whooping cough. Henry hoped that his parents were hearing from the two boys, since there was no blockade of northern ports.

In case letters had been lost he would repeat various bits of information. As his parents knew, after he completed his year in internship and had received his diploma in medicine from the College of Medicine at the College of the City of New York, he was so fortunate as to be able to spend a year as resident physician at Brooklyn City Hospital. It had been a most worthwhile year. Politically things had been in a furor all year, with people arguing back and forth in regard to the Missouri Compromise, states' rights, and abolition. Finally Lincoln was elected to the presidency and in the following December, South Carolina had seceded. Henry was sure his parents must have heard all that and he did not go into it. He only said that all this roared about his ears but he was too engrossed with the fifty patients in his charge to get much involved. But when he heard the news that in February 1861 six more states—Missouri, Florida, Georgia, Alabama, Louisiana, and Texas had followed South Carolina's lead and had seceded, he was shaken to the core. These seven states met in Montgomery, Alabama, organized the Confederate States of America, and elected a president, Jefferson Davis. This meant that they had freed themselves from the Union and had in fact become a separate nation. War was imminent and Henry had to make up his mind on which side he would be. It was a bitter decision, for while his beloved kinsfolk were in the South his parents were not there. And in the North he had many friends and classmates from whom he wished no separation. His year's contract with Brooklyn Hospital was expiring, and the constant vilification of the South he heard made him realize that his love and allegiance were there and not with the North. As soon as his year was up in April he had left for Charleston.

There he applied at once to the Army Medical Corps and on April 10 had received a commission from the Surgeon General's Department. He was attached to the Palmetto Regiment and was to serve as assistant surgeon to Dr. Lynch at Fort Moultrie. His commission was signed by the surgeon general, R. N. Gibbes, M.D.—who happened to be a cousin of his father's. He reported for duty immediately and was put in charge of medical and surgical supplies to be delivered to the various forts which ringed Charleston Bay. General Beauregard was their commander. That very night the first shot of the war was fired! Major Anderson of the northern garrison on Fort Sumter held out only until the 13th, when the bombardment set fire to the fort and he was forced to surrender. There were no casualties.

Richmond, Virginia, was chosen as the capital of the Confederacy. After Fort Sumter fell Lincoln ordered a blockade of the southern ports and all sorts of boats—river steamers, ferryboats, and small craft as well as sloops and frigates—were appearing off the coast to prevent the South from using its harbors. The North seemed to be worried about Washington, D.C., and was sending troops into northern Virginia to protect the rail lines. Just a few days before Henry wrote there had been a battle at Manassas on the rivulet called Bull Run, which was only about twenty miles outside of Washington. There had been heavy casualties on both sides in this, the first serious confrontation of "The War Between the States," as everyone in the South was calling it. The Confederates under General Beauregard had won the day, but everyone was saying that it did not look as though the war would soon be over, as had at first been hoped. Henry had been transferred to an army hospital in Richmond and was writing from there. He would take his turn at various field hospitals but would be based in Richmond. War was terrible. He hoped his parents would not worry about him. He wanted to do his duty and help the wounded. What he was seeing was enough to make anyone heartsick. He hoped his parents were well and said he longed to see them.

William and Phoebe read and reread their son's letter for, old as it was, there were many pieces of news in it which they had not as yet heard. From time to time letters were received from the younger boys in New York but they knew nothing of Henry, and his parents did not have any further word from him. That the war continued they knew. A year went by. One winter afternoon in December 1862 Phoebe, William and Robbie were seated in front of the open fire at the tea table when the doorbell rang. Ah-Fong ushered in an excited-looking, immaculately dressed young American with sandy hair and beard. He came toward them with quick steps, supporting himself with a cane, and before they could recognize him he called out in a voice joyous with fulfillment, "Father, Mother!" His parents could scarcely believe their eyes. How could it be possible that Henry, whom they knew to be in South Carolina, was here in Shanghai? After the shock of surprise and the greetings were over Henry told them what had happened.

In the spring of 1862 northern troops under General McClellan had invaded Virginia with the slogan "On to Richmond." There had been many skirmishes and many were wounded, but the Confederate cavalry under General Jeb Stuart was swift and strong and on home ground. Those men had grown up on horseback! The Yankees were outsmarted by them and driven back again and again, but they did manage to get within four miles of Richmond. Again their army was outflanked and they were finally forced to withdraw. The wounded poured into Richmond any way they could get there, and the hospitals were flooded. All doctors were on their feet eighteen or twenty hours a day trying to save those they could. It seemed cruel, senseless to see a fine young boy who was smashed to bits and try to save him, knowing you couldn't.

Again Manassas was threatened, with General Robert E. Lee and Stonewall Jackson confronting General Pope, who had been guarding Washington. Again it was Henry's turn to help staff a mobile field hospital. The Second Battle of Bull Run, as it was called, was sharp and severe. On the second day of the battle Henry said he was binding up the shoulder of a soldier on the field, just as the battle seemed over, when he himself was hit in the leg just below the knee. The bullet traced downward and lodged in his ankle. He got off the field and onto his horse and back to their base hospital. Here they probed the ankle and removed the bullet, and he was sent back to his own hospital in Richmond. Staying in bed was the hardest thing he had yet had to do. It had been a long time since he had had time to think about anything except his patients. Now he had nothing to do but think, and the more he thought about the war the more it sickened him. Was any cause worth all this bloodshed and desolation? There were good and conscientious men on both sides, as he well knew. In the North he had heard people calling all Southerners inhuman tyrants; then in the South they were calling all "Yanks" tyrants and devils. It didn't make sense. Each side was fighting for something they called their "honor" and their "rights." What honor was there in turning their beautiful country into a slimy field of blood and tears? Slavery was seldom mentioned as an issue anymore. The Negroes had shown themselves too brave and loyal and had helped the South in innumerable ways. The North was even starting to shut them up in war camps when they were captured to keep them from helping their masters. While he was lying there in bed Henry had made up his mind.

As soon as he was able to get about on crutches he had gone to the surgeon general's headquarters in Richmond and had put his case before Dr. Gibbes. Henry stated that he had come to the serious conclusion that his own views were at variance with those of both North and South. He thought war wrong. Differences of opinion should be settled by negotiation and not by fighting. He still wanted to be of use to his country but not as a partisan. He asked to be released from the Army Medical Corps and assigned work, dangerous work if needed, so he could serve the cause of humanity rather than the South alone. The surgeon general had come across such views once or twice before. He listened patiently to Henry but did not try to argue with him. When he gave his judgment it was that this case was beyond his jurisdiction and that Henry would have to go before the colonel of his regiment. This he advised him to do at once. As soon as the colonel had the leisure to see Henry he went before him. This was a much more peppery interview than the one with Dr. Gibbes. Finally after a good deal of questioning and recrimination he was told he must appear before the highest military court to be court-martialed.

The trial came at an early date and to his surprise was not as difficult an ordeal as the interview with the colonel had been. The officers were evidently well briefed on his case. He was asked if he had any change in his views and he answered in the negative. In the end the court offered him two alternatives. He could either enter Castle Thunder, the prison lately established in Richmond to incarcerate political recalcitrants and miscreants, as resident physician for the duration; or else he could undertake for the army a dangerous mission for which he was qualified—but after the mission was completed he must not reenter the country until after the war was over. It turned out that a secret mission was in the making to attempt to slip by the blockade and send a ship to England for needed medical and other supplies. The ship would carry a cargo of cotton to be sold and the proceeds could be used for the supplies. Two emissaries would also be on board to try again to present the cause of the Confederacy to England and seek their support, but Henry would have nothing to do with that. The ship would set forth as soon as arrangements could be completed. Henry said he chose the second of these two offers with no hesitation whatsoever.

Because Charleston harbor was so strategic, the Union navy had seen to it that it could not be used by the Confederacy by sinking fifty ships and boats laden with stones across the mouth of the harbor. Beaufort was a less functional port and less closely guarded so it had been decided to try to slip past the blockade from there. Henry was taken to Beaufort at once, having been instructed to tell his associates at the hospital merely that he was being transferred to another sector of the war. The moon was on the wane so arrangements for departure were speeded up, and one dark night Henry and the other two gentlemen, whose identity Henry did not as yet know, were hustled aboard the dark bulk of some kind of a craft and slipped out of Port Royal and into the sound. They passed all too close to an enemy sloop but were not detected, and all breathed more easily when they were fairly away from the coast and out in the Atlantic Ocean.

They headed for the Bermuda Islands and from there turned northeast and on directly to England. They were not intercepted and arrived safely at their destination. Since Henry was anxious to fulfill his mission as promptly as possible he set about at once getting in touch with medical and surgical supply companies. He found the British gentlemen with whom he dealt most courteous and generous. There was no delay in selling the cotton, as it was much in demand for the mills. His task was soon completed and Henry was free to go his way. He began looking for passage to China via the overland route through Egypt, which was much quicker than the ocean route. The first ship took him as far as

Egypt. Then there was the slow, hot trip overland to the Red Sea on the back of a camel. Their route took them just south of the new Suez Canal, where they were told swarms of Egyptians were at work under the direction of de Lesseps. It would be a jolly good thing when it was finished and would save lots of time and perspiration. From the Red Sea it was all the way to Shanghai by ship, with a change to a Jardine merchant vessel at Calcutta. So here he was!

It was not long before Henry found out that a doctor was a person heartily welcome in Shanghai. With the departure of Dr. Lockhart for Peking the needs of the growing foreign community were not being met. The London Mission had a small hospital for Chinese on Shantung Road, and Elliot Thomson was trying to maintain a very small clinic in Hong-kew, but he was not a medical man. Dr. Boone was promptly invited to take charge of the embryo Port Hospital, which ministered to the needs of seamen, adventurers, and solid citizens of the foreign community of all nations of which Shanghai's international settlement and French concession were composed. In addition, the doctor opened an office where he could see private patients. He soon found himself more than busy, but he was not content until he had opened a clinic where, on certain days of the week, he could see patients in the native city. His old friend and study-mate, the Rev. Wong Kung-chai, lived in rooms next to Christ Church with his wife and daughters and was glad to prepare a room at the church—vacated by Schereschewsky—for his use. Henry lived at home and relaxed into family life with his father and mother and delightful six-year-old Robbie. He had not felt as much at ease since he left Shanghai at the age of ten. Everything seemed right: the smells—not always savory, the sound of the Shanghai dialect spoken on the street, the shout of the roasted-peanut hawker calling *"Tsang-zunk-ku,"* the chant of pile drivers, the sight of blue-clad figures in comfortable attire—this was home.

St. Luke's Hospital, Shanghai. Gift of Mr. Li to Dr. Boone.

CHAPTER 11

"IF IT DIES,
IT BEARS
MUCH FRUIT"

Although both William and Phoebe were constantly at work—the bishop with overseeing the two churches, the day schools, and two or three new outstations and always with the study of Chinese, Phoebe with household matters: teaching Robbie, tending her garden, and holding Bible classes for the women of the church—their son's professional eye noticed that they did not look at all well. They were aged far beyond their fifty-one years. He noticed that at the table they scarcely touched the dishes upon which he and Robbie feasted hungrily. Upon questioning, his father told Henry that Dr. Lockhart had diagnosed the trouble they both had as the tropical disease sprue. There was no particular pain but the whole lining of the intestinal tract seemed to be in a raw condition and very few foods could be eaten without distress. Poor nutrition resulted in anemia and emaciation but there seemed to be no help for it. The medical profession did not as yet seem to have found any remedy for the malady. Young Dr. Boone, not having studied tropical medicine, did not know how to cope with it either. When she returned from the last furlough, on the voyage back to Shanghai

Phoebe had tenderly cared for a variety of plants from her friends' southern gardens. Since the climate of Shanghai, except for its mugginess, was much like that of Virginia, she hoped they would grow. Among others, her strawberry plants had flourished. Strangely enough, she found that during their short season she could eat strawberries with no ill effects. For the bishop, never too well, this added illness, though not as severe as Phoebe's, added a heavy cross. He was glad to have the energy of Henry at hand to relieve him of small duties. Robbie was entranced at having an older brother who would play ball with him.

Henry soon found that the Germans and the French in Shanghai stayed pretty much to themselves in their two communities. The Germans had their Club Concordia and the English, the Shanghai Club; but the young Americans among whom he soon had friends had no form of organized recreation. They enjoyed watching the horse racing and the cricket matches, but Dr. Boone saw that they needed active exercise. A few of the livelier ones got together and under his leadership organized the first baseball and rowing clubs. Henry was twenty-three years old and full of enthusiasm, which proved contagious; the clubs were a success.

For Phoebe the highlight of each month was the Saturday when all the women of Christ Church and the Church of Our Saviour and some of the neighbors came to the mission house for Bible study and tea after a service in the adjoining church. Mrs. Wong Kung-chai led the women from Christ Church and brought along her two lively little daughters, Soo-ngoo and Ah-mei. Mrs. Yen, Mrs. Wong Vong-fee, and Mrs. Woo were there with their youngest children and many of the wives of former boys' school students who had insisted that their betrothed attend the girls' school before they were married. They had much to chat about concerning both old and new times and enjoyed showing off their children to each other. Mrs. Yen was their leader. They called it simply the Fu Nu Wei or "Women's Meeting."

But all through that year Phoebe's health steadily declined.

Her family and friends were very much worried about her. During this period she wrote letters only to her two boys in New Jersey, for there was no assurance that letters posted for any of the southern states would ever reach there. The very few letters which reached Shanghai carried distressing news. One came from William's favorite sister, Mary. Since Major Pickens, at nearly fifty, was entering the army, he had taken Mary and the children down to her brother Tom's farm, "Woodlands," near Carrollton, Georgia, thinking it to be a safer place. Not long afterwards Tom had decided to emigrate to Texas, taking the family and the slaves along. As Mary did not care to go so far, he had left the farm to her and departed, charging his brother, George-Fraser Boone, who lived in Macon, to keep an eye on his sister. (Later Fraser also moved to Texas.)

Mary was having a difficult time, finding it very hard to obtain necessary supplies such as salt. She was raising bees and selling the honey, and the children, Andy and Mary, were braiding palmetto-leaf hats which she sewed together for them. The children had sold one hundred hats. Mary had a young baby and found little time for the weaving she wanted to do. She was not complaining and knew that every man strong enough to stand had to be in the army, for the Yankees were drawing nearer. She said, "I trust God will open a way for us to live honestly and owe no man anything but good will." It was well that William never heard that later when General Sherman's armies swept across the land, though Mary pled with them to leave one cow for the sake of the baby, they slaughtered it before her eyes, resulting in the baby's death.

By the fall of 1863 it was evident that Phoebe needed help. It was thought that if she had a change of scene it might do her good. The Rev. Channing Williams wrote from Nagasaki that the weather was bracing and the fall leaves beautiful. He invited the Boone family to come over for a visit. Henry had not taken a summer vacation and offered to go over with his mother. So on a bright day in September he and Phoebe and Robbie, along with Phoebe's amah, set forth on a small ship for Japan. They were given a welcome and settled in at the mission house for a visit of indefinite length, depending on whether Phoebe improved or not.

On their second day there Phoebe did not yet feel able to go out, so the Rev. John Liggins proposed that he take Henry to have a look around Nagasaki. They were in for a bit of an adventure. They were walking up a shopping street when shouts were heard ahead, and everyone in sight scurried for shelter. A passing man said something in Japanese to Mr. Liggins, who took Henry's arm and said, "We had best get into a doorway." No one seemed to mind when they pushed open a gate and stepped into a small private dooryard, closing the gate behind them. There was a great deal of shouting and the thwack of swords as the fray drew nearer. It was evidently a fight between the henchmen of two clan lords or *diamyos*. The two foreigners were not noticed and it was just as well, for hatred of foreigners still existed in no small degree. The scuffle passed on down the street. Only a short while before, Liggins told Henry on the way home, an Englishman named Richardson had been out on horseback with three friends when they met the lord of Satsuma returning from Yedo to his own estate. The foreigners should have drawn to the edge of the road until the great man passed, but with British stubbornness failed to do so, and Richardson was killed by the lord's retainers.

After a few days rest Phoebe seemed a trifle better and wanted to see something of Nagasaki. Her hosts suggested that they get a boat as that would perhaps be the least tiring mode of travel and the bay was very beautiful. They all boarded a Japanese sampan having a covered area and were rowed on the first trip of several over to the historic island of Deshima, where the Dutch had been permitted to reside and carry on a limited trade as early as the sixteenth century.

But Phoebe did not seem to improve, and in November she and her two sons returned to Shanghai. It was not possible to return to the United States but she was declining so rapidly that William felt he must try to get her to a doctor who understood her disease. He had word of one in Singapore and determined to take her there. He would place his wife under good medical care and return to Shanghai as soon as possible, for with the much-reduced mission staff he was sorely needed. Henry would remain at the mission house and look after things there. They embarked in the latter part of November on one of the P. and O. steamers. Phoebe wrote her two boys in the United States:

Singapore
Dec. 15, 1863

My dearest Sons,

I seem so transported from place to place without much volition on my part, that it is hard for me to realize where I am and what I have done or left undone. I wrote you that Japan did not benefit my health although I enjoyed my visit there and was able to go about in the country in the boats more than many people did who had more physical strength to boast of but who were restrained by their fears, from trusting themselves among the natives.

If it had not been for this trouble in America, it would have reconciled me more to the separation from your Father to think I could go and be with my children. But you are in different places and it might interfere with arrangements made for your good by an attempt to gratify my great desire to have you near me. Your Father wants you to finish your college course where you, Willie, are [Princeton University]. Unless you are drafted I hope you will do so. If it were possible for you to come to me for vacation, that would be delightful, but we must wait and see how I reach Europe and what arrangements we can make. If Tommy should not have gotten a situation he might come and study modern languages for six months. But all this we can write of later. Only be economical *now* so as to not make it more difficult to carry out these schemes.

Singapore is a lovely place I think and I would enjoy being here if I could only do and make use of the good things within my reach. Delicious fruits are spread wild around but I cannot touch one or a vegetable of any sort and this envolves more self-denial than any one would think until they have had to practice it. I smell the pineapples, oranges and lemons and when the weather is warm you want the juices of fruit, especially when the tongue is dry and parched and it is a great privation to have to refuse that which is pleasant to the taste. However, I have many mercies to be thankful for connected with my sickness and I always try to remember these. I have no bodily pain except that which grows out of weakness. Sometimes I seem to have a keener power of enjoying nature and natural objects than ever. I always was fond of traveling and I have lost none of my relish for it—for you must not think of me as a person sick in bed all the time.

Your fondly attached mother,

P. C. Boone

It was the last letter Phoebe ever wrote.

Not finding the needed help in Singapore, the bishop decided to go to Europe. While in Singapore the Boones had come in contact with an Englishwoman anxious to return home. She had come out a year before with an English couple as nanny to their young child. The little boy had recently died, and her employers were looking for a suitable escort for the nurse to travel with, at least for part of the way. The Boones were glad to take her under their wing, so Jane embarked with them. She proved to be a very great help, as she was fond of children and kept up with the active Robbie by the hour. Phoebe was tucked into a steamer chair on deck, with William at her side, and this made it possible for the tired couple to have long quiet periods together. They reviewed their twenty years of happy married life and spoke much of the children. One day William said to his wife, "My beloved, God has led us through the sun and the rain but always we have felt his hand guiding us. When so much around us seems to have perished of late the words of Saint John have often been in my mind: 'Jesus answered them, saying, The hour is come, that the Son of man should be glorified. Verily, verily, I say unto you, Except a corn of wheat fall into the ground and die, it abideth by itself alone: but if it die, it bringeth forth much fruit (John 12: 23–24, KJV).'

"I have pondered much on that verse. Seed lying in the dark earth must think that the end has come. But there is life within it which responds to moisture and warmth and light. Out of seeming death it germinates and, casting off the parent wrappings, rises again into new life with its potential of fruit bearing. When we first came to Shanghai it struck me as almost a miracle that, although the Roman Church missionaries had been expelled long since and Chinese converts had lived a hunted existence for many years before our coming, yet there were Christians to be found in Shanghai. Do you remember that old building used as a Buddhist temple that was said to have been a Romanish church before the persecution? Bishop Bessi reclaimed it and it is again a church. What I am trying to point out is, and it greatly encourages me, that though the Christian church has been persecuted and has had to go underground and lie in the ground as seed over long periods of time, it has always risen again. This is due to the fact that it was planted in the minds and hearts of living men and women to whom it was precious. It meant so much to them that they passed it on to their children. Sometimes, because there was no one left to cultivate it, the new plant almost perished in the choking weeds of a heathen environment, but still it persisted.

"It has seemed to me that much more of the seed would have survived to grow into healthy plants if the Roman Catholic missions had devoted more of their time to the cultivation of Chinese Christian leadership. Where were the Chinese priests and teachers when they returned? Their foreign priests and brothers had undertaken too much of the leadership. It is hard not to be paternalistic when the society in which we live in China is totally without the knowledge of God. But I believe there must be a converted, trained, and dedicated Chinese Christian leadership in the church in China if it is ever to thrive and become indigenous. That is what I strive for but we missionaries are in too much of a hurry. We forget Saint Peter's words: 'But, beloved, be not ignorant of this one thing, that one day is with the Lord as a thousand years, and a thousand years as one day. The Lord is not slack concerning his promise (2 Peter 3:8–9).' The word of God contains the truth and the life, and it shall one day overcome and the world find righteousness, justice, peace, and love. But, my darling, I should not tire you like this with all my talking. Rest now."

A few days later the ship arrived at Suez, where Phoebe was carried ashore and taken to the Ship's Company Hotel, where they were to stay. William posted a letter which he had written on shipboard.

> P. & O Steamer Monetan
> Red Sea near Suez,
> January 15th, 1864

My very dear friend, Miss Haines,

The hurried line which is all that I can send you must be full of sad news. Of my poor patient I have no good news to tell you except that her mind is kept in perfect peace. She grows weaker every day—she is reduced to a mere skeleton. All we can venture to hope for is to get her comfortably and safely ashore at Suez. It may please God to work wonders in her case by the climate and to call her "out of Egypt," but my fears are that she will be called from Egypt. Her decline is very gradual, very gentle like her own nature, quiet, persevering, nothing violent about it, yet the disease has done its work effectually upon her poor frame. She has no pain. All her distress arises from nausea, abhorrence of food and weakness. This last symptom is very distressing. It is irksome to move. Every time we have to get her up we fear fainting. We have all we can want except for warm nourishment during the night. Our cabin is large and airy and everybody on board is ready to do everything he can for us. But, oh my dear friend, you will comprehend the burden I

have to bear. Jane is very helpful and watches part of every
night while I am asleep in the same cabin. I can't bear to be
away from her. It may please God to spare her precious life
and I will not give up hope. I don't think I shall be able to
write to the boys. You must inform them of their mother's
condition. There is an excellent hotel at Suez, I am told,
kept by the Company. Direct a letter c/o Charles Shaw,
No. 4, Copthall Court, London, E.C., until you hear from
me again. I shall keep this open if possible, to say how she
bears the landing. Poor soul, it is such an exertion to her to
move that the bare thought fills her mind with horror. She
said this morning she wished she could fall asleep and never
wake again.

> As ever your affectionate friend and
> brother,
>
> W. J. Boone

Phoebe was not able to leave her bed after arriving at the
hotel. Everyone there was most kind and her room was filled
with flowers. She told William she was glad because she
wanted Robbie to think of death as something beautiful. She
confided that she had been afraid of death herself until her
visit to Japan. There she and Robbie had stayed for a while
with Dr. and Mrs. Hepburn. She and Mrs. Hepburn talked
of death, and her friend gave her much encouragement and
left her with the verse, "As thy days so shall thy strength be."
Phoebe said she had been resting on this promise ever since
and that now she faced death with no fear but with faith in
God's good promises. On the afternoon of the 20th, four days
after they reached Suez, she died.

Two days later William wrote to his sons:

> Suez Hotel
> Jan. 22nd, 1864

My beloved sons;
  Your dear mother departed this life at this place on the
20th inst., at 4.43 p.m. I am sure you have heard from Miss
Haines as to her illness. Nothing could be more placid and

calm than her end. She often expressed the wish during her extreme weakness that she might fall asleep and not wake again. This wish was granted to her, for she literally fell asleep in Jesus. I was sitting by her side watching her and yet knew not when her spirit took its flight. She died in an Inn but she wanted for nothing that human hands could supply and your father and little brother and the faithful Jane were by her side.

She had lived as she died, a Christian woman possessed of the ornament of a meek and quiet spirit. She was always gentle and earnest and persevering in whatever she undertook. We buried her in the cemetery for foreigners at this place. A quiet, retired spot on an Island in the harbor. There being no clergyman at this place I read the service myself. There were about 25 persons present. Poor Robbie was sick in bed from fever but Jane was present. We have met with great kindness at this place, Mr. West, the English Consul, took charge of all the funeral cares for me. She was carried to the cemetery in his boat and, though seven thousand miles from China, was borne to the grave by four Chinese who composed the boat's crew. This seemed a remarkable providence to me as there was no design on Mr. West's part in appointing these men to bear the coffin. She had devoted nineteen years of her life to serve their nation and they were appointed to carry her to her last resting place. I shall, D.V., leave this place tomorrow en route to Southampton, I would return to Shanghai immediately to take care of my duties, but I cannot take care of Robbie there, and must proceed to England to make arrangements for him. It was his mother's wish, and is mine also, that Miss Emma Jones should take care of him for a time, at least until the affairs in our poor country are settled. She is, as you know, retired and living in Wiesbaden. Write to me soon and address me in care of Charles Shaw, Esq., No. 4, Copthal Court, London E.C.

I am feeling very unwell and cannot write more today. God Almighty bless you both.

Your affectionate father,

W. J. Boone

William went first to London to make some financial arrangements for the boys. From there he and Robbie proceeded to Wiesbaden, where William proposed to leave Robbie with "Aunty Jones." While there he wrote to his uncle in Charleston:

Wiesbaden, Germany
March 5, 1864

My very dear and venerable Uncle:

It is a long time since I have heard from you. This cruel war has been a dreadful destroyer of domestic intercourse. God in his mercy grant it may soon cease. Phoebe and I left Shanghai in November for the sake of her health and now we longed to turn our faces to the dear native state and see the beloved friends of our youth, but it could not be. We had had a consultation of three of our best physicians in Shanghai and they all decided she must leave Shanghai for two years. We made up our minds to the separation and prepared for the journey. Cold was regarded as her enemy and we were to linger awhile in the tropics. We staid a month in Singapore and hurried on to Egypt. We reached Suez on the 16th of January and she died on the 20th. I have written several letters in regard to her death and feel sure that you have seen some of them, in spite of the blockade.

It is a great comfort to think that everything was done to prolong her precious life that the best advice could suggest. Notwithstanding all these efforts it has pleased God to take her unto Himself. From the bottom of my heart I say, "The Lord gave and the Lord taketh away, blessed be the name of the Lord." I used to look at her as she lay in her extreme weakness and say to myself, "Kept in perfect peace because she trusteth in Thee."

Her earthly remains are interred at Suez and I have ordered a plain, substantial monument to be sent on from Liverpool with this simple inscription:

Sacred to the memory of Phoebe Caroline Boone:
Daughter of the Honble. Stephen Elliott of So. Ca. &
Wife of Rt. Rev. Wm. J. Boone D.D. of

Shanghai, China. Who died at the Suez Hotel
Jan. 20 A.D 1864.
Kept in perfect peace because she trusted in Thee. Isa. 26:3.

Robbie and I are now in Wiesbaden where I have turned over his care to Miss Jones who was formerly a member of our Mission. Robbie is now eight years old and a promising boy but of a highly nervous and sensitive temperament. He broke down entirely the night I took him over to her and he realized he was not to sleep with his Papa. I find my chamber inexpressibly solitary since he is gone out of it.

My children, through God's blessing, appear to all be doing well. Willie is in the Junior class at your old Alma Mater. Tommy has gone into business with one of our old China export houses, Messrs. Oliphant & Son Co. They very liberally allow him $200 a year. Miss Haines writes me that Willie has lost his friend Mrs. Hope, with whom he took his meals in Princeton and that it has much quickened his religious sensibilities. She was the widow of a China missionary, a friend of mine, a lady of the utmost refinement and a great loss to him. He has promised to do his best and is very proud to have left the Sophomores behind him.

Tommy gains golden opinions of all men. He shows interest in his religious duties and is correct in his deportment. He resides with Mr. and Mrs. Nixon, a fine family which makes a delightful Christian home for him. Mrs. Nixon is a sister of Miss Haines. They have a son in Shanghai who has staid at our house, so we have reciprocated kindnesses.

Henry is correct in his moral deportment and is attentive to his business and has been rewarded with a fair measure of success. By my last letter from Shanghai [Jan. 7] Mr. Thomson, our missionary there, writes that Henry has just had a conversation with him stating his earnest desire to be a thorough Christian. God help the poor boy.

My expenses during the past year, as you may well imagine, have been enormous. The travelling by P & O steamers is very expensive and my expenses when I get back to Shanghai for our travelling since we left home will be over 1000 pounds. The Committee will pay part of this but I cannot put it all upon them. Miss Habersham of Savannah, Ga. managed to get sent over six bales of Sea Island cotton to Liverpool from their church for our Mission. I was so fortunate as to pick it up in Liverpool while in England and sold it readily making $1273; which will be of great help to the Mission. While in London I also received a letter from daughter Mary which she had sent in care of my agent there. I had written her to call upon you for help from any funds of mine in your hands. She writes, dear child, to say that the parish takes such good care of them that she prefers it should be put up for her dear father: I told an English clergyman of this as proof that people were not starving in the Confederacy as the Northern papers say, and asked him if he knew of a curate in England who would decline 50 to 100 pounds from his father-in-law? He said he did not believe there was such a man within the four seas.

My deepest sympathies are with you in all your afflictions. My tears often flow for the miseries of my dear native land and my beloved kindred. Give tenderest love to my dear Aunts and to all my cousins and relations. And to all my friends in Camden and Columbia. May the Lord God Almighty have you all under His gracious care and keeping and deliver you speedily from the scourge of war.

As ever, my beloved Uncle, your gratefully attached nephew,

Wm. J. Boone

On April 10 William again wrote his sons a short note saying that he had come to Paris three weeks earlier with the intention of sailing from there for China. His doctor there had given him permission to set sail and he was to leave the next day. The next letter they had from their father was postmarked Aden:

P & O Steamer Candia at Aden
May 6th, 1864

My beloved boys:
The incidents of our life are very checkered. Instead of

being at Point de Galle on the Island of Ceylon, as I had expected to-day, I am here again at Aden which we left ten days ago. On April 29th we encountered a severe cyclone and were obliged to put back. For many hours we were in imminent danger. We were near the center of the cyclone and when we got out of that were in danger from floating onto the lee shore until the wind shifted to the South. We nearly foundered for at the height of the gale we took on board an immense amount of H_2O. It was seven feet in the engine room and put out all the fires. From this danger we were rescued by all hands on board, passengers and crew, bailing and pumping. I never saw a ship on board of which everything was so complete a wreck: The water was so deep in the cabins on the lee side as to float the trunks and they were beaten to pieces. I was on that side and my things were knocked to pieces. All my clothes were spoiled and my new robes, just purchased in London for twenty pounds, ruined. But what I care most for is what money cannot replace, my Bible with its thousands of associations connected with it and other heart treasures. I assure you, however, that there is no murmuring on board. There is such a lively sense among us all of the great mercy of God in sparing our lives that earthly goods seem as naught.

It is solemn to stare death in the face and this I did for two hours with only one care in mind, the fate of my precious little Robbie. For myself it seemed to offer nothing but a welcome release from a weary warfare. I was journeying to a desolate house, with a diseased body that will probably never be well again, whose daily aches and pains are a heavy burden. But, sinful as I am, I have no doubt that I am accepted by my Heavenly Father in His Beloved Son and that He knows what is best. All you children seem old enough now to get along, with God's blessing, without my further care, except my precious little Benjamin. You can conceive, my darling boys, what a precious comfort it is to me to regard you both as sincere believers, those who with Mary have "chosen the better part"—the good portion which shall not be taken away. If I arrive in Shanghai I shall immediately prepare a new will, now that your mother is gone, so you will all be provided for. I have a strong impression on my mind that I have only a short time to live and I desire to set my house in order.

I shall be very anxious to hear from you both on my arrival at Shanghai, as I regard you both in a very important crisis of your eternal history. I am much in prayer for you and think of you both constantly. Do not, dear Willie, relax into idleness. Gird your loins for a long and earnest life work. Let my dear Tommy strive to become daily more and more confirmed on the faith of our Lord Jesus Christ. My kindliest love to Miss Haines and to all at Mrs. Doremus' and Mr. Nixon's. God Almighty bless and keep you both. Write me fully of your progress and tell me fully of all our friends North and South—but don't take up your precious space on politics!

Your affectionate father,

Wm. J. Boone

P.S.   Our ship is repairing and we expect to be able to go on in four or five days. To add to our troubles pestilence broke out on board. You have no idea of the smell from the masses of decaying leather from the trunks and bags added to which were the dead rats and poultry. To crown all, three of the crew were taken down with small-pox.

You will be anxious to learn how my health has fared during all these troubles. Strange to say I have been better since the day of the storm.

On June 13 Henry was notified at the Port Hospital of the arrival of the ship *Candia* and at once sent a messenger to Elliot Thomson and Wong Kung-chai. There was not time to notify others. Indeed, Mr. Thomson was the only foreigner left on the mission staff in Shanghai, for Samuel Schereschewsky was in Peking and Miss Fay had left on a short furlough. The passengers from the battered *Candia* went ashore at the customshouse jetty, and the three friends who were there to meet them were shocked to see how the bishop had aged and how thin and worn he appeared. Henry's brougham was waiting and they got in and drove along the grassy Bund, across

Soochow Creek, and up to the mission compound. The familiar streets had the look of home, but William dreaded entering the mission house which had been such a haven and was now empty and desolate as far as he was concerned. Henry had kept the servants and they gave the bishop a grave yet friendly welcome. William was glad to find that his tongue slipped back readily over the tones and phrases of Chinese. The anguish of sitting down at the table for that first meal, with the empty place at the table's head, was somewhat softened by the presence of Wong Kung-chai, Elliot Thomson, and his son.

In the course of the conversation at the table Mr. Thomson mentioned that a gentleman had come down lately from Peking and had told him that Mr. Schereschewsky was the best speaker of Chinese among all the foreigners in Peking and that he had good rapport with the Chinese. He was engrossed in translating the Old Testament directly from the Hebrew, with which he was so familiar, and had already finished Genesis and the Psalms. Burdon, Edkins, Martin, and himself had recently formed a committee to translate the New Testament into Mandarin. All of them were eminent scholars—Burdon later becoming bishop of Victoria, Hong Kong, Edkins publishing grammars and other books in Mandarin and the Shanghai dialect, Martin becoming president of the government diplomatic school of the Imperial University, and their associate Blodget leading the American Board Mission in Peking for many years with wisdom and tact. Thomson felt it a privilege to have met each of these outstanding men.

Wong Kung-chai, who regarded the bishop as his father, reported the progress of the church in Shanghai. The Taiping rebels seemed to be petering out and had given Shanghai no more trouble. The citizens of the native city, who had fled as refugees at the last raid, had all returned and had repaired or rebuilt most of the houses destroyed by the rebels. The Christ Church building was again in good repair and there seemed to be a much more friendly spirit since the people had returned. Chai had found many ways in which to assist his neighbors and they were appreciative. Many came to his instruction classes in the Christian doctine and several were asking for baptism. What the people appreciated most of all was the clinic Henry ran certain afternoons a week at the church.

The attention turned to Henry, who remarked that he enjoyed the work at the clinic better than the work at the European hospital. He only wished he had more time to devote to it.

When the rest of the clergy and the parishioners learned that the bishop had returned they planned a feast of welcome for him at the Church of Our Saviour, which was so near his home. It was delightful to the bishop to see so many of his old friends, many of whom were the boys and girls who had graduated from the two mission schools. Now they were men in responsible positions in the community and women who were the mothers in Christian homes. As he talked with these intelligent and consecrated men and women he felt how right his policy had been to work intensively with this group, small though it was. They were thoroughly instructed in the Christian way and had a good classical Chinese education as well; they were destined, he felt sure, to take places of leadership not only in the church but in the life of the community.

But his ill health and the terrible experiences of his hair-raising journey had left him very weak. It had been a great but worthwhile effort for him to attend the feast his friends so generously provided. He had been able to eat almost nothing, to his hosts' disappointment, but they saw how much he enjoyed being with them all. The next day the bishop was not able to rise from his bed.

On July 16, 1864, Henry wrote the following letter to his brother.

My dear Willie:
Three days ago Mr. Thomson gave Father the Holy Communion and a few friends came to join in the service.

Rockwood

17 Union Square.(West)
N.Y.

The Rev. William J. Boone, Jr., while on his first furlough, New York, 1878.

He made the responses and joined in all the prayers. After the service was over he said he wished to speak a few words to us all. He said his life had been that of an unprofitable servant, but he looked forward to passing from this world as going to join those who had preceded him to the world above. That he had neither a doubt nor a fear but put his trust in God. He then urged us all to care for our eternal welfare and not to allow the things of this world to draw us off from religous duties. That night his mind began, for the first time, to wander and since then he has slept a good deal and talked to himself at times, but when addressed rouses up and understands what is said to him. Oh, it is a great comfort to me that I am here with him to nurse and watch over him. He has had all the comforts that he wishes—I have seen all his food prepared and have given him the best of everything. He has an excellent nurse and Mr. Thomson, Mr. Wong Kung-chai and I are with him all the time.

Your fond brother,

H. W. Boone

On one evening his beloved Chai was sitting beside him and the bishop asked him to read the Order for Evening Prayer. Chai read it in English and when he came to the beautiful Nunc Dimittis William was listening with a look of radiant peace on his face.

Lord, now lettest thou thy servant depart in peace,
   according to thy word.
For mine eyes have seen thy salvation,
Which thou hast prepared before the face of all people;
To be a light to lighten the Gentiles, and to be the
   glory of thy people Israel.

The bishop said, "Amen," and drifted off into a quiet sleep. On July 21 Henry wrote another letter to his brother:

My dear Willie:

Since my last letter was sent to you our beloved father has gone from this to a better world. On Saturday night, the 16th, I was sitting up with him when he made an exclamation. I leaned over him and he looked at me, took my hand and pressed it. This was the last time that I think he knew anyone. At ten minutes before two p.m. on Sunday, the 17th, he breathed his last without a struggle. Monday eve he was buried. The funeral services were held in his own church and we went to the cemetery followed by a very large number of the community—for many persons here sorrow over his loss. My brother, I feel drawn to you in our loss.

Your attached brother,

H. W. Boone

The tender-hearted Elliot Thomson wrote the sad news to the Mission Board, ending his letter with the words: "Thus our dear brother, our beloved Bishop, our Father in the Lord, our Staff and Stay is taken from us, in joy and peace it is true, but how sad and bereft I feel and all feel you cannot realize. I felt it was the Lord's will. I should have liked to have gone too."

A few days later there appeared in the local Shanghai newspaper, the *North China Herald,* the following obituary:

During the past week the foreign community in China and more especially the residents in Shanghai have experienced a loss which will be long and severely felt. The inexorable hand of death has snatched from amongst us one to whom all classes and all sects looked as the impersonation of what is most lovable in the Character of a Christian gentleman and most admirable in the walk and practice of a Bishop and Pastor. After a life of zeal spent in the most arduous duties connected with Mission work, the Rt. Rev. William J. Boone has at length been gathered to his rest. The crowds of friends who on Monday last stood bareheaded around the tomb and with no feigned demonstrations of sorrow listened to the solemn words which consigned the body of our deeply loved and respected friend to the earth, attested the universal feeling of grief which his removal has caused. No lengthy notice of the late Bishop Boone's life is demanded of us. For the past twenty-five years he lived in the sight of the Chinese and foreign residents in China. His high positions in the church kept him prominently in the foreground whenever affairs of importance were being transacted on the neighborhood of his see, and when his kindly nature became well known, his active participation in every scheme for the spiritual or secular advantage of the native or foreign residents was in all cases counted on as a matter of course. Plans are being made by his Chinese and foreign friends to erect a handsome tomb at the Shantung Road cemetery, just beside the Cathedral which he helped to build.

A memorial service was held by his Chinese friends in his own Church of Our Saviour. Large numbers of both Christian and non-Christian friends attended. The Rev. Wong Kung-chai, Bishop Boone's beloved spiritual son, gave the address. After he had spoken the Rev. Yen and others of the clergy, both of the Episcopal and other churches in Shanghai, spoke briefly. When Deacon Woo, who loved the bishop, started to speak, he could not. Only his tears gave the tribute he desired to offer.

When the news of Bishop Boone's death reached the United States many memorial sermons and minutes were spoken or written. The Foreign Committee of the Protestant Episcopal Church recorded in their minutes a long account of the life, character, and work of Bishop Boone. But the warmest testimony was given in a sermon preached by William's friend of medical school days, the Rt. Rev. William Bacon Stevens, assistant bishop of Pennsylvania, in Calvary Church, New York. He said in part:

Bishop Boone's love of his missionary work was intense. From the time he gave himself to Christ for service in heathen lands, to his death, he never faltered in his zeal and perseverance, never tired of the work; but with an ever growing consciousness of the importance of it, he gloried in spending and being spent in the holy service. His eye was single, his aim was single and guided by faith; nerved by hope, impelled by love, he pressed toward the mark for the prize of his high calling ever looking unto Jesus. He no more doubted that the Sun of Righteousness would, through missionary instrumentality, shine on China, than that the next day's sun would rise in the East.

Unquestioning belief in God's word, unfailing obedience to God's command, unwavering hope in God's promises and unfailing love to God were the controlling elements of his life and made him an eminently faithful missionary and an eminently godly man. So intensely active was he, even when by reason of sickness and debility he might have claimed repose, that it seemed as if his motto was, "Wist ye not that I must be about my Father's business?" To such an extent did he carry this that, when unable to preach, he would place one of the missionaries or the native Deacon Wong Kung-chai in the pulpit, while he would stand at the street gate and ask the people as they passed by to "turn in and hear the doctrine of Jesus," declaring that he had "rather be a door-keeper in the house of the Lord than be altogether laid aside."

He was pre-eminently a Founder. He had scarcely anything prepared for him, neither did he build on another man's foundation. He began at the beginning and by years of toilful study, through months of tropic heat and burning fever, amidst intense physical suffering and family afflictions, during periods of war and rapine and anarchy, he faithfully laid his foundations, and piled up one course of Christian masonry on another, until the great Master-builder called him from toil to rest in the bliss of Paradise. So far, then, from Bishop Boone's work being either worthless or a failure, it was great and successful. It is impossible for any human mind to judge of the results of missions this side of eternity—and the reason is that we have not all the elements of the equation or all the factors necessary for the right calculation of the product. We can only see the human side of the results.

Tomb of the Rt. Rev. William J. Boone, Cathedral Cemetery, Shanghai.

We can only see the temporal aspect, because the work is done for eternity. We can see only the physical and material products; there are also spiritual products which are known only to the Father of Spirits, and where we are ignorant, therefore, of so much that is needful to be known before we can correctly judge, let us not dare, in our short-sightedness and narrow-mindedness, to call that a failure which, could we compute all its elements, would prove to be a glorious success. Nothing is a failure which is done at God's command and in God's way. It is not for the church to make results but to do her appointed work. It is for her to sow the seed, for God to give the increase; for her to send forth laborers; for God to furnish the harvest; for her to preach, for God to make men willing. It was in this spirit that Bishop Boone labored.

Faith tells us that results will come and that "they who go forth weeping, bearing precious seed, shall doubtless come again with joy and bring their sheaves with them." The carping spirit that pronounces the China Mission dead because of apparent small results and temporary declension, that judges of the whole work done and to be done by present appearances, such a spirit would have pronounced our blessed Lord's mission to earth a failure, when all his disciples forsook him and fled and he gave up the ghost upon the cross. The whole history of the church is a history of triumphs after apparent defeats; and its greatest conquests have ever been preceded by its greatest humiliations. Learn to look at the work with the eyes of him who hung there on the cross—before whose view the whole grand scheme unrolled itself as one steady progression of his Church—until the kingdoms of this world shall have become the kingdom of our Lord and his Christ. "It is not by might, nor by strength, but by my Spirit, saith the Lord of Hosts."

CHAPTER 12

RENEWAL

Henry's desolation would have been almost complete if it had not been for his father's friends, both Chinese and foreign. They rallied around to give him what strength and comfort they could. He had come home to be with his family and now there was no family. He was amazed at how many people sought him out to say they had loved and respected his father and mother. Of the mission staff, only Miss Fay and the Thomsons were left. They urged Henry to stay on at his parent's home in Hongkew, as they both lived at the other end of the city. Miss Fay had some time previously taken her twenty boys and joined forces with the school of the English Church Mission. This was an economy move, since the war had dried up funds from the United States.

In one way this shortage of funds proved a blessing, for there emerged a spirit of self-reliance which marked the history of the mission throughout its development. As Chinese friends saw the benefits they derived from church, school, and medical work they gave liberally and often anonymously. The work became self-supporting to a great degree. The respect in which the Chinese leaders, Wong Kung-chai, Yen Yung-kiung, Wong Vong-fee, and other Christians, both men and women, were regarded had a lot to do with this attitude. The number of people who attended services both at Christ Church and the Church of Our Saviour increased in a healthy manner.

Henry closed off some of the rooms of the bishop's residence. When he signed off in the evenings after a busy day at the European hospital and the Christ Church clinic, he often visited for a while at the home of Chai and his wife and two little girls, for he felt at home there. He sought the company of those who had known his parents and failed to find the same keen enjoyment in his young friends of the Baseball and Yacht Clubs as he had before his bereavement.

All of his activities, however, were cut short when disaster struck in September. Asiatic cholera had been unusually prevalent during the past summer. Intravenous technology being unknown, Henry and others of the medical profession were able to save only a small proportion of those struck down. The young doctor himself contracted the disease. Dr. Magowan of the London Missionary Society attended him and did his best to pull Henry through. He miraculously succeeded in doing so but his patient was utterly prostrated. His doctor prescribed a long sea voyage as the only hope of his being fit again. As soon as he felt strong enough, Henry parted reluctantly from his many friends and from the only place on earth which he felt was home and sailed for Europe. It was a long time before he would see Shanghai again.

By the time he reached London he had regained a good degree of strength and felt the need to be at work. Henry loved the sea and upon receiving an invitation to become ship's surgeon with the Pacific Mail Steamship Company he decided to accept the offer. He found the life and work so agreeable that, although he had intended to return to China as soon as he regained his health, he decided to stay with this opportunity for a while and see the world. The next few years were full of interest, for he met charming people, touched at many ports, and learned a great deal. He laid up a store of amusing and adventurous tales which, years later, gained him the reputation of a spirited storyteller at Shanghai dinner tables.

Two years elapsed after Bishop Boone's death before the mission again had a bishop to offer leadership. The Rev. Channing Moore Williams had been working in Japan for the past few years. He felt consternation when a letter came from New York with the news that he had been elected missionary bishop of China and Japan. He knew it to be ridiculous to think that any man on earth could handle as wide and diverse an assignment as that. But upon returning to the states on furlough he was assured that there was no one to take the job, so reluctantly he allowed himself to be consecrated to the office in October 1865.

Bishop Williams returned to Shanghai and joined the Nelsons, who had returned and were living in the Bishop's House. But Bishop Williams had no intention of staying in Shanghai and had no need of the house, being a bachelor. He and Mr. Nelson soon set out on a trip to explore the possibility of opening a mission station at one of the cities up the Yangtze River. They visited the triple cities of Hankow, Hanyang, and Wuchang at the very heart of China. Hankow they found largely in ruins following the Taiping Rebellion. They were much attracted by the literary center of Wuchang across the river. It was clean and had an air of life about it. Every three years thousands of students came to Wuchang from every part of the country to compete in the examinations for the advanced degree of Chu-Jen. Those who passed the grueling test, sealed for three days in a tiny airless cell, were honored men, marked for government appointments and eligible to try for the highest degree of all, that of Chin-Shih. So the city was full of learned men. The bishop determined to open a mission center there: he was able to rent a building and hoped to see a Christian school opened as soon as he could find men to man the station. Two new recruits answered the need. One of them was young William J. Boone II, second son of Bishop William J. Boone.

William had followed his mother's advice in her last letter to him and had completed his studies at Princeton University. From there he had gone to the theological seminary and upon graduation had applied to the Foreign Committee of the Episcopal Church to be sent as a missionary to China. The two new recruits arrived in Shanghai in January 1870, and it was inevitable that Bishop Williams should assign them to work in Wuchang. The bishop, Mr. Hohing, and Mr. Yen had already taken up residence there. The arrival of William and his young wife, Mary Caroline De Saussure, enabled the bishop to leave to visit other of his far-flung charges. A month later Mr. Yen Yung-kiung and William Boone were both ordained to the priesthood in the Rev. Griffeth John's London Mission Church in Hankow. All was not roses, however. Mr. Yen and Mr. Hohing were stoned on the street one day by a group from the local military school. But the literati deplored such an act in their city and reprimanded the offenders.

Such acts were not countenanced by the government at that time. In 1868 an edict had been issued in the name of the young emperor and circulated throughout the nation. It read:

Whereas the preaching of religion is sanctioned by treaty and all persons are at liberty to become proselytes thereto, as it suits their convenience, without compulsion either for or against; We therefore issue this proclamation to give the population, civil and military, to know that it is required of them that they carefully observe the treaty which has been concluded by our most gracious sovereign the emperor, and that they must not annoy religious establishments, nor raise pretexts; nor must they treat foreign travelers with wanton disrespect. Every willful offender will certainly be visited with heavy punishment, without hope of pardon. Obey with trembling:

A special proclamation, 27th day, 9th month, 7th year of Emperor Tung-chih.

One wonders how this edict was screwed out of the empress

dowager, the power behind the throne, in light of her attitude a little later, during the Boxer Rebellion of 1900.

It was only in the port cities and in Peking that people, for the most part, had as yet seen a foreigner. They had heard rumors aplenty of their dastardly deeds and felt hatred for the breed. Life went on in the age-old ways. Confucian ethical teaching had permeated all classes of society, laying stress as it did on right relationships between people. It was responsible for the high quality of morality, honesty, and courtesy that made the Chinese people great and lovable. Not that there were not thieves and rogues, as there are in any country. The common people did not go far from home, for transportation was rudimentary. Ties of sentiment to the ancestral home were strong and the attachment to home and family deep. The ancestors were revered and were a living force in controlling the morals and actions of their descendants, who had no wish to bring disgrace on the family name. Tradition, custom, and superstitition were strongly entrenched. Old ways were best. If a new way was suggested one had but to say, "It is not the custom," and that settled it. Why should foreigners come in thinking they could introduce strange ways?

Foreigners were coming in, and in greater and greater numbers, especially among the missionaries. Both Catholics and Protestants were sending out new people to fortify missions already started and denominations which had not had work in China before. Among them was a young Englishman, Hudson Taylor, who started a new venture, the China Inland Mission. He had already spent several years distributing scriptures south of Shanghai, dressed in Chinese clothes and mingling intimately with the people. Ill health forced his return to England, but so impressed was he by the urgency of taking the gospel to the people in the hinterland of China that he spent his time in the homeland recruiting people to go as missionaries. His requirements were not stringent. A member of any denomination was welcome to join his China Inland Mission, just so he was willing to undergo any hardship for the spreading of the gospel of salvation in Christ

Jesus. He met with good success and in 1866 landed in Shanghai with twenty-four new workers.

The political situation was quiet after the violence of the Taiping Rebellion. At the death of the emperor, Hsien Feng, in 1861 the languishing Ching dynasty had been given fresh impetus by the taking over of the reins of government by the empress dowager, Tzu Hsi. By clever manipulation she succeeded in having the empress and herself, a secondary wife of Hsien Feng and mother of the heir apparent, appointed coregents. As the young prince was but a tiny child, power rested in the hands of the dowager, his mother. At the time, she was engaged in affairs in Peking and left the government of the eighteen provinces largely up to the appointed viceroys.

In 1866 Hudson Taylor, therefore, found it possible to send his missionaries to preach in unevangelized provinces of the hinterland. The mission had phenomenal growth. In 1895 it reported 641 missionaries in the field and 462 Chinese workers. They evangelized in 260 stations and had a membership of 5,000 believers. They went in for almost no educational or medical work but concentrated on evangelism. Individual missionaries lived frugally and integrated themselves as much as possible with the people among whom they worked. Dressing in Chinese clothes and eating what their neighbors ate, they won the attention and respect of the common people.

All this while Mr. Schereschewsky was in Peking hard at his work of translating. But when he received an enthusiastic letter from his friend Elliot Thomson telling of the arrival in November 1868 of an intelligent and refreshing young lady, Miss Susan Mary Waring, to join the mission, he pricked up his ears. A few days later he said to his housemate, Henry Blodget, "I am going to be married."

"Have you met the lady?" his friend asked in astonishment, knowing that "Sherry" had not stirred from his desk long enough to meet anyone.

"No," was the reply, "but I am going to Shanghai to marry her." In the dead of winter the usual way of travel, by cart to Tientsin and thence down the coast by steamer, was out.

No steamers were running because of ice. Schereschewsky decided to walk the nine hundred miles to Shanghai! When he reached the Yangtze River after seven hundred miles he was glad to accept an invitation to go the rest of the way on an American gunboat bound downriver.

Supposing that Miss Waring was staying with the Nelsons at Bishop Boone's old residence, Sherry knocked at their door. Mrs. Nelson opened it and before she had time to greet him he asked, "Where is she?"

"Who?" queried Mrs. Nelson.

"Miss Waring, the woman who is to be my wife."

His astonished hostess told him that Miss Waring was staying at the Thomsons' but that he had better not start out by informing her that she was going to marry him. He was most persuasive and it did not take long. In two weeks they were engaged and on April 21 they were married in Shanghai by the Rev. Elliot Thomson, who had started it all.

The couple returned to Peking, where Sherry once again immersed himself in his Hebrew and Chinese and his wife delved courageously into the mysteries of Mandarin study. The wind and dust of Peking depressed her, and she was unhappy that her neighbors were afraid of her and ran at her approach. But as she learned to greet them in Chinese and invite them to come to see her, curiosity induced a few bold ones to come. When nothing worse than a cup of tea and the offer of simple medicine happened to them, others ventured in. It was not long before she was able to open a day school for boys. She wrote home asking for a cosmoscope, a large globe, and a map of the world, "for," she wrote, "while our main efforts are addressed to give the scholars that instruction which shall, by God's grace, lead them into eternal life, we are also desirous that they should not be utterly ignorant of the rudiments of Western science." Susan Mary also made friends with several women, holding a weekly meeting for them as long as she was in Peking.

The Episcopal Mission in China was blessed in the faithful and fruitful services of a number of single women: Emma

Jones, Mary Morse, and others. But perhaps the one who entered most deeply into Chinese life and thought was Miss Lydia Fay. She came out to Shanghai to join the mission in 1851 and remained in its service with only one furlough for twenty-eight years. With the financial stringency imposed by the War Between the States removed, Miss Fay left her temporary post with the English Church Mission and returned to the Episcopal Mission compound in Hongkew to gather up the pieces of the school for boys that had been so flourishing in Bishop Boone's time. She had already won the respect and admiration of Chinese scholars who knew her. They sent her their sons to be educated. Her mind and heart were centered on bringing out the very best potentiality in her dear boys. Her genius as a teacher brought marked success. Her two boarding schools were named Baird School and Duane Hall and formed the nucleus of the well known Saint John's College (afterwards Saint John's University), founded in 1879 after Miss Fay's death.

Lydia Fay died less than a year before the college opened. Many warm words about her life and character were written at the time by those who loved and admired her. One of the most perceptive was written by the noted Yale scholar S. Wells Williams, who had gone to Peking as secretary to the American minister, the Hon. Anson Burlingame, in 1862. He had spent much time preparing his Chinese-English dictionary, and Miss Fay and her teacher helped him in the final preparation. He wrote:

I first became acquainted with Miss Fay in 1856 and soon saw that the tuition and training of the lads under her care was a heart work which drew out all her strength, thoughts, time and hopes in its full accomplishment. That it was well done is now to be seen in the character and position of many of her pupils who have long since entered on their life work. When she took the school she entered upon the thorough study of the language and literature of China, in order to fit herself for teaching them the better in all knowledge. She soon became interested in the pursuit and to the end of her life her appreciation of the works of Confucius and Mencius increased. All that was true and good in those writings, she regarded as coming from the Infinite Source of truth and goodness. She led her pupils to make comparisons and give a juster value to their own authors, as they learned the perfect Word of God. Miss Fay's interest in Chinese literature was subordinated to the improvement of her scholars but when increasing weakness laid her aside from active teaching, these early researches furnished constant enjoyment to her mind.

My intimate acquaintance with her began when I came down from Peking in November, 1871, in order to print my Syllabic Dictionary. She arrived from America during the next month and willingly agreed to my proposal to aid in the revision of the manuscript, which we examined together so that she would know just what was to be done. Her old teacher, Tsang Chu-Kwei, happily was able to reenter her service and soon became much interested in making the work both accurate and full. Nineteen months soon passed away in this manner. The feeling that Miss Fay and her assistant had revised every one of the 60,000 phrases in it, removed much of my anxiety lest numerous slips and errors should slip in unnoticed.

Last July I received a letter from Miss Fay which told of the death from apoplexy of her teacher; I quote:

"Did I tell you of the very sudden death of my Teacher, Tsang, who had been my friend and guide in Chinese studies for more than fifteen years? He was the one who read the manuscript of your Dictionary with me and knew by heart every character and every definition in it! He had a wonderful memory and was so amiable too. I depended on him so much for my Chinese knowledge that his sudden death was a great grief to me. He was with me on the first of October, seemingly in good health, but as I waited for him the next morning, his brother rushed into my study to say he was dead. It was a terrible shock. There lay his open book and his half-closed fan, just as he had left them the evening before, and his empty chair. I could not believe I should never see him again. I can never hope to get another teacher like him; nor have I tried nor even opened a Chinese book since, in the way of study. I fear I was all too fond of it and perhaps studied when I ought to have been teaching or looking after the hundred boys I had in different schools."

In that unconscious biography which we are constantly writing of ourselves when we write familiar letters, Miss Fay delineated many of her traits of character and motives.

Internal affairs in China during the decade 1870–1880 were in a comparatively peaceful state but the Ching dynasty, which had been so illustrious under the great Emperors Kang Hsi and Chien Lung, was crumbling. Under the firm hand of his ruthless mother, the empress dowager Tzu Hsi, the young emperor, Tung Chih, had little power even after he came of age in 1873. Luxury at court had weakened the fiber of the once hardy Manchus. He had not the strength of character to undertake any of the reforms which cried out to be implemented and died in 1875, after a short and dissolute life. Again acting in a high-handed manner, Tzu Hsi placed on the throne a nephew who was still a small child, giving him the title of Kuang Hsu. Strong willed, able, and aggressive, yet not understanding the profound changes which contact with Western nations was forcing upon China, her long regency kept the Manchu dynasty on the throne longer than the times seemed to indicate.

As merchants, diplomats, and missionaries spread out through the country they were the cause of both benefit and irritation to the Chinese. Provinces that had been laid waste by the Taiping Rebellion laid the blame on foreign doctrines. The humiliation of defeat in the Opium Wars and their subsequent treaties with western nations was fresh in the minds of the people. It seemed wise to the literati to hold to the old ways, which had been the bulwark of the nation over the centuries. Why should foreigners with barbaric customs be permitted to upset them? Therefore when people from other countries, especially missionaries (who did not tend to cling to port cities as the merchants did, but penetrated inland) appeared asking to rent a house or buy land, local riots were met with not infrequently. The strange-looking foreigners, pale as ghosts, were looked upon with fear by the inhabitants. Rumors that they snatched children and extracted their eyes for medical purposes and that they disregarded all rightful religious ceremonies and moral practices, such as ancestor worship, brought abhorrence to right-thinking people. Few saw that the old ways were crumbling and that there were new values to replace them.

There were those who did see good in the new ways. Some of them were youths who, enrolled in mission schools by forward-looking parents, found their foreign teachers kind and interested in them. Curiosity about the subjects studied turned to interest. Articles made abroad were now easily available and seemed better than Chinese ones. The prefix *yang*, meaning "overseas" or "foreign," stuck to the names of many articles which came to be commonly used, such as matches, pens, calico, silver coinage, and a great many other things. Students learned of the political, social, and economic structures of other countries and began to wonder about their own. Christianity taught of one supreme God omnipotent—a Spirit, always present, all-wise and withal, loving.

These ideas appealed to many who came in contact with them. Mission clinics and hospitals offered relief from physical ills, especially to the poor. The Chinese, ever courteous and grateful, offered their thanks with gifts and aid. "Help your neighbor" was taught in mission schools as a Christian duty. In Shanghai the boys in Miss Fay's school responded by opening two day schools for poor boys and a little later the girls' school took in an abandoned baby girl and cared for her. She was followed by another orphan and then another, housed in the school storeroom. It was more than the girls could manage, so the mission took it over, providing a proper building, nurses, and teachers.

In the literary center of Wuchang, the new upriver mission station, no difficulty was found in entering students for the Bishop Boone Memorial School, opened in 1871. It grew and flourished in central China and later became Boone University and then Central China University. Bishop Williams, however, found it increasingly difficult to spend much time in Wuchang when his jurisdiction was so huge. He made frequent trips to Shanghai, to the outstations, to Japan, looking after the work and making plans for its development. Finally, in 1874 he wrote to Board of Missions in New York stating his difficulty and requesting that a bishop be appointed for China so that he himself might be released to give his whole attention to the church in Japan. The suggestion was approved, and in October of that year Bishop Williams was assigned to be "Missionary Bishop of Yedo, having jurisdiction in Japan." So Bishop Williams, the most saintly of men, made the long two-thousand-mile move from Wuchang to Tokyo. He lived and worked in Japan, becoming much beloved, until at an advanced age he returned to the United States. The House of Bishops looked about for a successor to Bishop Williams in China.

Before leaving China Bishop Williams had urged Samuel Schereschewsky to take a furlough, for his health was beginning to show the strain of his ten years in China without a home leave. But he kept putting it off, wishing to complete the various translation projects on which he was working. He wished to see the Old Testament translation into Mandarin through the press and remained in Peking until 1875. In 1873 Susan Mary had borne him a son whom he named Joseph Williams after his father and his friend Bishop Williams. The next year the family added a daughter, Carolina. In April 1875 they left for Japan, where they spent three weeks with Bishop Williams, and then proceeded to the United States. They remained there for two years, and both Mr. and Mrs. Schereschewsky were in great demand as speakers on missions in China and Japan. He was warmly commended by Bishop William Bacon Stevens of Pennsylvania who was reporting to the Board of Missions on progress abroad.

"Great things," he reported, "have been done by our Mission in China." He had recently received Bishop Williams' annual report. It told of the two churches and nine outstation chapels in and near Shanghai where regular services were conducted and reported on the three boarding schools with 68 pupils and the fifteen day schools in the same area with 368 pupils. There were 141 Chinese communicants in the diocese. Besides this there was the work in Wuchang with its school and two chapels; also a new chapel in the city of Hankow, across the Yangtze River, with hopes for a school.

He continued:

> A native clergy and catechists have been trained, a religious literature started and the Word of God translated into the court language of the Empire. But much of this will be lost if the present headless state of the Mission is permitted to continue. There is needed a bishop possessing a well-trained and cultivated mind; of poised and disciplined judgement; of earnest, self-sacrificing zeal; of quick perceptions and prompt action; of broad sympathies and of a devout and humble heart.
>
> The Committee rejoices to know that the Rev. Dr. Schereschewsky has completed his translation of the Bible. He, returning with bound copies of his translation, is more worthy than any victor who ever returned to Rome with the spoils of conquered provinces. He has made the Bible speak to nearly half a hemisphere.

It was scarcely a nomination but it was a broad hint and it is not surprising that two days later, on October 29, 1875, at a meeting of the House of Bishops at Trinity Chapel, New York, Schereschewsky was elected "Missionary Bishop in Shanghai, having jurisdiction over China." At first he refused, feeling himself unfitted for the responsibility. He envisioned returning to China or Japan and there making a translation of the Bible into the literary Chinese style of the Wen-li and another in Mongolian. But the House of Bishops assembled again in 1876, just a year later, and again elected Schereschewsky. He wrote to his friend Bishop Kerfoot shortly after his election:

For the first three or four days [after the election] I was in great misery of mind about this whole matter. I wished and still wish the Church had elected somebody else and left me to finish my course in the service of my Master as I began, a simple priest. However, I begin to feel a little more calm on the subject, a little more resigned to submit to a combination of circumstances which has all the appearance of being brought about by Divine Providence. And may He who is the strength of the weak and the Guide of the perplexed be my Strength and my Guide in this very solemn matter, and give me light to see my path of duty clear before me. And if it is His will that I should be a bishop in His Church, may He give me grace so to fulfil the duties connected with it as to justify my election, and not disappoint the expectations of the bishops who have appointed me to this very responsible and holy office.

He was of the studied opinion that the time had come in China for the establishment of a mission college to carry on the work of the schools in various parts of China that had already been established by missionaries. His plan was that along with the Chinese classics, modern science and Christianity should be taught. There was no Christian college at that time and this was a new and daring idea. There was no money with the board for such a project. He spoke so forcefully to the point, and his judgment was so trusted, that with the enthusiastic backing of Bishop Horatio Potter of New York, chairman of the Foreign Committee, and others, forty thousand dollars was raised for the projected college before Schereschewsky was consecrated to the bishopric. This ceremony took place on October 31, 1877, in Grace Church, New York. The new bishop then prepared to return to China but was asked to delay so that he could attend the second Lambeth Conference, which was to be held in England the following summer. The family sailed in April and arrived in Liverpool after a rough passage. Going on to London they secured an apartment at Clapham Common and awaited the conference. Mrs. Schereschewsky was glad of a time to rest and gather a

little strength, for she had worn herself out on their furlough
in America with the care of the two babies and constant calls
to speak before various church groups. The bishop sailed
forth to see the sights and had the pleasure of meeting eminent scholars, among whom were the savant from China James
Legge and Max Muller, the great Orientalist. These two men
knew of and admired the bishop, for Max Muller remarked
to Bishop W. S. Perry in 1888 that Schereschewsky was one
of the six most learned Orientalists in the world. (See Perry's
Bishops of the American Church, 1897, p. 251.)

While the Schereschewskys were still in London young
William Boone and his wife and three small children had
arrived there from China. They had come on sick leave, as
neither of them was well. The voyage had improved their
health, and they looked the Schereschewskys up and joined
the bishop in his forays about town. Mrs. Boone wrote:

> It was my very good fortune to meet both Bishop and Mrs.
> Schereschewsky in London in 1878 while they were en route
> to China and my husband and myself were coming home.
> The Bishop's wife was taking a much needed rest after a very
> fatiguing year in the United States. We spent about six
> weeks there and occupied ourselves in sight-seeing. I recall
> my gratification in having so tremendously well-informed a
> companion in our rambles. It mattered not what we saw
> or where we went, the Bishop knew all about everything.
> One's first visit to London always includes the Zoo, and
> there I can see the Bishop now in memory, enthusiastically
> expounding the habits of the snakes, pointing out their
> beautiful coloring; and so it was with everything, historical,
> horticultural, artistic—he had real knowledge of all he saw,
> not ostentatiously displayed, but naturally, in an ordinary
> conversation.

Since William's health already showed so much improvement the bishop recommended that the couple proceed to the
United States for a short period and return to China as soon
as it seemed advisable. This pleased the Boones, for they
were anxious to get back to their work after they had seen

their relatives and friends in America. The bishop sketched his plans for the new college and Boone was impressed with his practical suggestions and farsightedness. This time spent together was the beginning of a happy and steadfast relationship between the two families who were to work together in Shanghai through the coming years developing the first Christian college in China.

It was a coincidence that both Miss Emma Jones and Miss Lydia Fay, who had spent so many years in educational work for boys in Shanghai, succeeding each other in the boys' schools, should lie ill—one in Baltimore and the other in Chefoo, China, while these plans for the college founded on their work were being drawn up. They both heard of the plans with joy and satisfaction but did not live to see them carried out, Miss Fay dying in October 1878 and Miss Jones just five months later. Miss Jones' girls' school was renamed after her death the Emma Jones School for Girls. It afterwards was removed to the new St. John's College compound and became one of the best-known girls' middle schools in China under the name of Saint Mary's Hall.

When the Schereschewskys arrived in Shanghai in October 1878 they found that during their absence the work had gone forward in Shanghai with the very small missionary force left there. They would have been hard put if it had not been for the work of the four already ordained Chinese clergymen, Wong Kung-chai, Y. K. Yen, K. S. Ting, and H. N. Woo, plus eight candidates for holy orders. These eight men were studying in a Theological Department which had been added to Miss Fay's school, now called Duane Hall and Divinity School. Rev. Wong assisted by a catechist, Tan Ping-lin, had been living in one of the village outstations and had recently baptized thirty-three persons there. The Nelsons, the Thomsons, and Miss Fay, together with the Boones (who had come down from Wuchang to help after the Schereschewskys left for furlough), were the only missionaries left in the Shanghai station—reduced still further when the Boones went on home leave.

The Wuchang station was even more decimated. With the departure of the Boones and the sudden death of Mrs. Bunn, Dr. Bunn was left to carry on practically alone. This he did with phenomenal results. His report for 1877–1878 shows 9,649 patients treated. Since over two thousand of these were women and children he felt the need for a separate women's hospital. After the death of his wife he was able to rent a building and there opened the Elizabeth Bunn Memorial Hospital for Women and Children. As the bishop remarked, it was the quality and not the quantity of men which had kept things not only going but advancing.

Five miles out from the waterfront of Shanghai, past Bubbling Well Road, there was a beautiful place of rolling lawns and shade trees which formed the setting for the home of a wealthy Shanghai merchant. He called it Jessfield Place and it covered an area of thirteen acres. This property came on the market in January 1879, and the bishop decided at once to purchase it for the campus of the new college. Funds came in locally: eight thousand taels given by former students of the mission schools. On Easter Monday, April 14, 1879, the cornerstone was laid. A large company of people, both Chinese and foreign, was present, including members of the various missions stationed in Shanghai: Presbyterian, Baptist, the London Mission, the China Inland Mission, and others. The Rev. H. C. Deane, chaplain of the Holy Trinity Cathedral, and the Very Rev. Dean Butcher of the Church of England joined in the service. Construction was started at once and by September 1 the college was ready for occupancy by the students of the two boarding schools, Baird and Duane Halls. On that day college opened with an address by the bishop and by Mr. Yen. The Schereschewsky family moved into the residence already on the grounds and Mr. Yen and his family into a new house erected for him. The Boones returned from the United States in November and were also assigned a residence on the campus.

At the first faculty meeting the bishop, Mr. Yen, William Boone, and Daniel Bates, a new arrival, were present. It was decided that the bishop would head the college and be head of the Chinese Classical Department; mathematics, physics, chemistry, and astronomy would be taught by Yen; history, geography, and evidences of Christianity by Bates. Boone would be chaplain and teach English, philosophy, logic, and international law. All instruction would be given in Chinese but English would also be taught. There was a Theological Department in which the Revs. Thomson and Nelson also taught. Four Chinese teachers were added to the Chinese Classical Department. The sixty-two students in residence were put under the supervision of the Rev. Mr. Yen. Thirteen of them enrolled in the Theological Department. Saint John's College was a reality! There were few buildings, few textbooks—for many had yet to be written in Chinese, no chapel, no library, no scientific instruments, no money with which to purchase such things. But it had a dedicated faculty, promising students, a high purpose and faith in the rightness of that purpose for China's future, led by God.

In the meanwhile Henry Boone had grown tired of roving about the world as ship's doctor, as he had been doing for seven years. He thought he would enjoy work on land and in October 1872 accepted the post of assistant surgeon to the U.S. Army. He was sent to the headquarters of the Army Depot of Arizona at Prescott. The army was at that time occupied in negotiating treaties with the Indian tribes. This carried Henry into Arizona and New Mexico, and he sometimes found himself in the midst of sharp skirmishes.

Henry stayed with the army for four years and then resigned. Shortly afterwards he met and married a young and vivacious widow, Adelaide Meacham. She had one son, two years of age, who was named George Elwell after his father. Happy days followed for Henry, with his beautiful wife and little son making a satisfying family life for him.

The next year he entered the service of the U.S. Pacific Coast Geodetic Survey and embarked under Captain Taylor on the official survey ship *Hassler*. This service carried Henry to the Isthmus of Panama, where the canal was under construction. Here he contracted tropical yellow fever, but with his wiry constitution survived this often-fatal disease. Another uncultivated spot explored and surveyed was Catalina Island, off the coast of California. Its wild beauty and the fact that it was as yet populated only by wild goats impressed the survey party. Henry enjoyed the outdoor life with the survey and was distressed when on June 1877 he received a letter from the commander of the *Hassler* saying that by order of the superintendent of the Coast Survey, the ship had been taken off. All on board were "laid off except for those Naval Lieutenants not paid by the Coast Survey." The letter went on to say:

I am therefore obliged to annul your appointment as the Surgeon of this vessel to date Jan. 31, 1877. It is with great regret that I am forced to this action, a regret not so much on your account, for your high ability will always command a position; but for the "Hassler" and the Coast Survey which will lose so much in losing your valuable services. I am confident also that I express the sentiments of all officers of this vessel when I say how much we shall miss you as a messmate and a friend. Permit me, therefore, my dear Doctor, to express to you my high opinion of you as Surgeon, officer and gentleman. My thanks to you for the excellent manner in which you have always performed your duty; and finally my best wishes that, in the future, success, which you well deserve, may attend you.

I remain with high and sincere regards,

Respectfully yours,

H. C. Taylor, Lt. Commander, U.S.A.

Henry and Adelaide had a home in San Francisco, where his wife had many relatives. He decided that, since the break with the Coast Survey had to be made, he would seek a position where he could be nearer home. Therefore, when the Board of Health of San Francisco offered him the job of resident physician of the City and County Hospital, he accepted. The work was heavy and confining and the thought, long suppressed, that he really wanted to return to China for service there kept recurring. He thought the atmosphere of the hospital "too political" and did not enjoy it. After consultation with Adelaide and obtaining her consent, Henry wrote the Foreign Committee of the Episcopal Church submitting his application to be sent as a medical missionary to Shanghai, China.

Bishop Schereschewsky was delighted when he heard that Henry W. Boone, M.D., had been appointed to the mission. He had long hoped to include a medical department in the new college and now foresaw the fulfillment of this dream. With his usual promptness Henry and his family sailed at once upon receiving his appointment, arriving in Shanghai in August 1880. They received a warm welcome.

It had been fifteen years since Henry had left that city and he saw many changes. The most striking was the lovely campus at St. John's. But he could not help mourning the fact that just a year earlier Bishop Schereschewsky had sold a good part of the mission property in Hongkew to make way for commercial progress in that part of the city and to provide desperately needed funds for the purchase of the property at Jessfield. Bishop Boone's residence had but lately been torn down and there remained only the Church of Our Saviour, a warehouse, and the small building now used as a clinic and tiny hospital which Elliot Thomson and the Rev. Woo were trying to maintain in that now-busy section of the town. To this institution Henry soon offered his services and developed it into what became St. Luke's Hospital.

Soon after Dr. Boone took over the responsibility for this small institution an incident occurred which opened up its future. A young countryman was found lying in the street very ill, and police carried him to the hospital. He was unconscious and no one knew who he was or where he came from. His was a severe case of typhoid and it took weeks of devoted care before he was strong enough to return home. A month after his departure the sedan chair of a gentleman appeared and was set down at the door. A well-dressed man of middle age was ushered into Dr. Boone's office. After the customary tea and polite phrases the visitor came to the point. "A few months ago, did you," he asked, "admit a young man from the country and, unaware of his identity, nurse him back to life when death was already upon him?" Thinking of the typhoid patient, Henry answered, "We did." "Why should you do such a thing?" the caller persisted. Henry explained that he was a believer in the one God whose love extends to all and that as a disciple he too must aid anyone in need.

The gentleman was silent for a moment, then added, "That patient was my nephew. Now I want to express my thanks. I am a man of some means. What do you need for your hospital?" The doctor explained that they needed more room—a new building—and would be glad of a contribution toward it. His guest replied, "Draw your plans; I will come in a month to see them." He departed, but, true to his word, returned. When he saw the plans he said, "Good. I will give you the whole sum needed. You may commence building at once." This gave Henry the hope that the medical work could be supported locally. By obtaining contracts for the care of their patients from the police and other civic departments and from many organizations and firms in Shanghai, this became a reality and he never asked for funds from the U.S. other than for the salaries of American staff members.

The doctor was happy when informed that there were already nine students applying for admission to the medical school. He asked the bishop to allow him to reside in Hong-kew so that he could attend his patients before riding out to St. John's daily on his pony. He enjoyed the five-mile trot, which gave him enjoyable exercise. Henry did not feel he would have time to participate in baseball, but renewed his membership in the Yacht Club and took up duties again at the Masonic Landmark Lodge, of which he had been a charter member of its founding on May 9, 1864. After classes Henry took lunch almost daily with his brother William,

whose three older children were away at school in America.
William and his second wife, Henrietta, had an infant son,
Elliott, born after Henry and his family reached Shanghai.
The bond between the two long-separated brothers grew
closer.

When Wong Kung-chai saw Henry, now a mature man of
forty-one, his mind went back to his little charge of long ago.
Henry had sideburns and a beard in the fashion of the day,
and his mouth was partly hidden. But when Chai saw his
quick actions and the twinkle and warm glow in the blue
eyes he knew it was the same Henry and took him to his heart
once more. Chai thought of his own long sea voyage to the
United States with the Boone family and of his distress upon
returning home to find his parents so ill. He saw himself
again a bereaved and penniless boy finding at last the Boones'
residence in the Old City of Shanghai, taken in to become a
part of the family by Henry's generous and loving mother,
Phoebe. Chai had no son but he thought lovingly of his two
fine daughters: Soo-ngoo, in charge now of the mission girls'
school and little Ah-mei, who had declared her determination
to study medicine. He would be a father to Henry as Bishop
Boone had been his father.

"I am nearly sixty now," mused Chai, "a short span of
time but I have seen much suffering for myself and my country. Instead of holding to the great precepts of the ancients
and acting on them, China has forgotten them. We have
been clinging to rotten branches instead of to the sturdy
green tree. Customs and superstitions have taken the place
of the great truths that came down to us. As boys we all
learned the words of the classics from the Li Chi, *The Book
of Rites*: 'When the Great Way is followed all under heaven
will work for the common good. They will choose the virtuous
and able. They will advocate sincerity and cultivate peace. . . .
Idleness on the part of those who can work will be frowned
on. No one will be for himself.' What did they mean to us?
Words! Good words and true but they lacked motivation,

life. But I have seen men among us motivated by the word that has life, the word of God.

"Now is the time of seed sowing and the seed is the word. One day when the seed has died to itself, as the Li Chi agrees, it must, it will rise into life by the power of our Lord Jesus Christ and then our country will be truly great. It is for us today to sow the precious living seed."

Memorial window for Bishop Boone, chapel, The Protestant Episcopal Theological Seminary in Virginia, Alexandria, Virginia, of which Bishop Boone was a graduate.